The Boston Massacre

The
Boston Massacre

A FAMILY HISTORY

—◆—

Serena Zabin

HOUGHTON MIFFLIN HARCOURT

Boston New York

2020

For information about permission to reproduce selections from this book, write to trade.permissions@hmhco.com or to Permissions, Houghton Mifflin Harcourt Publishing Company, 3 Park Avenue, 19th Floor, New York, New York 10016.

hmhbooks.com

Library of Congress Cataloging-in-Publication Data
Names: Zabin, Serena R., author.
Title: The Boston Massacre : a family history / Serena Zabin.
Description: Boston : Houghton Mifflin Harcourt, 2020. | Includes
bibliographical references and index.
Identifiers: LCCN 2019026089 (print) | LCCN 2019026090 (ebook) | ISBN
9780544911154 (hardcover) | ISBN 9780544911192 (ebook)
Subjects: LCSH: Boston Massacre, 1770. | United
States — History — Revolution, 1775–1783 — Women. | United
States — History — Revolution, 1775–1783 — Social aspects. | United
States — History — Revolution, 1775–1783 — Causes. | Great Britain. Army.
Regiment of Foot, 29th — History. | United States — History — Revolution,
1775–1783 — British forces. | Families of military personnel — North
America — History — 18th century. | Military dependents — Great
Britain — History. | Army spouses — North America — History — 18th century.
| Boston (Mass.) — History — Revolution, 1775–1783.
Classification: LCC E215.4 .Z33 2020 (print) | LCC E215.4 (ebook) | DDC
973.3/113—dc23
LC record available at https://lccn.loc.gov/2019026089
LC ebook record available at https://lccn.loc.gov/2019026090

Book design by Chloe Foster

Printed in the United States of America
DOC 10 9 8 7 6 5 4 3 2 1

Dis Manibus

Jan Ellen Lewis, 1949–2018

CONTENTS

LIST OF ILLUSTRATIONS

Paul Revere and Mellen Chamberlain, 1770 (Map reproduction courtesy of the Norman B. Leventhal Map & Education Center at the Boston Public Library)

Insert: *page 1 top* "The Bloody Massacre Perpetrated in King Street, Boston, on March 5th, 1770, by a Party of the 29th Regiment," engraving by Paul Revere, 1770 (Collection of the Massachusetts Historical Society. Used by permission.), *bottom* "British troops on the march," watercolor, 1790 (Anne S. K. Brown Military Collection, Brown University Library. Used by permission.); *page 2 top* "View of Boston Common," embroidery on linen by Hannah Otis, c. 1750 (Photograph © Museum of Fine Arts, Boston. Used by permission.), *bottom* "A View of Part of the Town of Boston in New-England and Brittish Ships of War Landing Their Troops! 1768," engraving by Paul Revere (Courtesy of the American Antiquarian Society); *page 3 top* "A Prospective View of Part of the [Boston] Commons," watercolor by Christian Remick, c. 1768 (Courtesy of the Concord Museum, Gift of Mr. John Brown, Jr., www.concordmuseum.org), *bottom* "A Military Encampment in the Green Park," watercolor by Edward Eyre, c. 1780 (Anne S. K. Brown Military Collection, Brown University Library. Used by permission.); *page 4 top* "English Barracks," drawing by Thomas Rowlandson, c. 1788 (Anne S. K. Brown Military Collection, Brown University Library. Used by permission.), *bottom* "The Camp Laundry," mezzotint printed for R. Sayers and J. Bennett, London 1782 (Anne S. K. Brown Military Collection, Brown University Library. Used by permission.)

March 1770

B ending over the sheet of copper in his Boston workshop, Paul Revere wielded the sharp burin and thought about how the town had been buzzing over the past three weeks with rumors, stories, and contradictory accounts. Revere was a man who kept an ear to the ground, especially when it came to politics. He was a longtime member of the "Sons of Liberty," an informal network of men opposed to the Massachusetts governor. Revere had heard a great deal about the killings in King Street. Five Bostonians were dead; eight British soldiers were in the town jail. Now he wanted to say something about it.

By his side lay young Henry Pelham's vivid sketch of the shootings. It was good, and Revere was happy to copy it closely, but not slavishly. He would have to engrave a mirror image of Pelham's sketch in order for his own print to come out properly. Beyond the technical challenge, however, Revere wanted to heighten some points and make his engraving tell an even clearer story. He understood the political implications of this shooting; it was time to explain them to a bigger audience.

He kept Pelham's neat line of soldiers and their officer with his sword, giving the signal to attack. The crowd of unfortunate but neatly dressed Bostonians was well drawn, as were the three men sprawled on the ground. Even the little dog was perfectly placed, though challenging to engrave.

Henry Pelham created the drawing on which both his engraving and Revere's less subtle one are based. Pelham chose Psalm 94, "A Prayer for Vengeance," as his text below the image.

He would make one clear addition. The story needed a strong title; other changes could be subtler. In the meantime, what else should he do to tell the right story? Perhaps assign the name "Butcher's Hall" to the Custom House? Was that too much? Certainly it was no more extreme than William Hogarth's recent title "Gin Lane," applied to his moralizing print of disintegrating buildings and a drunken, syphilitic mother, highlighting the evils of alcohol.

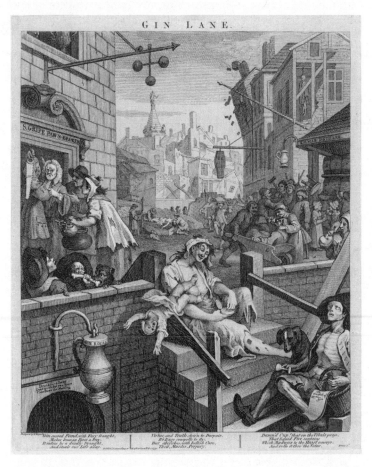

Hogarth's "Gin Lane," a scathing political commentary, was a model for Revere's own engraving.

Revere would leave that sign on the Custom House building, and his viewers would understand that, while the bloodthirsty soldiers pulled the trigger, the tax-collecting customs officials were ultimately responsible for the violence and the deaths. "Butcher's Hall" would make it quite clear that if the imperial administration back in London had simply allowed the colonies to contribute money to the empire's upkeep exactly as they had done before, this disaster would never have happened. Soldiers and politicians, not civilians, were at fault for this shooting.

Revere liked how Pelham's picture drew the eye to the center of the conflict; he wanted to keep viewers' attention on the people in the town square. The lightly sketched buildings, with smoke curling from their chimneys, indicated location without detracting from that focus. The image of warm homes was appealing, a contrast to the inches of snow still covering the ground in raw weather. He also retained the steeples of the nearby churches; it never hurt to point out that Boston was a town of God-fearing churchgoers.

He would, however, highlight that single woman in the crowd. Her presence would make it clear that the locals were not hooligans, but respectable citizens. Unlike the men around her, she would not look at the soldiers. There was no need to suggest that she might well have known them, rented a spare room to some, or that she might have flirted or slept with or even married one. He knew that part of the story, as did everyone in Boston. Nonetheless, it was not going to appear in this picture.

To tighten the visual focus, he would get rid of the two men fleeing in the background. No need to spend effort improving on the individualized faces of the soldiers. But that soldier at the end: he could lean forward into the crowd even more aggressively with his bayonet. And Pelham had not made it easy to count how many soldiers were involved; Revere could separate the two that had been half-hidden by smoke in order to prove that seven privates had fired on the crowd.

Gun smoke. A thick white line in the center of the picture divided the row of disciplined soldiers in red from the crowd of terrified civilians they were slaughtering. It marked the split between inhabitants on one side and soldiers on the other. Only a bayonet pierced the barrier between them. That wall of smoke could be used to clarify rather than obscure. It was the perfect dividing line.

Nothing left but to refine the title. Pelham's was far too long: "THE FRUITS OF ARBITRARY POWER, OR THE BLOODY MASSACRE: PERPETRATED IN KING STREET BOSTON ON MARCH 5, 1770 IN WHICH MESSRS SAML GRAY, SAML MAVERICK, JAMES CALDWELL, CRISPUS ATTUCKS, PATRICK CARR WERE KILLED SIX OTHERS WOUNDED TWO OF THEM MORTALLY." The death of civilians in a public square at the hands of the British government's soldiers was undoubtedly the result of unchecked political power—but it would be far more effective not to bury the lede. Revere retitled the engraving "THE BLOODY MASSACRE: Perpetrated in King Street, Boston on March 5, 1770 by a party of the 29th Regt." Now the title emphasized the gore, the central square, and, most of all, the guilty. Now it told exactly the story Revere wanted, the narrative of the Boston Massacre that would endure for centuries.

Two hundred and fifty years later, it can be hard to look beyond this iconic picture and its interpretation of the event. Yet its complete opposite—the image created in words by the young lawyer and future president John Adams as he defended the soldiers in court—also has its appeal. Adams's brilliant reversal of the message of Revere's print painted the townspeople as the aggressors and the soldiers as the innocent victims. In the end, however, there is no real difference between the stories Revere and Adams told. Both narrators focus on the conflict in the public square, both make the gunshots the center of the story, and both put the two parties, the soldiers and the civilians, on opposite sides.

But another story lies beyond Revere's picture and Adams's words. This forgotten world has been hidden in plain sight since the event. To enter it, we simply need to take seriously the humanity and complexity of Boston's denizens. Those who wore uniforms were not themselves uniform; soldiers were not bloodthirsty devils stuffed into red coats but rather a mix of hopeful bachelors, family men, scoundrels, and (in at least one case) an aspiring playwright. Some soldiers came to Boston with their families; others made new families when they arrived. For their part, not all Bostonians were steadfast opponents of British power. In 1770, they were not sorted into tidy factions of loyalist and patriot; they did not yet conceive of those terms as necessarily distinct, nor diametrically opposed. They were all Britons, although they did not all agree on the best way for Britain to rule.

For almost four years, these people lived together on a peninsula hardly bigger than a square mile. Along the streets of Boston, soldiers, their families, and local inhabitants met and mingled. In public thoroughfares and unpaved lanes, the people we now think of as foes on two different sides were actually entangled in a web of social and spatial relationships that would color their lives, the event that came to be known as the Boston Massacre, and the nature of the American Revolution itself. This is their story.

The Boston Massacre

I

Families of Empire, 1765

June 7, 1765. A young Irishwoman made her way through the crowded streets of Cork to the harbor. Following the red coat of her husband to the dock, Jane Chambers approached a man in uniform and gave him her name. To her relief, he let her pass. The name of her husband, Matthew, had also been checked off the list, but the uniformed man did not bother to note the name of the couple's child. At last, after weeks of waiting, Jane and Matthew Chambers, along with their child, boarded the HMS *Thunderer,* where they joined Matthew's mates in the British army's Twenty-Ninth Regiment of Foot. Three days later they set sail for America.

It may seem strange to begin an account of the Boston Massacre with a woman in Ireland, yet she and women like her are the threads that tie together the range of people and the complexity of the forces that led to that dramatic moment. The complete story of the death of Bostonians at the hands of British troops is more than the political upheaval that followed the shooting. It is also the story of personal connections between men and women, civilians and soldiers. Over time, the women and children associated with the eighteenth-century

British army have been forgotten. In the American imagination, most of the men too have been reduced to anonymous "troops" rather than considered as individuals.

Jane Chambers was not and is not famous. Her early life is lost to historians. We know neither when she was born nor in what year she married. Could she read or write? Was Matthew Chambers her first love? Had she ever dreamed of a life beyond Ireland? The sources are silent on these questions. But other parts of her life, including the choices she made, the family she created, and the voyages she took, have left traces. The everyday life of an ordinary woman would become part of an extraordinary moment.

The faint path of Jane's life events merged with the far better documented path of the army regiment with which she traveled, from Ireland to Canada to Boston, and beyond. This was the same regiment whose soldiers in 1770 would live with civilians in Boston, marry civilians in Boston, and finally shoot civilians in Boston. Jane's attempt to keep her Irish family together collided with British imperial politics in ways that few understood at the time and that no one in 1770 acknowledged. When she traveled with her husband's regiment, Jane would become an unwitting teacher to Bostonians, helping them understand exactly what it meant to be a member of the British imperial family.

As the wife of a soldier, Jane, like tens of thousands of other women, became a part of the British army. Where they went, she went too. In this way, the eighteenth-century British army was quite unlike a present-day fighting force. Early modern armies were family institutions, comprising women and children as well as men.

A watercolor dating from the end of Matthew Chambers's time in the army shows how army and family life were then one and the same. As far as the eye can see, a long line of red-coated soldiers marches through an empty landscape. In the foreground, with a splash of blue to mark her off from the reds and browns elsewhere, trudges a woman. She carries a baby in one arm and grasps an older child by the hand. Her husband carries a third child piggyback while leading a horse, on which a second woman sits, talking earnestly with the soldier at her side. The march looks long and slow. The woman in front hikes up her skirt to free her legs for walking, while the young boy whose hand she holds is burdened, like his father, with a large backpack. The older members of the family — mother, father, and son — all wear red coats like the hundreds of men ahead of them. Even as they stumble along behind the train of soldiers, they are part of the regiment, in appearance and in fact.

I imagine Jane's life resembled that of the blue-skirted woman. She too followed a regiment. Like her husband and other soldiers, she went where she was sent, not where she chose. Lugging a child in her arms, close by her husband, she was not a casual visitor to the world of the British military but a member of it.

Women like Jane who accompanied the army were — and still are — often dismissed as prostitutes or parasites. Their usual label is "camp followers," an undeservedly derisive term. But Jane and thousands of women like her tell a different story. Jane did more than accompany the army as part of a family unit; she was a genuine part of the army itself. As a rule, women did not fight in the eighteenth-century British army, but they performed vital support work for which they were often paid, housed, and transported by the War Office. Still more women who accompanied the army were married to soldiers but were not officially recognized by the War Office. The eighteenth-century British army was full of married men and women.

It is not easy to adjust our vision of these soldiers: not all were roaming bachelors, and many were family men. Yet many elites of their era despised them; high-ranking officers had little respect for enlisted men. A handbook written in 1761 by one officer-turned-colonial-governor characterized military recruits as the "scum of every county, the refuse of mankind." He vividly, if inaccurately, described these men as criminals who were "loaded with vice, villainy, and chains." Although very few of the men in the British army were in fact felons, this characterization was pervasive.

But just as women like Jane Chambers were not slovenly prostitutes, men like her husband, Matthew, were not "scum." The army offered an opportunity, and like many other young men, Matthew seized it. Born in County Down, some ten miles from Belfast, he had trained there as a tailor until he was nineteen. But in 1759, as recruitment intensified during the Seven Years' War, which Britain fought in North America, Europe, and India, Matthew, along with many other artisans and farmers, joined the army. The recruitment bonus might have persuaded him to join up, or perhaps it was the promise of steady employment, or even the possibility of a pension. It was unlikely that pure desperation made him do it. One Irish estate manager at the time bemoaned the difficulty of finding men to enlist, noting that "people are so full of bread, at present, that they care neither to work, nor be under any command of any kind." Army rations were certainly not a sufficient inducement.

Apart from the promise of a recruitment bonus or steady employment, there might have been an additional reason for Matthew to join the army. Putting on a red coat was one way for a young man to improve his chances at marriage. Tailors without regular work may not have seemed like much of a catch; soldiers, on the other hand, drew the attention of young women. As another recruit from County Down boasted only a few years later, "Soldiers in most quarters can without difficulty find wives; . . . in the north of Ireland, wherever the regiment was stationed, young women appeared to have a predilection for our men." And so it was for Matthew Chambers, who found a wife in his early twenties, within five or six years of joining the army. Ordinary men and women in the eighteenth century married for many reasons: for affection, for stability, for someone to share the labor, and for social standing. As a married man, Matthew would be entitled to more respect than he would receive as a bachelor, both at home and in the community. Soldiers in particular gained status from becoming a head of family, even if, as members of traveling garrisons, they rarely had an independent household to rule.

It was not necessarily simple, however, for Matthew to combine his marriage and his military career. The same military experts who sneered at enlisted men also discouraged them from marrying. Military handbooks suggested that noncommissioned officers and privates who wished to marry should obtain the permission of their commanding officer in advance. This measure was necessary, one former officer warned, because women who married private soldiers were a bad influence on the regiment: they were "in general so abandoned, as frequently to occasion quarrels, drunkenness, diseases, and desertions; they involve their husbands in debt; and too often are the ruin and destruction of a soldier." If a soldier insisted on marrying even after his commanding officer had refused permission, "he deserves a punishment, for his folly and disobedience."

In fact, officers may have had little hope that they could control the social lives of most privates. Despite the advice in officers' handbooks, there is scant evidence that any soldier in Ireland sought the advice of his sergeant before marrying, nor left his intended at the altar because of a superior's disapproval. Soldiers married when and whom they pleased, especially during peacetime, when there were no new deployments to expose the conflict between a soldier's family life and the army's penny-pinching budget.

In theory, even if a couple managed to get married, they did not have much opportunity to build a life away from the barracks. Advice manuals for officers recommended that "officers should frequently enquire into the married Soldier's manner of living." If the woman could not earn as much as the man's army pay, he had to continue to eat at the army mess with his mates; his wife clearly could not be trusted to put food on the table. Only soldiers who married "industrious sober women" would be permitted the "indulgence" of eating with their wives.

Pundits and former officers complained that married men, and especially their wives and children, were a drag on the army. During the Seven Years' War, General James Wolfe, leading troops in Canada, grumbled that "the service suffers by the multitude of women already in the regiment." From the perspective of these officers, women and children were expensive, slow, and unprofessional.

Officers especially objected to traveling with women. Women and children often ended up in the "baggage train" at the back of the army. Most of all, when women accompanied armies on the march, questions of money quickly arose. Who would pay for their transportation? Their rations? Would they receive wages for their work?

At the same time, despite their complaints and concerns about money, British army officials were willing to resign themselves to the presence of a few women in each regiment. Those had to be tolerated, as a British major general explained in 1755, because they were "necessary to Wash & mend." Even the former officer who contemplated punishing men who had married without permission was inclined to admit that "honest, laborious Women are rather useful in a Company." Although they tended to think of women as distractions, likely to spread venereal disease to soldiers or get them drunk, officers could occasionally appreciate the labor that women might contribute to the army. The army was even prepared to pay for it, up to a point.

It is easy for modern readers to adopt the attitudes of these aristocratic essayists. Under the influence of their writings, women like Jane Chambers have been denigrated for centuries. But when we understand soldiers' wives as a necessary component of the British army, rather than the disreputable inconvenience that officers' manuals implied, the army begins to look quite different. It becomes, in effect, a social world of families, friends, and children.

When Matthew enlisted in the army in 1759, there was no question of an overseas deployment. Desperate to find men that year, the military had promised that recruits would serve only a three-year term and not have to leave Ireland. Instead, these new soldiers were to guard the country against an anticipated French invasion, which never came.

Between the threat of the French invasion and the demands of the worldwide Seven Years' War, recruiters were everywhere in northern Ireland in 1759. Matthew might have had his choice of regiments: that summer, some half dozen recruiting officers were scouting for new soldiers. He chose the Twenty-Ninth, a British regiment that had been stationed in Ireland for the past nine years. In previous eighteenth-century wars, the Twenty-Ninth Regiment had seen action in Gibraltar, the West Indies, and Canada. But when it returned to Ireland in 1750, it stayed put throughout the Seven Years' War, even while the rest of the British army — which grew during the war from 35,000 men to 100,000 — crisscrossed the globe. Meanwhile, the Twenty-Ninth moved every year, but only around Ireland, from Kilkenny in the east one year, to Galway in the west the next. One year Matthew was stationed near his hometown in northern Ireland; the next year he was sent south to Dublin and then farther south still, to Cork. Soldiers had little to do besides putting down an occasional riot or an agrarian protest movement.

Life in the army was not unlike life outside the army during those years, for both men and women. Matthew likely continued to work as a tailor, since "the custom of the Army has established it part of the Duty of a Soldier, who is a Taylor, to work for his Brother-Soldiers." The red coats and other regimental clothing always needed alterations, and in theory tailors were to be paid a "reasonable" fixed price for their work and enjoy exemption from other army work while they were sewing uniforms. As for Jane, once she married Matthew, she too could find paid work. Army women, as we have seen, washed and mended clothes, an essential task, since privates were issued only one uniform each year (which they had to buy out of their own wages). All clothing was made by hand at the time; even officers had limited wardrobes. Army women also acted as nurses for the wounded, and sometimes as cooks. And they cleaned. They cleaned stockings and belts to a snowy white. They cleaned sickbeds and berths with vinegar and smoke. They cleaned ashes to make soap so they could begin the cycle of washing again. In 1756, one army recruiter pleaded, "If we could be allowed a certain Number of Women it wou'd Contribute greatly towards keeping the Men Clean." Cleaning up after the army was no easy job for a woman, even if it did allow her to stay with her husband.

The Twenty-Ninth Regiment was not fated to remain quietly in Ireland, however. During the Seven Years' War, Ireland had acted as a holding pen for trained soldiers who could be transferred to new regiments in order to bulk up depleted forces. But once the war ended, army officials began to move whole regiments from Ireland and send them throughout the Atlantic world. Within two years of peace, the Chambers family was swept up in a game of military musical chairs that would soon bring them to Massachusetts.

The Treaty of Paris, ratified by Great Britain, France, and Spain in 1763, completely shifted the political map of North America. France gave up all claims to land east of the Mississippi River, to six islands in the West Indies, and to mainland Canada. This enormously expanded empire would require careful oversight, starting with a British military presence. The government needed troops to control its new territory in Canada, but most of the regiments that had seen active duty there during the war were due to be replaced.

And so, in 1764 the British secretary at war put together a careful plan for rotating regiments around the British Empire. He imagined that, every two years, a regiment would be "relieved" and sent home. That year, four regiments left Ireland to go to the West Indies, while three regiments from the West Indies were sent home. For North America, the goal was to replace five of the fifteen regiments left on the continent in 1765, another five the following year, and three more in 1768.

The British had experimented with the idea of troop rotation before, in order to fight one of the most dangerous enemies of all: boredom. In 1741, the House of Lords discovered, with a certain embarrassment, that the government had left several regiments on the Mediterranean island of Minorca—which was little more than a stone fortress—for more than a quarter of a century. Those who could leave did: fourteen of the nineteen officers who were supposed to be on the island were absent. Privates, who had a much harder time escaping from unpleasant postings, were driven to desperate measures. The commanding officer admitted to the House of Lords in that year that "there have been a good many Instances of Soldiers upon that Island shooting off their Hands, and some of them shooting off their Feet, and some shooting themselves thro' the Head, of those that have been the longest there." Troops stationed anywhere, even on sun-drenched islands in the Mediterranean, lost their will to live after too much time in isolation.

By the end of the Seven Years' War, in 1763, the British were determined to be more mindful of how the country deployed troops in peacetime. Compared to Minorca, Canada seemed less likely to drive soldiers to suicide, but nonetheless few were eager to go. Rumors that Irish regiments, including the Twenty-Ninth, were to be sent there began swirling in the winter of 1765. On the last day of

February 1765, Thomas Waite, the Irish undersecretary, dashed off a frantic note to his superior, Robert Wilmot: "Dear Sir . . . I find by a letter . . . that three Regiments are immediately to be sent from here to America . . . I assure you that this new Measure will alarm and frighten and give vast Discontent. Is there no possibility of putting a stop to it?" Canada's cold climate was a byword in the Twenty-Ninth. The regiment had last been in Canada twenty years earlier, fighting the French and their Native allies during King George's War, and the winter of 1747 had been particularly grim. Troops in Nova Scotia were "froze to death," and sixteen-foot drifts of snow buried soldiers inside their guardrooms. It was not a happy memory.

The real problem that made soldiers hesitate to leave Ireland, however, was not the Canadian weather. It was personal. Privates who had joined the Twenty-Ninth Regiment after its return from abroad in 1750, and whose families were in Ireland, keenly felt how distant Canada was from their homes and loved ones. Especially for those who were illiterate and unable to write to their families once they left, America might as well be the moon. Matthew Chambers, for one, never learned to sign his name.

Even for officers, an overseas deployment could wrench families apart. Thomas Waite had not been mistaken about the "vast Discontent" that would sweep over the Irish regiments once they heard a trip to North America was on the horizon. In the spring of 1765, the Crown's representative in Ireland (known as the Lord Lieutenant) was disgusted by the hordes of officers trying to resign their commissions when they learned they would be sent overseas. He wrote angrily to his undersecretary, ordering him to stanch the flow. The undersecretary responded with the story of an officer who had attempted to resign. When confronted with the Lord Lieutenant's refusal to accept his resignation, the officer claimed that he had made it "at the Request of his Wife, & but for her would never have made it at all."

Most men did accept their fate, but the personal costs for them and their families were high. A surgeon's wife named Isabella Graham willingly accompanied her husband to Canada when he was sent there with his regiment in the late 1760s. Graham left her infant son at home with her mother when she left, and her voyage to America left her feeling torn. She wrote to her parents as soon as she landed in Canada: "I had left behind all that was dear to me except one dear friend — that one was constantly with me — . . . but though I love my husband even to extravagance, yet my dear friends whom I left behind have a large share of my heart." To her great sorrow, Graham never again saw either her mother or her son.

And yet Isabella Graham was one of the lucky ones, in one respect. As the wife of an officer, she knew she would always be allowed to accompany her husband. The wives of noncommissioned officers and privates had no such assurances. The British government was reluctant to pay for the travel and sustenance of more women than were thought absolutely necessary for the maintenance of the troops. As a rule of thumb, the army administration decided that each regiment of roughly six hundred men required about sixty women to clean, nurse, and do laundry. That calculation meant that only one man in ten could bring along his wife. What would happen to the families of soldiers who had been in Ireland for most of their lives was of no concern to the royal administration in London. Most historians have never wondered about those women and children either. But their story is key to understanding the British military and its impact on Britain's colonies.

Not every administrator ignored the hundreds of families under his own nose. Lieutenant General Robert Rich, for example, kept a close eye on the embarkations, and worried about the fate of the families who were left behind. His concern was practical rather than sentimental. When rumors that the Twenty-Ninth Regiment might be sent overseas began to circulate in 1765, Rich was both the governor of Londonderry and Castle and the president of the board of overseers for a new charity school in Dublin. In February 1765, the charity school governors claimed that in Dublin alone there were "above four hundred boys, all orphans, or destitute children of soldiers." When the board met with Rich in April 1765, they decided that there were so many children in need of poor relief that they would have to begin to support daughters as well as sons of soldiers as soon as they could find the funds to do so. Even as they were considering the hundreds of children whom they were already trying to support, the overseers were well attuned to the movement of troops out of Ireland. They knew that the numbers of needy children could swell even more once three regiments were sent to Canada. Rich resolved to make a personal appeal to try to nip the problem in the bud.

Rich fervently hoped that he would be more successful than military officers had been in 1764, the year before, after four regiments had been ordered to the West Indies. It had been the first peacetime deployment from Ireland in a decade. Imagining the reaction to the news that only sixty women would be allowed to accompany each regiment had galvanized the commanding officers. The four lieutenant colonels sent a petition to the Lord Lieutenant, begging that he would "take the Case of the married Soldiers into Consideration." They assured the Lord Lieutenant that when the soldiers learned about the limits on families, it could not "fail of occasioning a very considerable Desertion and will even fill the Breasts of those who Embark with discontent." Morale of soldiers sent to the West Indies would be bad enough; to force them to abandon their families would be disaster. The officers proposed instead that each regiment be allowed to bring two hundred women. That increase would allow four men of every ten to bring his family, rather than only one in ten.

The Lord Lieutenant politely sent the petition on to the secretary of state, but without an endorsement for the plan. The Lord Lieutenant's secretary, however, quietly indicated his support for the officers by noting in a cover letter that two ships already in Cork's harbor could be pressed into service as transport ships if the ones that the admiralty was sending were too small to hold the additional families.

But neither the officers' heartfelt warnings of troop discontent nor the secretary's pragmatic suggestion swayed the ministry. Cloaking his refusal behind "His Majesty's Pleasure," Secretary of State Lord Halifax curtly rejected the petition altogether. He warned the officers that deviating in any way from the "Regulations long since established" would only encourage other regiments to ask for an increased family allowance. The whole proposal would create nothing but "great Expense and Inconvenience." The decision was final: no increase in families.

A year later, the result of the 1764 failed petition was all too evident to Rich and other men concerned. The enrollment of Ireland's charity school was burgeoning. Rich and others worried about how women and children would survive without turning to "Popery, Beggary and Idleness." The Cork city council regularly had to allocate money to send to their "respective homes" the wives and children of soldiers who had set sail from Cork's harbor. If the new deployment of three regiments to Canada was not to make hundreds more women and children destitute, Rich would have to try a new approach.

Rich laid his plans through the spring of 1765 as the Twenty-Ninth Regiment began gathering in Cork. Once the transport ships HMS *Thunderer* and HMS *Belle-Isle* arrived in the harbor in May, General Rich approached the three most powerful officeholders in Ireland and made a proposal. He assured them that this was a recommendation "very much for the good of His Majesty's Service." The general's plan was even more expansive than the one put forth in the 1764 officers' petition. Rich advised the army to allow an unlimited number of families of private soldiers to accompany the regiments to North America. This time, he secured the enthusiastic support of the Irish officials. They wholeheartedly agreed with Rich, urging the captains of the naval ships assigned to bring the troops to Canada to pack in "as many of the Wives and children" as wanted to go. They did not ask for approval from the secretary of state this time. The proposal may have gotten to Lord Halifax through back channels, but if he heard about the scheme, he chose to ignore it. Newspapers in Britain and America widely reported this unusual circumstance in which "women and children were permitted to go." Several reports added also that "the Men . . . went off with great Chearfulness," perhaps a contrast to the regiments that had set off for the West Indies the year before.

Robert Rich's determination to send as many families of soldiers as possible to North America was not the outpouring of a generous heart. Unlike the commanding officers of the regiments sent to the West Indies, Rich showed little concern for the emotions that might "fill the Breast" of a soldier. Keeping military families intact was not his goal; he was far more worried about the impact of destitute women and children on Irish towns and their budgets. But whatever Rich's intention, the result was a happy outcome for the regiments that were sent from Ireland in 1765. As the soldiers of the Twenty-Ninth Regiment set off for North America, their families came with them.

Inseparable Interests, 1766–67

J ane and Matthew Chambers, with their child, spent five weeks on the *Thunderer*. When the ship reached Halifax in July, its arrival made the newspapers in the colony of Massachusetts, four hundred miles south. All three Boston newspapers noted that the seventy-four-gun ship had crossed from Ireland "with 500 Troops, to relieve those which have been in Nova-Scotia several years." Neither the rotation of troops nor the size of the regiment came as real news to Bostonians; they were keeping an eye on both.

Massachusetts readers had more than an idle interest in the British army and in the British Empire's recent victories in Canada. In 1765, American colonists were thrilled to be part of the newly enlarged Britain. The Seven Years' War had not been easy on Massachusetts — nearly a third of its men between the ages of thirteen and thirty had served in the war alongside British regulars — but it had all seemed worth it, once the 1763 Treaty of Paris was signed. James Otis Jr., the new speaker of Boston's legislative body, the town meeting, had crowed in that same year, "We in America have certainly abundant reason to rejoice. The Heathen are not only driven out, but, the Canadians, much more formidable Enemies, are conquered and become Fellow-Subjects." By expelling indigenous Americans, Acadians, and the French government from Canada, the British army had done its job. Now it was time to allow the colonies, as Otis continued, "to begin so glorious an Empire as British America is rising to." It was the dawn of a splendid new age, and Bostonians could not wait for it to begin.

Even beyond the shared glories of world domination, colonists had reason to look forward to a joint future with Great Britain. Most of all, Otis concluded, the war made clear that the colonies and Great Britain were part of the same family. To make his point, he turned to the language of kinship. Appropriating the well-known phrases of the Anglican marriage ceremony, Otis said emphatically, "The true interests of Great Britain and her plantations are mutual, and what God in his providence has united, let no man dare attempt to pull asunder." As in any good eighteenth-century marriage, both parties shared a goal of economic stability as well as affection.

Colonists had been imagining themselves as part of the imperial family for decades. For them, the most fundamental element of that relationship was the great advantage that living in this family conferred on its members — including subordinate ones. As early as 1720, the governor of Massachusetts celebrated the "Wealth, Power, & Glory" of "Our Mother-Country, Great Britain." At the same time, he reminded his subjects that "these blessings reach us, tho' in a Lower and Remote sphere." The ruling member of the family was always Great Britain, while the colonies perched on a lower rung of the ladder. Unequal as the relationship might be, however, all the imperial family shared in its benefits.

The "Mother-Country, Great Britain" was by far the most common way that colonists talked about their relationship to the imperial family. Even in 1763, some Bostonians mocked Otis's grandiose ideas that the colonies might become Britain's wife rather than its children. A few months later, Otis's father revived the idea of colonies as children. "We love, esteem, and reverence our mother country," Otis Sr. claimed in 1764. As direct descendants of Great Britain, he continued, colonists were entitled to the same rights and privileges as any Briton. And so, when the colonists protested the new taxes that paid for the presence of troops in Canada and elsewhere after the war, they did so by calling out Britain's neglect of its responsibilities to its children. "Britannus-Americanus," writing in the *Boston Gazette*, assured his fellow colonists that "it will be always the interest and consequently the *wisdom* of a mother country, to retain the *good will* of her colonies." Editorialists hoped that the mother country was listening.

But the seamy underside of Britain's empire was apparent to anyone in Boston who chose to look. Destitute Acadians passed through Boston's streets. Enslaved Africans were offered for sale in every Boston newspaper that reprinted Otis's speech. Native Americans launched massive attacks on British forts, understanding that the British meant to "hem them in, and in the end extirpate them," as one British official reported. "Pontiac's War" came to a close in 1765 only after the Ottawa chief sent a peace pipe to the British diplomats, with a message stating that he had "taken the King for my father." Perhaps the Treaty of Paris that had ended the Seven Years' War was not an entirely unambiguous gift.

Certainly government officials in London quickly recognized the new challenges. As they thought about how to organize and admin-

ister the new British colonies, Massachusetts colonists began to wonder whether the newly expanded empire was going to be as glorious
as they had hoped. The king's ministers needed to raise money and
centralize management. Parliament had already paid for the war and,
now that it was over, was hoping for a peace dividend in England. It
was clear that money would not come from Parliament to pay for the
administration of empire. But North America still needed troops, and
moving whole regiments around this larger empire was expensive.
Raising taxes on colonial trade seemed like a good start.

In the summer of 1765, as the *Thunderer* was sailing the Atlantic,
Bostonians were feeling distinctly underappreciated. Having paid for
the war in "blood and treasure," they did not see why the new costs
of empire should fall on them. The British prime minister had recently announced that the army in America would be funded by a
new revenue stream—a tax on stamped, or embossed, paper, produced in London and used in the colonies. Parliament had already
declared a new tax on sugar the year before—the immediate cause
of James Otis's 1764 pamphlet, in which he tried to remind Britain of
its parental obligations to its colonies. The Sugar Act had provoked
grumbling; the Stamp Act would produce riots.

This new levy applied to many kinds of official paper: newspapers,
pamphlets, legal filings, bail bonds, and even college diplomas and
playing cards. By insisting that colonists purchase and use stamped
paper for official business, the Crown's officials would collect a tax
for every liquor license, every bill of lading that listed the goods in a
ship's hold, and every newspaper advertisement. The prime minister
had hoped the tax would be uncontroversial. He was completely mistaken. As a tax, the Stamp Act seemed perfectly designed to anger the

most vocal, most literate, and best-connected colonists in America: lawyers, journalists, and merchants. Their protests found plenty of support among their fellow colonists.

Among their supporters was a Boston merchant named John Rowe. In 1765, Rowe was about to turn fifty years old. He was hale, wealthy, and extraordinarily sociable. Almost any day of the year found him drinking at taverns, dancing at assemblies, riding his horse, fishing with other sportsmen, or entertaining at home with his wife and niece (whom he and his wife had adopted as a daughter). The merchant's friends spanned the political spectrum, from the cautious Massachusetts governor, Francis Bernard, to the governor's archenemy, the passionate Samuel Adams. Rowe had come to Boston as a young man from England and immediately launched his mercantile business. He had been cultivating his connections in Boston ever since.

For a merchant like Rowe, the Stamp Act was both a political and a financial problem. The act was to go into effect as of November 1, 1765. Rowe had until then to decide whether he would pay the tax on his bills of lading for his ships and the legal papers he needed to collect debts, or whether he would refuse, in an act of civil disobedience. Meanwhile, the merchant applied himself to protesting the proposed legislation. In September 1765, he worked with elected local representatives, including James Otis Jr. and Samuel Adams, as well as several Boston merchants to compose a letter of thanks on behalf of the town of Boston to the members of Parliament who had spoken out against the Stamp Act. The Boston Town Meeting, which had appointed Rowe to this committee, emphasized that the writers should thank the members of Parliament for their support of the "Rights and Privileges" of the colonies due to them as members of the imperial family. Their goal was to remind Parliament of their loyalty and connection to the British Empire.

Massachusetts was not alone in writing to Parliament. In the fall of 1765, representatives from nine colonies met in New York at a "Continental Congress" to write a formal petition to the king and Parliament, asking that the tax be rescinded. Angry as they were, the petitioners continued to stress their "warmest sentiments of affection and duty to His Majesty's Person and Government." Still pointing emphatically to their place in the imperial family, these representatives reminded the king that they were entitled to the same "inherent rights and liberties of his natural born subjects within the kingdom of Great-Britain." And as the king's children, they had a "duty" to their "mother country" to push back against any form of taxation that was passed without their representation in Parliament.

In Boston, however, not many people were willing to wait for the slow, deliberative process of holding a convention and signing petitions. By the summer of 1765, Bostonians were no less loyal than they had been at war's end in 1763, but they were angry. Many felt disrespected—especially those men who thought that they were entitled to be treated like any Briton when it came to taxation. And so, Bostonians took to the streets. In mid-August, Rowe awoke to find that protesters had hanged an effigy of the man who had become the official Massachusetts distributor of stamped paper. A notice pinned to the sleeve read "What greater Joy Can New England see / Than Stamp men hanging on a tree." Crowds ceremoniously burned the dummy figure of the stamp distributor, then pulled down the building designated as his office. They also did some damage to his house. The day after watching his effigy tortured, the Crown official re-

signed. Two weeks later, another crowd did further damage to the
man's property. In his diary, Rowe lamented the "mischief" done to
the stamp distributor's house but was studiously silent on the street
protest itself.

This sort of "controlled rioting" was in fact a common and even
acceptable part of British political life. In a time when many decisions
were made in private meetings between ministers, and even parlia-
mentary debates were not necessarily open to the public, most Britons
—rich and poor, male and female, young and old—made their political opinions known through parades, placards, and street theater.
Yet although Britain's political culture permitted mass protests, the
government also reined in potential violence with official shows of
force. Mayors, magistrates, and other political leaders regularly asked
the government to send troops in to control the people in the street.
And America in 1765 was no different.

Within a month of the Twenty-Ninth Regiment's arrival in Canada, colonial governors began considering whether to request troops
in the wake of the summer Stamp Act disturbances in Boston and
elsewhere. Matthew Chambers and his mates, now in Halifax, had
had some experience facing hostile crowds; two summers earlier,
two Irish magistrates had requisitioned Captain Pierce Butler's company to put down a riot of several thousand men. That time, Butler
boasted, the mere presence and "intrepidity" of his company terrified
the crowd so much that they ran away. A lieutenant from the same
regiment, Jeremiah Meara, was awarded a generous pension for sin-
glehandedly capturing the two ringleaders of the protest, who were
marching "at the head of some thousands of insurgents, completely
armed," and thereby breaking up the riot. Officers and soldiers alike

from the Twenty-Ninth Regiment were more accustomed to facing rioters than engaging enemy soldiers. The Massachusetts governor certainly could not turn to the Boston militia to control the protesters; they were among the agitators. Turning to the British military seemed a better idea. The Twenty-Ninth Regiment went on alert.

The Massachusetts governor, Francis Bernard, was certainly tempted to call for troops. His neighbor to the south, Lieutenant Governor Cadwallader Colden of New York, had already done so, the month before. Twenty-five years earlier, white New Yorkers had executed over thirty enslaved men and four whites, convinced that they were part of a plot to free slaves and hand the city over to their Spanish enemies. In 1765, Colden was not quite sure whether he needed the soldiers "to quell Tumults amongst the Populace, or Insurrections of the Negroes." Apparently, a slave revolt and a political protest seemed equally dangerous, or equally likely, to the New York governor. At any rate, Colden knew that he wanted soldiers in New York early in the summer, despite the lack of any actual riots. For permission, Colden needed to turn to General Thomas Gage.

The general had been stationed in North America since the beginning of the Seven Years' War. As he made his way up the ranks of the army, he settled into life in America, marrying a wealthy and well-connected New Jersey woman named Margaret Kemble. When he became commander in chief of all the British forces in North America, Gage oversaw the use of the American garrison to control both the colonial trade with Native Americans and the political upheavals in the port towns.

Gage did not begrudge Colden the troops, but he did warn him that using soldiers for civil policing was a delicate job. "It is needless for me to tell you," he reminded the New York governor, "that the Military can do nothing by themselves; but must act wholy and solely in obedience to the Civil Power ... they are no longer under my Command, or can the officers do any thing with their Men, but what the Civil Magistrate shall command." In other words, the buck stopped with the governor, not the army. It could not be clearer that Gage was washing his hands of the whole business. Perhaps Gage foresaw a disaster brewing by dispatching troops to New York. If so, his crystal ball was a little cloudy; he should have been looking farther north, toward Massachusetts.

After two rowdy protests in August 1765, Governor Bernard panicked. The day after a second crowd tore down parts of the house of Thomas Hutchinson, the lieutenant governor of Massachusetts, Bernard went to pieces. He fled to Castle William, the fort on an island in Boston Harbor, feeling completely powerless and "extreamly weak" in the face of a popular uprising. "I had not the least authority to oppose or quiet the mob," he remembered. He was sure his government had completely collapsed. "In short, The Town of Boston is in the possession of an incensed & implacable Mob," he scrawled in a desperate letter to Gage, which he did not dare to send; he knew that his advisory council opposed undertaking this correspondence. If only, he lamented privately, the general would send some troops to restore his authority.

But when, a couple of weeks later, in September 1765, General Gage finally did offer troops to police Boston (an offer Gage made unasked, surmising correctly that Bernard was "affraid to demand them"), Bernard turned them down. The immediate crisis seemed to be ebbing. Nonetheless, Bernard insisted that the situation was still

dire. "Indeed," he warned the general darkly, "the Power & Authority of Government is really at an End." Bernard hoped, however, that
he could exploit the protests for his own political ends. Certainly,
he thought that he would have more luck positioning himself as the
victim of protests than as the man in charge of a small company of
soldiers who would likely do nothing more than "irritate the people
and not protect the government." Besides, he knew that he had to
get the approval of the Governor's Council before he could agree to
accept troops as a police force, and the council would never permit it.
By exaggerating the threat to the royal government, Bernard hoped
to compel the ministers in Britain to simply send over a large force
and take all the decisions out of his hands. In part, at least, he would
get his wish.

Meanwhile, the Twenty-Ninth Regiment, cold and bored, had settled in Halifax. On the positive side, there were no rioters there for
them to face down. By the next year, 1766, it seemed as though most
of the conflicts in the American colonies had blown over. Parliament
had retracted the Stamp Act. Although the problem of wresting taxes
from the colonies remained unresolved, the imperial relationship
seemed to have healed. In 1766, Bostonians filled the newspapers with
extravagant promises of "subordination to the Mother Country,"
which arose from "a natural and warm affection." Once again, they
celebrated their familial ties to England.

John Rowe was an especially enthusiastic booster of these ties. The
letter he wrote to the members of Parliament, thanking them for
their support in arguing against the Stamp Act, was only one of many
that he wrote on behalf of the Boston Town Meeting in the 1760s.
He penned notes constantly, thanking famous Britons for funds, for

portraits, even for the "behavior and good services" of a naval captain who regularly stopped at Boston Harbor.

This last expression of gratitude must have seemed insufficient to Rowe, or at least a little dry. The day after the town meeting had charged him and several others with first writing an "address" to Captain John Lewis Gideon of the HMS *Jamaica* and then offering him in person the thanks of the town of Boston, he put together a far more elaborate tribute to the naval captain. In December 1766, he and forty-five other merchants gave Gideon a goodbye party that allowed Rowe to express, very fully, exactly how he hoped Massachusetts would be included as part of the British imperial family.

Rowe himself presided over the dinner, and "a very Genteel Entertainment it was," he noted in his diary. Rowe's primary responsibility as host was to be the toastmaster, and he recorded in his diary the twenty-seven toasts that he had given, to which the other men had drunk. Eighteenth-century toasts were both lengthy and carefully scripted. Rowe started with the loyal toast to George III. He offered the next toasts to "2. The Queen & Her Family. 3. The Parliament of Great Britain. 4. His Majesty's Ministry." The men, colonial merchants and naval officer alike, drank heartily. Even more than the letters, protests, and pamphlets in which colonists declared their undying affection to their fictive mother, drinking allowed them to share their feelings of loyalty publicly and enthusiastically. In the decades to follow, some of the men at that dinner would come to see their interests and affections in opposition to Great Britain's. But at that moment in 1766, no one could foretell the future.

After drinking to twelve separate English politicians, to administrative boards like "the Lords of Trade" (toast number eighteen), and to "the Army and Navy" (toast number twenty), Rowe turned to more abstract ideas. He urged the men to drink to "the United and Inseparable Interest of Great Britain & Her Colonies." If they were still sober enough by the twenty-second toast to understand the sentiment, the merchants were giving their approval to their dependence on the British Empire. By the time Rowe and his friends sent Gideon off, with a final toast to "A Good Voyage to the *Jamaica,*" they may not have been able to express many rational ideas about the ideal colonial-imperial relationship. Nonetheless, they staggered home in harmonious goodwill as fellow Britons.

That same winter of 1766, as Rowe and his friends drank to "the Army and Navy," more members of the British armed forces were settling into Halifax. As part of the Crown's plan to keep the regiments circulating around the empire, five new regiments were supposed to move into North America in 1766, and the Fourteenth Regiment would be one of them. From 1752 to 1759, the Fourteenth Regiment had been in Gibraltar, until its return to England. Gibraltar's weather may have been more pleasant than Canada's, but it was a deadlier posting, only in part because of its proximity to the French invasion of Minorca.

To fill out its rolls again once back in England, the regiment's recruiting officers advertised for "All Gentleman Volunteers that have Spirit and Resolution" and who were drawn by the generous wartime bounty of a five-guinea enlistment bonus. In England, the Fourteenth Regiment spent the rest of the Seven Years' War moving around the country, occasionally guarding the coast at Dover Castle or Plymouth against possible invasion. Unlike the Twenty-Ninth Regiment, the Fourteenth had spent no time putting down rioters or acting in any other way as backup for civil magistrates. In 1766 the War Office put the regiment on notice that its pattern of marching around England was about to shift. In April, orders came down that they were "to hold themselves in readiness to embark speedily for America." They could not know that they would not return to England until after the American Revolution had begun.

On June 30, the entire Fourteenth Regiment, along with "women, servants, and baggage," embarked on four transport ships from Portsmouth. Taking command of the regiment was Lieutenant Colonel William Dalrymple, thirty years old, with ten years of military service under his belt, including a stint fighting against the Spanish invasion of Portugal four years earlier. His promotion from major had come only the year before, and he was still figuring out how to administer his regiment. One of his first gaffes involved military wives.

Like the Twenty-Ninth Regiment, the Fourteenth brought far more than the standard sixty women from Europe. When the *Dolphin,* the *Eagle,* the *Sally,* and the *Neptune* sailed from England, Dalrymple had allowed many families to embark. Apparently in the six years since the regiment had returned to England (and bulked up its rolls with "Gentleman Volunteers"), men had found English wives. Privates such as Samuel Marsh, for example, married Elizabeth Beckley while he was stationed at Dover Castle in 1765. With little formal discussion, Dalrymple allowed the "whole" number of women, including Elizabeth, to sail with their husbands. He had even, until the Crown accountants caught the error, charged their travel costs to the regimental budget.

When the Fourteenth Regiment reached Halifax in mid-August 1766, its members and those of the Twenty-Ninth met for the first time. One officer's reputation, however, had preceded him. In February, the Halifax newspaper republished a bit of news about the Fourteenth Regiment from the time when it was stationed in England the previous year. A sergeant found drunk while on duty had been subjected to such unusually harsh flogging that he died a few days later. The event made such a stir in the nearby town of Winchester that a civilian grand jury had charged with murder the captain who had overseen the punishment. Although the *Halifax Gazette* did not name this captain, other newspapers identified him as Captain Brabazon O'Hara. In the end he was acquitted, but not until the secretary of state had ordered, in advance, a stay of execution for O'Hara, had he been found guilty. The stay made it highly unlikely that O'Hara ever would be punished for the man's death. Nonetheless, this story would come back to haunt O'Hara.

In the abstract, the British army, the "Lords of Trade," and even "the United and Inseparable Interest of Great Britain & Her Colonies" seemed worth celebrating with toasts and cheer in Boston in 1766. No army regiments occupied the town, and the Lords of Trade were far across an ocean. It would not be long, however, before both came to Boston.

3

Seasons of Discontent, 1766–68

One May day in 1767, after John Rowe had dined with nine of his close friends, he mentioned to his diary that "Mr. Dalrymple, an officer," had been with them as well. He made no comment on why Lieutenant Colonel Dalrymple of the Fourteenth Regiment was in Boston, rather than with his regiment, which had been stationed since the previous summer in Halifax. Possibly more important to this avid fisherman was the fact that, after dinner, he and two friends went fishing at Jamaica Pond, a few miles west of Boston.

Boston Harbor, with its convivial hubbub and luxurious dining, was a far cry from Halifax, and in fact there was no mystery as to why a regimental officer stationed in the latter would welcome time away. Three years earlier, when the Chamberses had sailed into Halifax's harbor, they found little merriment in Nova Scotia. One correspondent wrote a few years later of his own introduction to the town, saying, "The prospect appeared very discouraging and disagreeable; nothing but barren rocks and hills presented themselves to our view along the coast. This unfavorable appearance greatly damped the spirits of most of the passengers, and several of them began to wish them-

selves in Old England before they had set foot in Nova-Scotia." When
they landed in Halifax, they found a tiny settlement around a large
harbor. Overlooking the harbor, a citadel crowned a very tall hill.
Another fort marked off land farther down the hill. Besides these two
forts, a small cluster of warehouses lined the water and docks. That
was the entire town.

Not including the soldiers and their families, the town of Halifax
had a population of about three thousand. The great majority were
single white men: a census taken two years after the Chamberses disembarked recorded nearly twice as many white men as white women.
There was a small scattering of black families (thirty-five adults and
nineteen children), probably a mix of enslaved and free. Almost half
of the people were born in North America, but those were most likely
to be the children, who made up more than a third of the population.
An Irish family like the Chamberses might well have felt at home:
not including the nearly twelve hundred children, the majority of
the rest of the population was Irish by origin. All of the Irish were
Protestants: Irish Catholics were not permitted to join the army and
received no government support for immigration to Canada.

Once off the ship, the Chambers family tried to make a life for
themselves as they had in Ireland. They were safer than they had been
on the open ocean, and certainly healthier. But Halifax was both bor-
ing and uncomfortable. The War Office considered Halifax a holding
pen for soldiers, much like Ireland, but with worse weather. Armed
conflict with Native Americans seemed unlikely in eastern Canada, so
there was little need for extensive guard duty. There was nothing to
do but wait.

Officers too found this posting terribly tedious. The problem was not Canada itself: Quebec and Montreal were vibrant cities. There, members of an officer's family could find themselves in the midst of an endless social whirl. An officer stationed in Quebec while the Twenty-Ninth was in Halifax wrote home that his wife had found that "her taste is rather more refined since she came to town and turned a fine lady, every day dressed out as for an assembly, introduced to colonels, majors, and captains . . . in short, it is a very gay and extravagant place." By contrast, officers found Halifax, as one Irish officer wrote a few years later, "a shocking place of itself."

The ways in which young officers amused themselves in Halifax did not make them particularly popular. They used the locals' goats for target practice. They went fishing. And they drank heavily.

In one notorious — but not unusual — incident, young officers terrorized local tavern keepers and officials. On a May morning in 1766, four bored junior officers wandered into a tavern a few miles from Halifax. They ordered a dinner to be ready at midday, then began drinking. By two o'clock, when dinner was served, the four together had polished off seven bottles. By six in the evening, they had drunk even more. Then they proceeded to beat the tavern keeper with their swords and threatened a magistrate with a pistol. Twenty-nine-year-old Lieutenant William Monsell screamed at the magistrate that he was "a Rascal, a Scoundrel, and Villain" before he and the other regimental officers began punching the man. Another man tried to defuse the situation by pleading with the officers to have some pity on the magistrate's pregnant wife, who was standing in the doorway. Lieutenant Monsell, then still in the street with a drawn sword, swore that "if he could get at her, he would rip the child out of her." After trying to shoot the magistrate with his own pistol, the officers attempted to blow up the tavern with gunpowder, as the tavern keeper hid in the cellar with his terrified family. Passersby tried to defend the magistrate, and corporals and sergeants stood by, watching the actions of their commanding officers. The situation might easily have escalated to a full-scale riot. Only the fact that the officers were too drunk to set the powder on fire prevented a massacre.

When hauled into court on charges of assault, the officers apologized profusely to the judges, admitting that they were "intirely insensible of what we might have done." The officers did not mention their assault on the tavern keeper but expressed regret for attacking the magistrate. In a nod to the police work that many of them knew would be part of their regiment's assignment as peacetime soldiers, they admitted that they were "fully sensible that by our Profession, we are obliged to support the Civil Magistrates in the Exercise of their office and not to insult them." The court accepted their apology, but the local judges were not feeling indulgent. They fined the offending officers the hefty sum of fifty pounds apiece. Halifax officials were not antimilitary rabble-rousers (in fact, the governor later remitted the fines), but they had no interest in allowing the army to wreak havoc.

Drinking and brawling were not every officer's favorite way to while away his posting in Canada. In fact, most simply left, if they could. "Regimental disputes" drove a Captain Steele to take the first boat he could find back to Europe, once his commanding officer gave him permission. The following winter, Ensign Alexander Mall pleaded with General Gage to give him a leave of absence "to visit his friends in Virginia." Most officers eager for escape from Halifax sailed to Boston. Captain Thomas Preston was on a schooner to Boston within three months of his arrival in Halifax; Captain Mallows and three servants sailed the following June. Captain Ponsonby Molesworth lasted until November 1766 before he left for Massachusetts. Officers' wives fled to Boston too, if they could manage it.

One major from the Twenty-Ninth Regiment was determined to make his home in America, but he hoped for something rather more comfortable than Halifax. We have seen that Major Pierce Butler had, back in Ireland, acquired experience in putting down a riot of several thousand protesters. While posted to Canada, Butler made a determined effort to find a wife in South Carolina, a colony he had probably visited during an earlier posting, with a different regiment, in 1761. There he hoped to elope with a fifteen-year-old heiress, but her stepfather intervened. After a winter of soap-opera-worthy drama, the following spring the heiress married the governor's son. Butler unsuccessfully challenged her new husband to a duel; when the young man refused to fight, Butler simply assaulted him. The major soon found himself overstaying his leave from his regiment while also facing an assault charge in the South Carolina courts. It took Butler another three years to find a wealthy woman willing to marry him. Despite the duel —and losing out on his first attempt to find a rich wife—Butler did manage to avoid staying in Canada for most of his Canadian posting.

Officers who could not leave were miserable, often physically. A typical complaint was made by an Irish officer who wrote home to Dublin, "I've been very ill with Biles & the Scurvy." Scurvy was the bane of eighteenth-century armies, especially in Canada. Ten years earlier, during the siege of Quebec, great numbers of British soldiers had died from vitamin C deficiency. Fresh food, especially fruits and vegetables containing vitamin C, were hard to come by in winter. The newest medical research at the time held that scurvy was really a form of body rot (or "putrification") that could be slowed by a proper diet, made up of fruits, vegetables, fermented food and alcoholic drink, including wine. Experts also claimed that it was necessary to rid one's body of potential putrefaction by sweating. When fresh vegetables were not available, soldiers made do with vinegar or wine. A Lieutenant Colonel Leslie wrote home that he had had "no Vegetables but Madeira all the Winter, I've really been very sober, but the severe Cold shut the Pores and stops Perspiration — I hope to be able to pass my next Winter at New York." Another winter in Halifax, he feared, might kill him.

If his substitution of Madeira for vegetables kept Lieutenant Colonel Leslie moderately sober and scurvy-free, he was more fortunate than others in Canada. In 1766, one soldier explained that at St. John's in Newfoundland, "it is no uncommon thing to behold Men that have only remained a few Years here, reduced to mere Ideots by Drink and Debauchery. When a Soldier sees no Prospect of being speedily relieved from such a Country as this, his Spirits become depressed and he flyes to Liquor to raise them, which soon grows into a habit, and the Man of course good for nothing."

Those who had come from the more moderate climate of Ireland or England were shocked at the cold. Newspapers throughout North America reported that in January of the first winter that the Twenty-Ninth Regiment was in Canada, the temperature fell to seven degrees below zero (Fahrenheit) and never rose above three degrees. The newspapers insisted that even Native Americans could not remember such cold weather over the past forty years. It froze even the brandy and rum.

The privates of the Twenty-Ninth Regiment had far fewer op-

portunities for travel than did their officers. A rising birthrate, however, suggests how they might have spent the chilly winters. In two
years, a town of 3,000 people had about 300 births. After three years
in Halifax, the local minister claimed that there were 250 men of the
Twenty-Ninth Regiment in the settlement (the rest were scattered
among rural outposts throughout Nova Scotia), and the same number
of women and children. A few men married local women. In 1767,
for example, a private named William Clinton married the Nova Scotian Ann Dixon. William apparently grew so attached to Halifax that
twenty-five years later he asked for an army discharge to move back
to Canada. But overall, most of the regiment's children were born to
women who had traveled from Ireland. Jane and Matthew Chambers
too welcomed another child, a daughter.

The meager food, drafty housing, and harsh weather were hard on
children. Jane's infant was sickly, but luckier than others. One of her
shipmates on the *Thunderer,* Catherine Charloe, was one of several
army women whose child died during a Canadian winter. Catherine
and her husband, James Charloe, were no strangers to harsh conditions. Both had been born in the West Indies and had come to Ireland late in the 1750s. Both were black; both were free. A year and a
half after they had disembarked in Halifax, they buried their daughter
Catherine.

Privates could make a little extra money building roads or helping
to bring in the harvest. When it came to building the barracks, they
were paid also, but the army regulated the rates strictly. Except for
the foreman, a soldier could earn only nine pence per day "on the
King's work." Working for the province of Nova Scotia or individual farmers, however, meant that soldiers could negotiate their own

prices. The province was so grateful for the extra hands that its assembly offered the two commanding officers a vote of thanks for "their generous regard to the Interest of the Province." Knowing full well that he himself had done nothing to warrant the assembly's thanks for the troops' "ready and cheerful aid," the commanding officer, Lieutenant Colonel Maurice Carr, wondered if the fulsome gratitude was due to the fact that the soldiers were willing to work for less than the market price. At the very least, he told Gage, he had "never heard the Gentlemen or country People Complain that the Soldiers ask'd more Wages than the Customary price of Labour in the Province."

But General Gage warned officers against becoming too chummy with local officials. "You are to consider Halifax as a Station for the Troops till His Majesty's Service shall require them to be transported, to any other part of the World, not posted there for the sake of the Province of Nova Scotia."

Halifax's population grew during the summer of 1766, when the Fourteenth Regiment joined the Twenty-Ninth in the citadel. For privates of both regiments, life in Halifax ground on, in its tedium and unpleasantness. The week before Christmas 1766, one private from the Fourteenth Regiment, carrying a load of wood, slipped on the ice-covered street and smashed his skull on his own load of kindling, dying almost instantly.

Unsurprisingly, like the officers of the Twenty-Ninth Regiment the year before, the newly arrived officers of the Fourteenth tried to leave as soon as possible. After he suffered through one winter in Halifax, Lieutenant John Stanton took a vacation to Jamaica for the next one. Similarly, twenty-five-year-old Captain Edmund Mason decided to spend his winter in New York City.

Lieutenant Colonel William Dalrymple joined the general exodus of officers to head for the pleasures of New York, where he stayed for the winter of 1767–68. But come springtime, he had to return to Halifax. On his way back, in May 1768, he stopped once again in Boston to greet the local notables.

John Rowe once more noted Dalrymple's arrival in his diary, and invited him to dinner a few weeks later, just one year after their first get-together. A few days later, Dalrymple sailed again for Nova Scotia.

Bostonians' ability to socialize across political hostilities was on full display that summer of 1768. Nonetheless, Dalrymple's dinner with the Bostonians might not have been so easily convivial if it had occurred only a week later. By then hostilities in Boston had begun to boil over. The troubles had started a half year earlier, and John Rowe again found himself in the thick of things. The new Chancellor of the Exchequer, Charles Townshend, had decided a new round of import taxes would serve the dual purpose of raising funds and making it easier to administer the far-flung empire. When the news of Townshend's eponymous customs duties became public in the fall of 1767, Rowe got involved with the resistance. The Boston Town Meeting appointed him and several other merchants to a committee to organize a boycott of those newly taxed goods. Rowe and others convinced over 660 people, including 53 women, to sign an agreement to stop buying those particular imported goods.

The following spring, Rowe organized an even more far-reaching boycott. Rather than simply ask consumers not to buy the taxed goods, Rowe and his fellow merchants agreed to stop importing them at all. By putting economic pressure on their suppliers, Boston merchants hoped their British counterparts would help agitate for an appeal of the taxes. Other towns, both in Massachusetts and in other colonies, soon also created nonimportation agreements.

Apparently unperturbed by — or perhaps simply unaware of — the resistance gathering in Massachusetts, Townshend decided to make Boston the headquarters of the customs service. That meant that the men responsible for overseeing the new taxes, known as the Board of Customs Commissioners, would be living in a town of only sixteen thousand people. Collecting import taxes in the eighteenth century was a face-to-face job, not buried beneath layers of impersonal red tape. Initially Bostonians accepted the customs officials socially, even if they resented their work. As Ann Hulton, sister of one of the newly arrived customs officials, explained to a friend back in England, "As Gentlemen [Bostonians] would treat 'em with great Civility, but as Commissioners most dreadful threatenings are denounced against all."

When the customs commissioners acted in their official capacity to seize the sloop of one of Boston's wealthiest and most politically prominent men, John Hancock, on accusations of smuggling, Bostonians reacted swiftly. They organized a large street protest that included stoning the houses of commissioners and burning, on the Boston Common, a commissioner's personal racing sailboat. After the riot subsided, William Molineux, a close political ally of Hancock, wrote a note of apology to the commissioner who had lost his boat. The destruction of his property, Molineux assured him, was nothing personal.

Unaccustomed to Boston's unruly street politics, the commissioners were terrified. Ann Hulton was surprised at the extent of property damage that the crowd was willing to engage in. "We soon found," she explained by letter to a friend in England, "that the Mobs here are very different from those in O[ld] England, where a few lights put into the Windows will pacify, or the interposition of a Magistrate restrain them." Governor Francis Bernard washed his hands of any responsibility for the customs officials' personal safety, so on June 11 the commissioners and their families fled to a British navy gunship, which happened to be moored in Boston Harbor. After nine days onboard (during which time, Hulton reassured her friend, they were "well accommodated, & very genteelly entertained"), the commissioners, their families, and their staff all moved out to the fort on Castle Island in Boston Harbor.

From the ship, Hulton's brother and the other commissioners penned a desperate plea to General Gage, who was in charge of all North American troops, in the hope that he would send troops to rescue them. They were sure that Governor Bernard would not put in a formal request "without the advice of his Council, which measure we do not imagine They will recommend." The commissioners knew they did not have the authority to request military backup, so all they could do was "write to acquaint Your Excellency of the very alarming State of Things at Boston, and leave it to your judgment to act as you shall think proper."

The customs commissioners were quite right that Bernard did not want to ask Gage directly to send in a regiment or two. As he had three years earlier, after the Stamp Act riots, Bernard still preferred a more indirect approach, hoping that the decision would be taken out of his hands. When he received the commissioners' letter in late June, Gage alerted Dalrymple, the commanding officer in Halifax, that he should start preparing soldiers to move to Boston. At the same time, however, Gage warned Bernard, as he had earlier warned Bernard's counterpart in New York, that Gage himself had no authority to order troops into a British settlement during peacetime; that was a job for the civilian authorities, not the military. A flurry of sealed letters among Gage, Dalrymple, and Bernard gave the governor hope that troops would come without his explicit request. Bernard was convinced that if anyone learned he had asked for troops, he would be stoned, or worse. He suggested to Dalrymple that the officer allow him to maintain plausible deniability if asked whether he had ordered the troops. Meanwhile, he wrote to Dalrymple, they should communicate by means of "private hints." Unfortunately for both Dalrymple and Bernard, this mode of conducting business did not make for effective planning. And so matters remained at a standstill for the summer, at least to the best of their knowledge.

But as Bernard was trying to communicate with Dalrymple by means of his too-subtle hints, the secretary of state, the Earl of Hillsborough, had already made up his mind that the Massachusetts governor needed help. In June, several days before the customs commissioners took refuge in Boston Harbor, Hillsborough had ordered Gage to send at least one regiment from Halifax to Boston to "give every legal Assistance to the Civil Magistrate in the preservation of the Public Peace and to the Officers of the Revenue in the Execution of the Laws of Trade & Revenue."

Once news of the commissioners' flight to Castle Island had reached England in July, however, Hillsborough agreed with the commissioners that one regiment would be insufficient to pacify Boston. He turned first to Ireland, where he deployed two regiments, the Sixty-Fourth and the Sixty-Fifth, directly to Boston. One thousand men embarked on September 1 from Cork. Hillsborough's orders included only the "usual allowances" for women. More concerned with rules and regulations than Lieutenant Colonel Dalrymple of the Fourteenth Regiment had been, the senior officer coming from Ireland—General Alexander Mackay of the Sixty-Fifth Regiment—was careful to request rations for only the sixty women permitted by the War Office.

The governor and commissioners may have been miserable, but their families seemed to be enjoying themselves. July on an island in Boston Harbor could be quite idyllic. To Ann Hulton, Castle William "appear[ed] delightful & a most Agreeable Summer Retreat." Part of the pleasure, she expounded to her friend, was that it was a hub of social activity. Castle Island was no deserted place "in a state of banishment, secluded from Society or the rest of the World." In fact, she thought her friend should imagine Castle William "rather like one of the Public water drinking places in England," like Bath or Tunbridge Wells. "We have a great many Visitors come every Day from Boston incog[nito], and are seldom less than twenty at dinner," she exulted. "We live luxuriously." Castle William might not have had all the pleasures of the Pump Room in Bath, but many enjoyed its social whirl. Even John Rowe, still leading the opposition to the Townshend Acts, brought a large party, including his wife and adopted daughter, out to the fort one fine afternoon. Politics rarely stood in the way of sociability at this time.

In fact, politics added a pinch of witty spice to Hulton's summer vacation. In July 1768, the Boston newspapers printed one of the colonies' first hit songs, John Dickinson's "Liberty Song." Sung to the rousing 1758 tune "Hearts of Oak," the lyrics took direct aim at the Townshend Acts that Hulton's brother was there to enforce.

> *COME join hand in hand brave AMERICANS all,*
> *And rouse your bold hearts at fair LIBERTY'S call;*
> *No tyrannous acts shall suppress your just claim,*
> *Or stain with dishonour AMERICA'S name*
>
> *In FREEDOM we're born and in FREEDOM we'll live,*
> *Our purses are ready,*
> *Steady, Friends, steady,*
> *Not as SLAVES, but as FREEMEN our Money we'll give.*

The song was so popular that even the pro-government *Boston Chronicle* reprinted it, along with an advertisement for the sheet music. Perhaps after hearing her dinner guests hum the catchy melody all summer, Ann Hulton had had enough. Given her sense of sly humor, her disgust at Boston mobs, and her sheer amazement at the rudeness of Boston politics, she might have written this parody, published a few weeks later:

> *Come shake your dull Noddles, ye Pumpkins and bawl,*
> *And own that you're mad at fair Liberty's Call,*
> *No scandalous Conduct can add to your Shame.*
> *Condemn'd to Dishonor, Inherit the Fame—*

[Chorus:]

> *In Folly you're born, and in Folly you'll live,*
> *To Madness still ready,*
> *And Stupidly steady,*
> *Not as Men, but as Monkies, the Tokens you give.*

It continued for another nine verses, each more biting than the last. The author of the parody never was revealed, but three clues point to Ann Hulton. The headnote on the newspaper publication clearly indicated that it was someone living at Castle William. It was printed with a note claiming that *"Last Tuesday the following SONG made its Appearance from a Garret at C—st—e W——m."* The parody's first place of publication was the anti-government *Boston Gazette,* an odd choice for a song mocking the anthem of the governor's opposition party. It could only have been printed there if one of Ann Hulton's friends from the oppositional liberty party, such as John Rowe, had brought it to the printer for her. Finally, directly beneath the parody, the *Boston Gazette* reproduced what it titled an "EXCULPATORY letter" from Ann's brother Henry Hulton, in which he warned that he had heard the newspaper planned to publish his name as the author of the parody. He angrily insisted that the newspaper would do so "at [its] peril." Perhaps Henry Hulton was responding to a rumor that the song's author was actually his sister?

Whether or not Ann Hulton actually penned the parody, the clever rejoinder reveals the sort of amusements that those summering on Castle William engaged in. Wordplay, singing, and sarcasm kept the commissioners diverted until the fall of 1768, when they decided it was safe to return to Boston. Moreover, the commissioners finally felt that they had some support that could be trusted more than Governor Bernard: four regiments of the British army.

By the end of August, Gage sent Governor Bernard a blank requisition order that he could use to call up to two regiments from Halifax, in addition to the two preparing to embark from Ireland. He sent the order for the Fourteenth Regiment's deployment to Bernard for his signature. "I . . . left a Blank in the Letter," he explained to Bernard, "to fill up with the like order for the 29th Regt. in case you shall . . . not think one Regiment as sufficient Force." Remembering Bernard's fears about what might happen if the Governor's Council were to find out that he had requested troops, the general added, "The Contents of this . . . will be kept a profound secret, at least on this side of the Atlantick."

Throughout September, Bernard tried desperately to enact his plan of deflecting blame for the request for troops, knowing how deeply unpopular their arrival would be. Less than a week after Bernard received Gage's letter with the blank order form, John Rowe noted in his diary, "The Governor told me in Conversation yesterday morning that he had Stav'd off the Introducing Troops as long as he could but could do it no longer." One wonders whether Rowe believed Bernard's disingenuous claim. After all, there had been rumors for months that troops were coming.

Neither General Gage in New York nor Lieutenant Colonel Dalrymple in Halifax was particularly pleased with the idea of sending troops to Boston. Both were disgusted by Bernard's spinelessness. Dalrymple blamed Bernard for the commissioners' fears in Boston, eagerly passing on to Gage the unflattering gossip he had picked up about the governor: "if what I hear of him is true, his timidity is in a great measure the cause of the present tumults."

Dalrymple also feared that Bernard's cowardice was going to hurt his own career. The instructions for his command in Boston, which Dalrymple had received from the War Office, seemed to imply the possibility that a major incident was brewing, something much larger than one might expect from a small provincial town. "They seem better calculated for a riot in London, than for directing the conduct of an officer in New England," the lieutenant colonel fretted to Gage.

Gage obliquely acknowledged Dalrymple's critical comments about Governor Bernard, while trying to reassure him that he would have the authority to do what was necessary. "As this appears to be a service of a delicate nature and possibly leading to consequences not easily foreseen, I think proper, relying on your Prudence, Resolution, and Integrity, to appoint you to the Command of the said Force."

For his part, Gage wondered how the presence of troops could support the government if the governor was too cowardly to call them out. Gage suspected that Bernard was getting cold feet even before the troops embarked from Halifax. In a letter to Lord Barrington, written as the troops were preparing to leave, Gage sneered, "Two Regiments are ordered to Boston from Halifax and some People who wished it, seem to be frightened now they are comeing." As for himself, he added, "I can't foretell any occasion to fear bad consequences."

Lieutenant Colonel Dalrymple and Lieutenant Colonel Carr began to organize the embarkations. There were naval ships already waiting in Halifax's harbor, several of which would travel regularly back and forth between Boston and Halifax. Using navy transports made the move easy for the commanders, since there was no need to haggle over hiring private ships. But it had a downside for privates and their families. Admiral Samuel Hood, in charge of the embarkations, would not put any families on the navy ships, leaving Dalrymple to find transport for the women and children. By September 20, two regiments, families and all, were on their way to Boston.

4

Under One Roof, 1768

The sun was rising through a fair blue sky in late September as the
flotilla got underway. More than a dozen ships, ranging from
the forty-gun *Launceston* to unarmed sloops, carried over a thousand
men and hundreds of women and children toward Boston. The journey took more than a week, and it would have been a relief to everyone to tack past the lighthouse that marked the beginning of outer
Boston Harbor, even if they were still four or five miles away from
Boston itself. From the ship rail, all that Matthew Chambers would
have seen in the distance was a handful of church spires on a hilly
landscape.

The next day, a Thursday, the flotilla sailed as far as the final pair of
islands guarding the entrance to Boston Harbor. At noon, each ship
dropped a single anchor in front of the flagpole of Castle William, the
large square fort on Castle Island. Chambers and other soldiers of the
Twenty-Ninth Regiment must have regarded the fort with curiosity.
The stone barracks looked far sturdier than the rotten wooden structures they had endured in Halifax. There, the damp had rotted away
most of their bedding, and for over a year Lieutenant Colonel Mau-

A view of Boston from the sea reinforces its connection to Britain's overseas empire.

rice Carr refused to order replacements, theorizing that they would simply rot again. It was not long before some of the men chose to make their beds out of leaves.

By contrast, the Castle Island barracks had been renovated a decade earlier, when the Massachusetts legislature, in the early days of the Seven Years' War, allocated nearly a thousand pounds to upgrade and winterize them. Chambers might have heard the rumor that General Gage himself had ordered the Twenty-Ninth to stay in these snug barracks. Lieutenant Colonel Dalrymple, now in charge of all the troops en route to Boston, had received the order in a letter from Gage, his commander, before they had sailed.

But as the soldiers waited on the ships all afternoon, they saw no dinghies coming alongside to bring troops to shore. The next morning Dalrymple and James Smith, the captain of the flotilla, hurried up the path to the fort. The lieutenant colonel expected a frustrating argument about where to quarter the troops and who would foot the bill; the Massachusetts governor had alerted him that agreement on these issues would not be simple, but Dalrymple hoped that a little diplomacy could smooth over the matter.

In the council chamber of Castle William, Dalrymple found the governor and his council. The latter consisted of ten men, all elected by the Massachusetts legislature and given control of the purse strings of the province of Massachusetts. They had the power to allocate the space and the funds for quartering troops. Recalling his previous two social visits to Boston, Dalrymple tried to win over his audience with warmth. He "hoped he was going among Friends," he began, and assured the council members that he wanted everything to proceed as smoothly as possible. Gage had ordered him to establish one regiment at Castle William and the other in the town. Boston's officials would not, he was sure, want to impede these orders, and if they would simply authorize access to spaces he might use for barracks in central Boston, the troops could begin to unload. Dalrymple's only desire, he concluded ingratiatingly, was to take care of the business of housing the troops in the way that was "most easy and agreeable to the Town."

The council refused to be swayed by Dalrymple's gentle approach. They gave him the same answer they had earlier given the governor: they had no objection to putting the Twenty-Ninth Regiment in Castle William, but they would not countenance the quartering of any regiment in the heart of Boston.

The Governor's Council had already consulted with the town's selectmen (including John Rowe) on this matter, and they had both an explanation and a reason for the refusal to let the army quarter troops in town. The explanation was legal, but the reason was emotional:

they were offended that the governor, the general, and the secretary of state himself considered Boston unruly and ungovernable, and they could view the order for a regiment to be housed in Boston only as a desire to punish the town. Governor Francis Bernard had defiantly admitted to the council that the troops were coming "in consequence of" the riots of the previous spring. The only reasons the ministry could have decided to order the troops to Boston, the council shot back, was if the governor and his friends — some "ill-minded persons" — were "disposed to bring misery and distress upon the town and province."

In the context of this angry exchange, the council and selectmen sent the governor an official letter stating that both regiments should be housed in the refurbished Castle William barracks. The officials based their recommendation on the 1765 Quartering Act, which held that troops were first to be quartered in existing barracks; only when those were full could other troops then be quartered in inns and public houses, and only when those inns and public houses became full in turn could troops be quartered elsewhere. Inns and other buildings were, moreover, to be rented out of the Crown's pocket, not the province's. In other words, the army could not simply appropriate housing from the town of Boston, at least not without paying for it.

Bernard and Dalrymple were infuriated by this reading of the Quartering Act. What was the point of stationing a peacekeeping force "Seven Miles by Land and three by water" from the center of Boston, even if the barracks were technically within the limits of the township? Having troops so far from the town could not, Bernard stormed to Gage, fulfill "the purposes intended by sending troops to

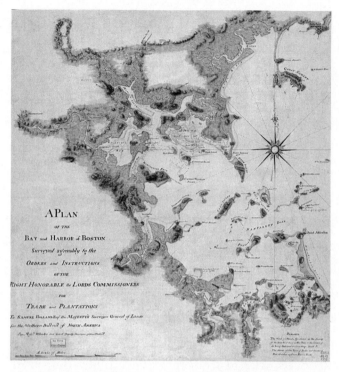

This chart illustrates the narrow channel available for ships to sail between Castle William and Boston's Long Wharf.

Boston." But try as the two Crown officials might to come up with compromises and alternatives, the council refused to budge.

Meanwhile, the regiments were stuck on the ships until Bernard and Dalrymple could resolve the dispute. Through the rest of Thursday and on into Friday morning, the ships remained anchored off Castle Island, until Dalrymple decided he had had enough. Far from following his original orders and putting one regiment in the barracks, he would put all the troops in Boston proper. He did not care if they had to camp out on Boston Common, among the town livestock, so long as those recalcitrant Bostonians understood that he was not to be trifled with. There was no point in lingering by Castle William; by ten o'clock that morning, the ships began to pull up anchor.

As the fleet traversed the three miles into Boston Harbor, the spires that Matthew Chambers had seen from Boston Light slowly came into view. They towered over a motley collection of some two thousand brick and wooden buildings. Despite the fog and drizzle, however, what stood out most was the Long Wharf: 1,586 feet of wooden planks and stone pilings stretching out to sea, lined on either side with warehouses and taverns and filled with pedestrians. Up to fifty ships could moor there at a time, bringing wares from around the world to the colony's shops and storehouses. The Long Wharf embodied Boston's affiliation with the British Empire, symbolically pointing east to London. When Captain Smith and Lieutenant Colonel Dalrymple ordered the fleet to set their moorings in a semicircle around the Long Wharf then, blocking it from the open sea, few Bostonians would have missed the point: it was meant, as Paul Revere noted, to look like a siege.

But Matthew Chambers was no Bostonian. As he gazed at the buildings ahead of him and the barracks behind him on Castle William, he must have wondered where his own family, once they finally disembarked, would sleep that night. The question was hardly an idle one, and the answer turned out to be far more significant than Matthew could have known. It was to change everything about Boston and its relationship with the British Empire.

It took several days and much work to disembark one thousand soldiers. From the ships moored out in the harbor, small groups of men were rowed on dinghies to the Long Wharf. To offset the tedium, Lieutenant Colonel Dalrymple decided on a grand display: at noon on Saturday he ordered the two elite companies from each regiment to disembark and march directly down the most prominent road in Boston. As these men from the Fourteenth and the Twenty-Ninth Regiments gathered on the eastern end of the Long Wharf, they unfurled their banners and fixed their bayonets to their muskets, an unmistakably martial gesture. The Fourteenth Regiment led the parade, marching up King Street, straight into the heart of Boston. Stopping at the east door of the Town-House and massing on the street in front of the Custom House, they waited until the Twenty-Ninth Regiment caught up. Then two hundred men marched together through the town center, their standards fluttering and the sound of fife and drum filling the air. They made, as the Bostonian John Tudor admitted, a "gallant appearance."

Impressive as the parade may have been, it did nothing to solve the problem of housing. With nowhere else to go, the Twenty-Ninth Regiment pitched tents among the cattle that grazed on the Boston Common; the Fourteenth managed to get under a roof in Faneuil Hall; and a detachment from the Fifty-Ninth Regiment, sent from Halifax with the Twenty-Ninth and the Fourteenth Regiments to fill out their numbers, found shelter in an empty warehouse. Over the next few days, Matthew and the other men began to disembark and join their regiment. The four smaller transport ships, stuffed with baggage, women, and children, were still out on the Atlantic.

As the troops landed, they started to unpack the provisions and gear they had brought from Halifax. Matthew's Twenty-Ninth Regiment had brought tents, which they liberally scattered over the Common. A watercolor painted that fall depicts the tents and troops in a rolling landscape, dominated at the back by the merchant John Hancock's enormous house and the tall beacon tower of Beacon Street. Couples and families stroll through the Common; townspeople and troops are sharing this central pasture.

Even more centrally located were the Fourteenth Regiment's temporary quarters in Faneuil Hall. The first floor of the building, rebuilt only five years earlier, was a public market, and the second floor provided meeting rooms for the town government, including the Boston Town Meeting and the smaller, elected Town Selectmen. Faneuil Hall was less than a five-minute walk from the Long Wharf, the Town-House (the home of the royal and the provincial governments), and King Street, the commercial, legal, and political heart of Boston.

This main street was dense with taverns, shops, and offices, including the Custom House and the Royal Exchange Tavern, a three-story building where merchants shared drinks and gossip. From here it was only a hundred yards to the beginning of the Long Wharf, where two more taverns served customers. At the Sign of the Ship, one of the two, the proprietor, Sarah Bean, also offered rooms for travelers looking to journey to the port of Salem on the stagecoach that stopped almost every day.

Next to the Custom House, a militia captain owned a tailor shop, and across the street Rebecca Payne sold customers the raisins, sherry, Jordan almonds, and delicate rose-colored silk fabrics that her husband, Edward, imported in his ships. From the very next house, Joshua Davis sold fresh lemons from Spain, and nearby were others selling cheese, coffee, and gloves. King Street even included a choice of wigmakers who catered to the fashion for powdered hair: Abraham Vernon across from the Custom House, Timothy Kelly across from the British Coffee House, and John Piemont farther down. The lieutenant governor bought his wigs from Piemont and retained him as his barber; so did other wealthy men, including the merchant and Son of Liberty John Hancock.

The whole range of Britain's trade could be found on King Street and the Long Wharf. Henry Lloyd's warehouse on the wharf displayed goods from all over the world: "French Indigo, Albany Peas, Connecticut Pork, Esopus Flour, new-York Butter-Bread, refin'd Iron, Pig Iron, Ship Bread, Cordage, Anchors, Spermaceti Candles, Cotton Wool, Silk Handkerchiefs, Feathers, Logwood, &c, &c." The same warehouse put humans up for sale as well: "One New negro Boy, three Girls: also a negro Man, that has been in the Country some Time." Just a few steps away, auctioneers sold people in the Royal Exchange Tavern, the Crown Coffee-House, and the Bunch-of-Grapes tavern. In summing up the power and the extent of the empire, King Street could not have been better named.

October in New England can be beautiful. On a fine Sunday two weeks after the troops had paraded down King Street, the sun sparkled on the shallow water of the Frog Pond, on the yellowing leaves drifting on the autumn breeze, and on the bright red of the Union Jack fluttering in the middle of the Boston Common. It illuminated the dull canvas of the army-issued tents grouped under that flag, a military encampment in plain sight of the townsfolk as they made their way to church that morning. Given this influx of more than a thousand new residents, Bostonians could not help but encounter military families at every turn: in the streets, in the churches, and eventually even in their own homes.

On that Sunday, the sun's warmth may have seemed like a good omen to Jane Chambers as she rocked her sick baby in a tent on Boston Common. Meanwhile, her husband, Matthew, pleaded anxiously with the minister of a nearby Congregational church to agree to an emergency baptism for his dangerously ill baby girl. Matthew may have guessed that many Bostonians, some of them members of this very church, did not want soldiers like him in Boston. Why would they allow their minister to baptize the sick child of a British soldier? Moreover, as a rule, Congregational churches insisted that parents had to be members of a congregation before their child could be baptized.

This particular Congregational church seems like a strange choice indeed. The West Church had, in the 1760s, a minister who had been a fierce opponent of the Stamp Act, and the church continued to oppose the political positions of Crown officials. That such a church would be willing to vote its approval for the hurried baptism of a "Daughter of Mr. Matthew Chambers, a soldier of the 29th Regiment, who has, as he says, had children baptized in Ireland," seems surprising. Yet in the midst of a fierce political battle over the abstract idea of "soldiery," a minister and a worried father found common ground.

A week after the baptism of baby Jane Chambers, named for her mother, the three-year-old child of the Boston merchant Benjamin Goodwin disappeared one afternoon. The child was kidnapped from his school by a Boston woman who had been released from jail the week before. The town crier was sent around to announce the child's disappearance. He began in the North End, where the boy was last seen. The child was eventually rescued at the edge of the Frog Pond on the Common, where the same Boston woman was stripping him of his clothes, pocketing the valuable metal buckles and buttons, and seemingly on the verge of drowning him. But it took the rest of the day for the news to reach the Goodwins. Late in the evening, the crier finally made it to the military encampment on the Common, where a soldier's wife told him that she had a child in her tent, brought there by "a woman belonging to the town." This wife had put the exhausted child to sleep until it could be "carried home to its Parents."

The kidnapper was identified that night in North Square. A crowd surrounded her and dispersed only when the night watch arrived and brought her to the workhouse. There she stayed until morning, when a justice of the peace committed her for trial.

The newspapers reported this incident as the lurid tale of a depraved criminal who preyed on innocent local children. But this same tale also includes an unnamed soldier's wife in a sympathetic role. The *Boston Gazette* reported that she took tender care of the little boy until he could be safely reunited with his mother. As the child traveled from the North End to Boston Common and back again, he wove a connection between two women based on their common care for a child. At this moment the divide between civilian and military did not matter.

Despite such moments of mutual understanding, the tensions created by the new military presence were real—and were only aggravated by Boston's culture of heavy drinking. On the morning after the troops disembarked, John Rowe strolled from his house to the center of town, and on King Street he entered his usual club, the British Coffee House, to do a bit of business. He found the coffee rooms and the hallways full of army and navy officers, while the two enslaved servers dashed around, serving them coffee, Madeira, and rum. Here Rowe encountered Ralph Dundass, the captain of one of the schooners that had brought soldiers from Halifax. The two had met before.

To Rowe's utter surprise, Captain Dundass spoke to him belligerently. "Hah John are you there Dammy I expected to have heard of your being hang'd before now for Damm you you deserve it." Rowe tried to laugh off the threat, but Dundass insisted that he was not joking. The captain repeated that Rowe was a "damn incendiary" who should be "hanged in his shoes." Although Dundass had not been in Boston since the previous year, when Rowe had spearheaded the merchants' boycott in response to the Townshend Acts, news had clearly traveled fast. Rowe looked around for his friends, in case Dundass became any more hostile, but though he saw a few drinking in the doorway, none rushed to lend support. The Bostonian decided discretion was the better part of valor, and went home.

Some army officers seemed to make trouble each time they drank. In every neighborhood, the men who served as the official neighborhood watch complained throughout November that officers "in Licker" harassed them frequently. The verbal abuse was seldom intense enough to be taken seriously, but it was common. One night, after midnight, an officer stormed into the night watch's little warming house near Dock Square, cursing "God dam you what do you think to do will you stand 4 regiments I will fetch them and set you all in fires in a menet and drive you all to hell and damnation." When other officers came back to the watch house two days later, "hollowing swearing and making a noyse," the constable threatened to lock them up until morning. At that point, the officers made extravagant apologies:

"They asked pardon for what they had done and ofered to [go] down on the [k]nee." The constable let them go home and sleep it off.

Before the end of October, an army officer named John Wilson made threats quite similar to those that Dundass had leveled at John Rowe. The *Boston Evening-Post* reported that while in a King Street coffee house, Wilson had "greatly insulted" two Bostonians by refer-ring to the locals as "liberty boys, rebels, etc." The incident made a big splash. The partisan news report known as the *Journal of the Times,* written anonymously by a group of liberty party supporters, sug-gested that the officer was not man enough to stand up to the Bosto-nians he insulted. Having shouted out "very indelicate threatenings," Captain Wilson apparently began to fear that one of them would beat him with a cane. The paper mocked him for summoning the sheriff to escort him home. The Boston shopkeeper Harbottle Dorr annotated the newspaper account, jotting in the margin that the "Captain of the Regulars" in question was known as "Bully Wilson."

Wilson's hostility revealed a fundamental conflict between Bosto-nians and some imperial agents. A week after the episode at the coffee house, Wilson was publicly drunk again, and this time his outburst struck deeply at the racial fears of some Bostonians. It was, as Joshua Henshaw explained to his cousin in western Massachusetts, "an affair of a blacker complexion," one that exposed a deep fault line within Boston's political culture: slavery. Henshaw succinctly described the incident: "Capt. Willson one evening last week, coming from an house at the South End, where he had drunk plentifully, met with several Negroes in the street, asked them whether their masters were Liberty Boys, they made him different answers, he told them to go home, be abusive to their Masters, & to cut their throats, then to come to him for protection, he would give them arms, & make them Gentlemen soldiers."

It was one thing for an officer to taunt another gentleman with charges of treason; it was something else entirely to incite a slave uprising. Was this a political move on Wilson's part? Was he simply trying to stir up trouble? Slaveholding crossed political lines in Boston. Sons of Liberty as well as supporters of the Crown held people in bondage. Boston slave owners were more than indignant; some were frankly terrified.

A few of those slave owners happened to be in the street that night. Nathan Spear, Zachary Johonnot, and William Foster heard Wilson's threat and rushed to complain to the selectmen. Town officials spent several days taking their depositions and then went into action. They started legal proceedings against Wilson. They also ordered the town constables to step up their surveillance of enslaved men, especially at night.

Wilson led the Boston sheriff on a chase around Boston for a full day; in the end, the captain hid in the warehouse barracks assigned to his regiment. Not until one of the justices of the peace threatened to raise a posse to help the sheriff arrest him did Wilson finally give himself up. A troop of constables led the captain first to the house of Justice Richard Dana and then to the selectmen's office in Faneuil Hall, an unusually public site for a simple bond hearing. The size of the bond was unusual too: four hundred pounds. Dana and other officials wanted to teach Wilson a lesson.

Wilson tried to mollify the selectmen. He assured them that he had not really meant anything by his speech to the enslaved men. Henshaw wryly wrote to his cousin that "his excuse was as usual & as good as usual <u>that he was drunk</u>." John Rowe, in his role as selectman, accepted the excuse, noting in his diary that the officer had been arrested for "some drunken behavior."

Whether or not Wilson had simply allowed liquor to get the better of him, slave owners fretted over the implications of his threat. Would the army give enslaved Bostonians ideas? There were already nearly a dozen free black men in the Twenty-Ninth Regiment, serving as drummers; they received regular wages and the promise of a pension at the end of their service. It would not take much imagination on the part of an enslaved Bostonian to see the attraction of Wilson's suggestion of freedom in the British army.

Even free black men in Boston did not have the same status as white civilians or black soldiers, especially when it came to patrolling other people. For most of the eighteenth century, black men were excluded from participating in either the militia or the watch. White legislators would not give them the authority to arrest other Bostonians or to carry arms. Instead, free black men were compelled to perform the civic duties of cleaning and paving public roads. Boston selectmen assessed each of them up to thirty days of unpaid work on the town's highways per year. Unsurprisingly, the black men engaged in constant battles with the selectmen concerning the completion of such unpleasant and unremunerated work. Their civic service looked far more like slavery under an overseer than did the sociable, alcohol-fueled "training days" of the local militia.

Nor could white Bostonians feel confident in the stability of slavery. Massachusetts law allowed enslaved people to sue in the courts and receive due process. From the 1760s into the 1770s, enslaved men and women brought cases against whites for unlawful imprisonment, for back wages, and, occasionally, for their freedom. Although the suits themselves did not spell the end of slavery in Massachusetts, they certainly made clear its shaky foundations in both law and custom.

Henshaw scribbled a hasty note to his cousin at the bottom of his letter: "Quere: whether it will not be prudent to keep the affair of Willson with the Negroes as secret as possible." What might happen if enslaved men like Cato Spear or Caesar Johonnot began to think that the British army might have the power to end their servitude? Would enslaved men and women, rather than wait for the British army to come to their aid, decide to take that power into their own hands?

Nathan Spear and Zachary Johonnot were right to be concerned about the precarious foundations of slavery in Massachusetts, and at some point amid the tumult of the following decade, both of them emancipated their slaves. But the "affair of Willson with the Negroes" made clear to everyone that even casual encounters between Bostonians and soldiers befuddled by drink touched on issues with enormous and long-reaching implications.

The army, the town, and the governor continued to argue over where to house the troops. Several officers had no intention of camping out in Faneuil Hall or the Town-House and had already obtained private leases for themselves. Less than a week after disembarking, two officers from the Fourteenth Regiment, Captain Brabazon O'Hara and Major Jonathan Furlong, rented houses on Essex Street from John Rowe, who charged them each the healthy sum of twenty British pounds per year.

The need for more permanent housing was felt not only by the

men, women, and children of the Fourteenth and Twenty-Ninth
Regiments. A detachment of the Fifty-Ninth, which had come along
from Halifax, had to be quartered as well, as did the Sixty-Fourth,
which arrived from Ireland soon after. It could have been worse: the
Sixty-Fifth Regiment, traveling with the Sixty-Fourth, were housed
in Castle William and so did not add to the press for housing in the
town. But the current conditions in Boston could not be allowed to
continue. Soldiers and families could live only so long among the
livestock on the Common or on the crowded second floor of Faneuil
Hall. This last place was particularly galling: the troops slept among
the town's stock of muskets and in doorways to the chambers used by
the Boston Town Meeting, the Boston selectmen, and the court.

For the most part, neither town officials nor many Bostonians
were willing to help. The troops attempted to take over one provincial building, the manufactory house, but the families living inside
mounted a four-day standoff, rebuffing and humiliating the soldiers.
General Gage himself came to Boston in mid-October to resolve the
impasse, but his presence produced no immediate results. A few days
after his arrival, the Boston minister Andrew Eliot wrote to a political supporter in Britain, "The present disposition of the people is to
treat the troops with civility, but to provide nothing." Understanding
the town's tactics, Bernard and Gage fumed that Bostonians seemed
to think that they could force the troops to leave if soldiers had nowhere to live but the Common. Though the army would not in fact
be forced out, its leaders were running out of housing options. Neither the governor nor the army officers could find a way to refute the
town officials' legal arguments.

Even the rental of warehouses and private homes was a financial challenge. To his great annoyance, Lieutenant Colonel Dalrymple found that the cost of these rentals would need to be borne not by the colony but by the army itself. Dalrymple justified the cost, however, especially in the rental of private homes, where soldiers and families could mingle with townspeople without supervision, by praising "the uncommonly good behavior of both officers & soldiers."

In long, self-justifying letters to the Earl of Hillsborough, Governor Bernard explained why he could never compel Boston officials to offer free housing to the troops. At last, Bernard and Dalrymple managed to avoid the town's political and legal challenges through the simple expedient of money. The army agreed to pay locals for the rental of private rooms, and the troops could finally move into more comfortable quarters. Historians have spilled a good deal of ink explaining the machinations of this compromise and noting, not without amusement, the speed with which moderates like John Rowe and hardcore liberty partisans like William Molineux compromised their principles for cash and rented their property to the army. But financial details and ideological ironies pale in importance compared to the profound social change created by the wide dispersal and mingling of troops with civilians throughout the town of Boston.

By the beginning of November, Gage's officers had found thirteen buildings—storerooms, sugar houses (sugar refineries), even a cotton warehouse—to refashion as barracks. John Rowe rented the military one of his warehouses. William Molineux rented one of his own and acted as an agent for three others on Wheelwright's Wharf. Dalrymple hoped that such buildings would keep soldiers in the heart of the town, yet isolate them from townspeople; his hopes were entirely unreasonable. As the drama over the kidnapping of Benjamin Goodwin's son showed, even putting troops in a military encampment could not segregate them from civilians altogether. Moreover, thirteen buildings were not nearly enough to house all the troops. By the time the Sixty-Fourth and Sixty-Fifth Regiments arrived, in the middle of November, there were roughly 2,000 men, 380 women, and 500 children who needed a place to stay.

The army was not looking for particularly luxurious housing. A full-size barracks in Halifax was about 160 feet long and 32 feet wide; divided into twelve rooms, it was intended to house 336 soldiers. By contrast, a typical Boston sugar house was only about one-third the size. Even with fourteen privates per room — senior officers got their own rooms, subalterns had to share two to a room, and privates had to share four to a bed — dockside warehouses would be insufficient, and Boston simply did not have enough vacant sugar houses. In the end, the army also rented private houses, rooms in private houses, and even outbuildings to house the overflow. As a result, the troops and the townspeople found themselves living very close together. Matthew and Jane Chambers managed to lodge their family in South Boston, renting a house near the Orange Tree Inn.

No sooner had members of the army started to settle in than some of them wanted to leave. Officers, in particular, wanted to flee this particular assignment. Urban policing had no opportunities for glory, but many possibilities for failure. The secretary at war himself admitted that it was "a most Odious Service which nothing but Necessity can justify." In the spring of 1768, as Secretary Barrington faced a major riot in London as well as mobs across England, he lamented, "Employing the Troops on so disagreeable a Service always gives me Pain; the present unhappy Riots make it necessary." The commanding officers in Boston could not have agreed more. When General Mackay's transport ship from Ireland was blown off course, and Mackay was forced to spend the winter in the West Indies, Colonel John Pomeroy of the Sixty-Fourth Regiment was given the temporary rank of brigadier general and the command of all the Boston troops (superseding Lieutenant Colonel Dalrymple). Pomeroy arrived in Boston in November and within four months was pleading with General Gage to allow him to return to England. When General Mackay finally arrived in Boston in the spring of 1769 and was forced to assume the top position, he lasted only six weeks before he began begging for a home leave. Other officers too applied for permission to escape; Mackay included four officers' requests along with his own. Even Dalrymple immediately asked Mackay for permission to leave for Canada as soon as possible. Suddenly, unexciting Canada did not seem so terrible. Any officer who could tried to leave Boston, knowing that this posting would likely ruin his reputation.

A week after the troops began to move into rented housing, William Cooper, the clerk of the Boston Town Meeting, wrote to a correspondent in London to say that "Boston is now become a Garrison town." Cooper did not mean only that one might come across soldiers in the street at any time of day or night. He meant that he felt the surveillance of the imperial state.

It was common custom for sentries anywhere in Britain to challenge people walking past a guard post, but Bostonians resented the practice. The merchant Lewis Gray, passing a guard post at midnight in early December, refused to answer the challenge, found himself detained, and retaliated by accusing the two sentries of assault and false imprisonment. Gray was not the only one who ignored the demand to identify himself. Colonel John Pomeroy complained to Governor Bernard of "many people, who refused to answer" and thereby created friction with the sentries. Bernard brought up Pomeroy's complaint with his council, but their only response was that any fault lay with the sentries for harassing "respectable people."

Samuel Adams, writing in the *Boston Gazette* as "Vindex," argued that such challenges were inimical to Bostonians' liberty. The very presence of troops was an affront; if the purpose of an army was to fight a war, an army that took up position within Boston could only be intended to deprive its free people of their liberty.

Richard Dana, Boston's justice of the peace, certainly subscribed to this philosophy. When three Boston men accused thirty-three-year-old Private John Duxbury of assault after he challenged them that winter of 1768, Dana wholeheartedly supported the plaintiffs from the bench. It was the principle of military challenges to which he objected, Dana explained: "The matter of the Soldiers challenging people in the Streets was in itself nothing," but such military practices were the thin edge of the wedge. Dana warned Bostonians not to respond to the challenges, "for if they once did that[,] other things would be introduced and steal upon them by degrees so as at last to reduce them to a state of slavery and make them subservient even to these Soldiers." According to Bostonians like Dana, the very presence of soldiers put freedom at risk.

It was not only political types who found the presence of troops unpleasant. As one merchant wrote to his suppliers in London, "We are in such a situation here at present with regard to trade money growing so scarce and like to be worse that we are at a stand — not only so but having more than three Regiments of soldiers quartered in the town and a number of men of war in the Harbour makes the town very disagreeable so that if we are not soon relieved I believe many will leave the town." The political liberty that Dana and others feared losing seemed to many Britons the foundation for their flourishing commerce. Letting soldiers wander around Boston streets seemed to put both trade and freedom at risk.

Citizens were right to be concerned about the effects of living in a "garrison town," but they were wrong to think that they knew what those effects would be. The great changes that they would experience were not the loss of liberty, the obstreperousness of the soldiers, or even the violent confrontations that they feared. Instead, the quartering of British soldiers in Boston created a fundamental shift in the relationships between colonial and imperial, between citizen and soldier.

A map of Boston that displays the homes of some of the soldiers demonstrates clearly how completely soldiers' families infiltrated the streets of the town. They lived in houses and outbuildings in every area of Boston. The family of Allan McGinnis, a member of the Sixty-Fourth Regiment, rented a house on Atkinson Street in the South End, while the wife of Patrick Walker lived in a house "in the yard of" James Cunningham on Orange Street, along with several other families from the Twenty-Ninth and Fourteenth Regiments. Richard Starkey of the Twenty-Ninth rented a house in the west side of Boston (known as New Boston) for his wife and two children. Hundreds of families needed homes; hundreds of Bostonians became landlords. As regimental families spread through the city, they created uneasy but definite connections between civilian and military communities.

The presence of some of these families could change a neighbor-

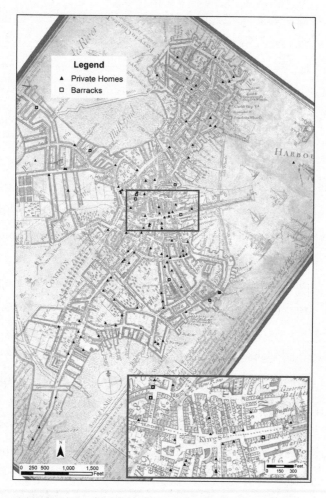

Military families lived in private houses and barracks scattered throughout Boston.

hood, and not always for the better. Neighbors along Marlboro and
School Streets complained about two military households, those
of the black drummer John Bacchus and the white private Edward
Montgomery. They had resided in Boston just a year when the neighbors protested that each "kept an ill govern'd & disorderly house, &

entertaine'd certain lewd Idle & disorderly persons, at all hours as well by night as by day, and as well on Lords days as on other days, suffering them to Tipple in his house and profanely cursing and swearing, being a great grievance & common nuisance." Eighteenth-century Bostonians' complaints against disorderly houses were as numerous as the disorderly houses themselves, but the language of this complaint deserves attention. First, the vices of Sabbath breaking, illegal drinking, and bad language are commonly alleged not against disorderly houses but rather against the British army, whose culture was well known both to civilians and New Englanders who had served with the regulars in the Seven Years' War. Second, John Bacchus was a black Jamaican, forty-three years old at the time of the complaint, and had already served sixteen years in the army. If his neighbors were offended by his race, they made no mention of it in their catalog of iniquities. Finally, the locals allege that this raucous behavior had been going on for the past six months. It is possible that these soldiers had lived elsewhere for the first six months of their time in Boston. It is also likely, however, that the first few months had not been so irritating. Perhaps, over time, Bostonians had begun to lose patience with their new neighbors.

Not every local relationship was so fraught. On the same date that seven Boston families complained about Bacchus and Montgomery, six different ones complained that John Timmins, another soldier from the Twenty-Ninth Regiment, was also keeping a disorderly house. Among Timmins's neighbors were Thomas Wilkinson and his wife. Although Wilkinson signed on to the complaint against Timmins, he did not seem reflexively opposed to all soldiers as neighbors.

In fact, he had an excellent relationship with Edward Montgomery and his wife, Isabella, about whom other Bostonians had complained. But Wilkinson had quite a different connection with Edward and Isabella: in the eighteenth-century equivalent of running to a neighbor's house for a cup of sugar, Wilkinson occasionally sent his children to the Montgomerys' home for coals to start his own fire.

Within the six months following the complaint, the Montgomery family had moved out of the city center into the North End, where Isabella Montgomery in particular continued to alienate many of her neighbors. After only a few months in her new house, Isabella had antagonized them to such a degree that one screamed at her that she hoped Isabella's husband would die.

Whether cordial or heated, these complex relationships between civilian and military were replicated throughout the town. After living in Boston for a year and a half, several soldiers and their wives seemed quite comfortable spending time in the North End house of the jeweler John Wilme and his wife, Sarah. When the Bostonian David Cochran dropped by one evening in February, he found several of them visiting with the Wilmes and speaking in a way that managed to combine threats with advice. Sarah reported later that a member of the Fourteenth Regiment "did talk very much against the town" that evening, boasting that in any confrontation with townspeople "he would level his piece so as not to miss." Ugly words, yes — but as Wilme explained it to Cochran, the soldiers also intended to warn Wilme and his family and friends to expect "disturbances." Another soldier took Cochran aside and claimed that "blood would soon run in the streets of Boston," but presumably not Cochran's own. Somehow, general threats of violence went hand in hand with neighborly concern.

For seventy years, historians have argued that one reason why soldiers and local men were at odds throughout these years of occupation is that the privates, permitted to freelance, were willing to work in Boston establishments for less than the going rate of pay. But though there were many well-documented brawls in Boston, none seem related to pay. Private Patrick Doyne, for example, worked in a wigmaker's shop with a few local apprentices. They seemed on good terms; the apprentices had a habit of dropping by to see Doyne and his wife in the evenings. Rather than creating enmity, shared workplaces could become venues where privates and townspeople could get to know one another.

There were limits to these friendships, however. Even as the Boston apprentices Richard Ward and Bartholomew Broaders visited in Private Patrick Doyne's rooms, other soldiers came in and out, discussing brawls with the locals. Individual connections did not necessarily translate into an easy acceptance across the military-civilian divide. While sharing the town's streets might have brought the two groups closer together—too close, some might have said—it did not incorporate soldiers completely into the civic community.

As their husbands and fathers met other apprentices and journeymen, military women and children were far more likely to see another side of Boston: its public institutions. In June 1769, the selectmen heard a rumor that smallpox had broken out at the regimental hospital that the army had established on the Boston Common. Worried that the infection would quickly make its way through the crowded city, they prevailed upon General Alexander Mackay to remove the ill man immediately to the Province Hospital, at the west end of Boston. It was too late. Although the town avoided a full-blown epidemic, new cases continued to crop up through the summer and fall. As smallpox made its way through the population, women and children related to the army came to know the town's selectmen, its doctors, and, in particular, its quarantine hospitals. Their experiences demonstrated some of the limits of neighborliness, even as they shared some of their most intimate moments with the inhabitants of the town.

Jane Chambers again had to navigate private grief as she dealt with one of Boston's public institutions. This time it was not a Congregational church. Less than a year after the terrifying illness of her child, disease struck again and forced the Chambers family into a strained relationship with the selectmen.

In the warm weeks of August 1769, Jane Chambers sat by one sickbed after another. Doctor Elisha Story came to see three of her children day after day, for four days. At last, yet another doctor came, this one sent by the town, and he diagnosed one of the children with smallpox, possibly the daughter who had already been so ill the year before. On August 23, a week later, Boston's selectmen determined that Jane and her child posed a risk to the town's public health. They sent the two not to the regimental hospital on the Boston Common but to the public hospital on the western edge of Boston, to isolate them from the others who shared their rented house. A week later, the selectmen's agent transferred them again, this time to Rainsford Island, another "Pest House," this one in Boston Harbor. Jane stayed on the island for a week, until she seemed to be out of danger. Then, on September 3, the selectmen ordered the director of the hospital to allow her to leave, provided that she had fresh clothes and was "suffi-ciently smoked," or fumigated with sulfur. Meanwhile, her husband, Matthew, stayed in their rented house with their other children.

The spread of smallpox in Boston in 1769 was not particularly extensive, but how it had arrived was still a source of speculation. Jane and her daughter were among the handful of residents sent that summer to the smallpox hospital on Rainsford Island. Of the twen-ty-three family groups—primarily mothers and children—brought there for quarantine, less than a third were associated with the army. The selectmen attempted to reassure the town that the outbreak was limited and that the commanding officers had guaranteed—wrongly, as it turned out—that there was no smallpox either in the garrisons or the regimental hospital. The Bostonian Harbottle Dorr was incred-ulous and infuriated, in equal degrees, by this announcement. "It was brought by the soldiers," he insisted. "Another article to be charged to the account of Gov. Bernard or who ever was the Instigator of Sol-diers amongst us!" Dorr's skepticism over the source of the outbreak was understandable, given the untrustworthiness of the army's other recent claim. Only two days after General Mackay had assured the selectmen that there was no smallpox in any hospital or barrack that he oversaw, he was forced to return and admit that there was, in fact, a man in the regimental hospital with smallpox.

The Chambers family was not the only one in the neighborhood with smallpox that summer. As the disease spread, Dr. Miles Whit-worth, who examined the ill for the selectmen, reported on sick sol-diers' wives and children on the western side of the city. In the middle of July, a Boston woman named Frances Tyler, who lived with her husband, Joseph, near the Orange Tree Inn, also fell ill. But the disease and the town treated the two families differently. Tyler refused to be quarantined in the public hospital; in response, the selectmen were willing to hang white flags around her house to warn others away. As the wife of a wealthy merchant, Tyler could push back against the selectmen's attempt to regulate her body. She was, ironically, better able to separate herself from the town (or at least from the scrutiny of its officials) than was an outsider like Jane Chambers. When their illness was announced, as a public health concern, the selectmen noted both Tyler and Chambers by name and address, and in terms of each one's relation to her husband.

Neither the Tylers nor the Chamberses escaped from smallpox unscathed, however. Frances Tyler died of the disease a week after her diagnosis. Unsurprisingly, this event merited a fulsome obituary in a Boston newspaper, an encomium to her "amiable mind and sweetness of her temper and disposition." When Jane Chambers was allowed to leave Rainsford Island, the selectmen's report made no mention of her child. But on September 2, the day before Chambers was released, a bill was submitted to the selectmen for the burial of six smallpox victims, including the "curing [putting in a tarred shroud and coffin] a sholyer's [soldier's] child and digging grave." The unnamed casualty may well have been Jane's child.

The few traces of these women in the public record reveal how strangely intertwined with and yet distant from the town of Boston and its officials soldiers' families could be. The bill the town sexton presented to the town for the burial of smallpox victims itemized local women by name ("for carrying Mrs. Beals to the grave"), but not military ones. These women and children were listed solely as "soldier's wife" or "soldier's child."

Soldiers' families found themselves living the most personal, and sometimes the final, parts of their lives both within and outside the civilian world. The sorrows that Jane Chambers experienced in Boston can hardly be blamed on the town meeting; the death of her child was not itself the direct result of the town's resistance to armed occupation. Yet that resistance created a world in which her family experienced occasional warm support but also heartless disregard and separation.

5

Love Your Neighbor, 1769–70

Sex and Courtship

Whife his comrades in the Twenty-Ninth Regiment were camping on the Boston Common or meeting their new neighbors, Private William Clark was spending his time with literature: his own. Two months after his arrival in Boston, Clark announced that his play, *The Miser. Or The Soldier's Humour. A Comedy of Three Acts,* was available for purchase by subscription. The broadside announcing the subscription included a brief and nearly correct Latin tag: *Non possunt placeto omnibus,* "I can't please everyone." Presumably, Clark acquired enough subscriptions to publish his play, since the following February, the printer Ezekiel Russell advertised in all the Boston papers that he had just published *The Miser* and would sell it, with a blue paper cover, for eight pence. Sadly, no copies remain for us to read today. Russell may not have printed many. The short run was likely read until it fell apart and then, like many cheaply printed pamphlets, reused as toilet paper. Such a fate might have been particularly appealing to some Bostonians. In the winter of 1769, not many residents were likely eager to read about "the soldier's humour."

. . .

Private William Clark seemed to have a flair for drama off the page as well. In May 1769, he had a shouting match with the Boston watch. When stopped on the street, he threatened to burn down the town workhouse and all of Boston with it. As the watchman arrested him and brought him to the local lockup, Clark swore he'd have his revenge on the entire town.

It took Clark only a month to stage an even more melodramatic scene with Boston locals. One June day in 1769, seventy-five-year-old Joseph Lasenby was shocked, upon entering his married daughter's house, to find Clark in bed with his twenty-year-old granddaughter, Mary Nowell. The elderly Son of Liberty ordered Clark out of the house, but the insouciant soldier declined to leave. He had every right to sleep with Mary, Clark asserted. After all, she was his wife, he told the astonished old man, and he was going nowhere without her.

Clark may have been stretching the truth a bit. Mary said they had been married one evening "by a person who was drest as a priest." In fact, they were not married until four months after being caught in flagrante. But married they were, much to the distress of Mary's parents. So devastated were they, the *Boston Evening-Post* claimed, that the news of the affair "much impaired their health." Two weeks after the marriage, Mary's father had a showdown with his new son-in-law. Clark shoved a loaded pistol into Joseph Nowell's chest, Joseph pressed charges, and after many adjournments, in April 1770 Clark found himself in jail until he could pay a forty-shilling fine.

William Clark's marriage meant more than family scandal; it became political fodder for Boston's Sons of Liberty. In fact, the story of Joseph Lasenby finding Clark in his granddaughter's bed was reported in newspapers sympathetic to the liberty party. Nodding to a sense of propriety, especially about sexual matters, the press usually replaced many personal names in its stories with dashes. But Bostonians obviously knew something of the Clark story before it was printed. When the shopkeeper Harbottle Dorr read the account in the *Boston Evening-Post,* he carefully annotated the article, recording that

These annotations by the shopkeeper Harbottle Dorr identify the young woman and grandfather involved in the William Clark seduction drama.

the young woman in question was Mary Nowell and her grandfather "Mr. Lasenby."

Boston's newspapers rarely printed accounts of sexual scandal for their salacious details alone (such earthy stories were much more likely to show up in fiction or in rhymed doggerel). The *Journal of the Times* used the story to point out the political implications of this illicit marriage, urging its readers to reflect on the inevitable impact of troops on Boston's families: "that the most *dear & tender* connections must be *broken & violated*." The ultimate blame for this seduction, the article concluded, must fall on those imperial officials "who have been the authors of those scenes of *public* and *private* distress." The old man stumbling in on his favorite granddaughter was only the preface to the primary protest: the "quartering of a standing army in times of peace." The author argued that in the world of occupied Boston, "*public* and *private*" affairs of the heart were one and the same.

It seems unlikely that Clark had thought of his seduction in terms of politics; he spent his time in prison imagining his next literary work. In August 1770, he took out another advertisement, this one for his new memoir, *A True and Faithful Narrative of the Love Intrigues of the Author, William Clark, Soldier in his Majesty's 29th Regiment of Foot* (and this is only the beginning of the extensive title). Clark's "love intrigues" exposed an eighteenth-century soap opera, complete with cameo appearances by various Sons of Liberty and British army officers, in settings ranging from prisons to bedrooms.

He clearly meant his sixty-page narrative to be a tell-all, and perhaps also a means of revenge, targeting his in-laws; unlike the *Journal* and other newspapers, Clark named names. The long title of his memoir concludes with these words: *in which is Given a Faithful Ac-*

count of his Courtship, Marriage and Bedding with Mary Nowel, Daughter of Joseph Nowel, Boat-builder at North End Boston; with a Description how much he suffered on said Account.

The memoir has not survived, so we can only imagine how Clark might have told his version of being found in bed by his lover's grandfather. We can assume from the title—and from its emphasis on Clark's suffering—that his version would depart from the narrative in the Sons of Liberty's *Journal.* The villain of Clark's story is his father-in-law, called out by name. This flippant young man was not troubled by the politics of the British Empire and its impact on his wife's family or hometown. Instead, his was the age-old story of young lovers and disapproving parents.

One imagines *A True and Faithful Narrative* to be the sort of tale that George Wickham, the charming rake of Jane Austen's *Pride and Prejudice,* might have written, had he been a literary soul. Seduction, clandestine marriage, and angry guardians were the main themes for both. Both in Austen's telling and in Clark's, the actual military work of the army is quite irrelevant: soldiers were lovers, not fighters.

Many Boston women and military men felt the same way. Mary Nowell was not alone in falling for a soldier. Boston's young women found the arrival of troops thrilling. White women outnumbered men in town by almost five to four, and the influx of eligible young men offered delightful possibilities. Young women across the social spectrum were eager to make conquests among the soldiers.

One middle-aged Massachusetts woman watched her young friends' attempts at courtship with a sympathetic eye. Seizing a quiet moment with her young ward, Charity, Christian Barnes did try to temper "the great raptures she expressed for the officers and soldiers." Barnes ruefully admitted that other young women, including Charity's older sister Dolly, might have undercut her advice. She wrote to the girl's aunt, "I am greatly mistaken if Miss Dolly is not as much pleased with the soldiers as her little Sister [Charity] is." Dolly herself seemed to be torn between her current love interest, a young cleric, and her attraction to the soldiers. Barnes wondered if she was trying to have it both ways by trying to persuade her clergyman beau to join the army. Barnes mused to Dolly's aunt that "I think it almost time to inquire whether she has yet boiled her lobster," a vivid image of the minister exchanging his black coat for a red one. In the end, however, Barnes decided that the relationship was still too delicate to withstand her prying, and stated that there was "enough said." In fact, both Barnes and Dolly's aunt were disappointed in the eventual outcome, Dolly's match with the clergyman, but found themselves helpless to say anything.

A year and a half later, Barnes demonstrated similar empathy for another of her young female friends. Having invited Polly Murray to visit her in Marlborough, some thirty miles west of Boston, Barnes was disappointed but resigned when Polly apologized, explaining that she could not possibly leave Boston in February 1770 just as the winter social season was getting started. She blamed politics for the slow start to the season, "for the party disputes ran so high they could not agree to have an Assembly till last month." Despite the inconvenience, Barnes justified Polly's decision: "I think Miss Polly would have made too great a sacrifice to have quitted the Town at a time when she was going to enter into (what all Young People think) the injoyment of Life."

Polly's cousin Sukey Inman was too eager to meet British officers to bide her time until the assembly. While Polly was waiting for the public dances to begin, Sukey convinced her aunt Hannah Rowe to host a dance ("a genteel one," according to her uncle) at which she would be the guest of honor. Her uncle John carefully noted the guests: fourteen men and ten women, excluding the hosts. All of the unattached men were officers, most of them closer in age to the uncle than to Sukey.

Her wealthy and extroverted uncle, John Rowe, would make it possible for his niece to meet many other military men. Rowe, as we have seen, spent his years tacking between Boston's political parties, drinking and dining with army officers and Sons of Liberty, often in the same evening. He was a "trimmer," as historians have come to call him. A man like Rowe understood how sociability both smoothed and reinforced political differences. And by the winter of 1770, his niece Sukey had already met the man she would eventually marry, an officer from one of the British navy ships that had transported soldiers from Halifax to Boston.

It was not always easy for Boston women to capture the attention of the soldiers. When Lieutenant Stanton of the Fourteenth Regiment attended a dance in 1769, he passed his time writing snide poetry about his potential dance partners there. His verse apparently circulated privately in manuscript, but once the young women heard about the insults, they, or their defenders, shot back in the much more public venue of the newspaper. Their poem, in an affronted tone, demanded, "Have Boston's Beauties, blest, belov'd, admir'd, / No Pow'r to please?" It then listed the charms of some half dozen of Boston's young elite women, which John Stanton somehow was too blind to see: Christian Amiel, "Smooth in the Dance"; one of the Sheaffe sisters, "Young, mild, and fair"; and Lucy Clark, "serene, yet gay." Lucy's father was in fact one of the most determined of the king's men, a tea merchant who would soon find himself in the midst of the Boston imbroglio over that beverage, but that fact did not make her any more attractive to the young lieutenant. Although the poem specifically took Stanton to task for his poor manners, addressing him pointedly in the first line, the goal of the doggerel itself was to highlight the attractions of Boston's women: "These, and yet more, whom Fame's fair List can tell / Please in their Movement, in their Charms excel." Countless Boston beauties floated through a ballroom, this poem maintained, even if one soldier was too dense to notice them.

These women, at least, were not prepared to allow a British officer to dismiss them as less than stellar potential mates. Lieutenant Stanton could not forgive the criticism, and the next week, he stormed the printing offices of the *Boston Gazette,* demanding the name of the poem's author in order to clear his own name. The paper refused to give it to him, and the *Boston Evening-Post* gleefully printed an account of Stanton's temper tantrum.

In Boston, courtship could never be hidden for long. Relatives, neighbors, and friends all kept an eye on the progress of a romantic relationship. But by the time the regiments had come to Boston, parents had lost much of their authority over their children's choice of a spouse. Increasingly, teenage and adult offspring began to decide for themselves whom they would marry, leaving parents with little influence in selecting who would become a daughter- or son-in-law. And sometimes the public nature of courtship made those choices even harder for some parents to swallow.

To a few deeply committed Sons of Liberty, the flirtations of the ballroom and the romantic fallout in the newspaper were not innocent amusements, but acts of war. Justice of the Peace Richard Dana fumed as he saw young redcoats in the streets and homes of his Boston neighbors. He took every possible occasion to show his rage at the presence of troops in Boston. In a proceeding that made a deep impression on several of the officers, Dana used his courtroom to inveigh against the regiments' practice of challenging passersby and to question the soldiers' right to be in the town at all. The justice spent most of his time on the job binding over miscreant soldiers for trial. In letters to his eldest son, Edmund, who was living in England, Dana found it hard to restrain his reflections on liberty and "arbitrary tyrannical principles," finally concluding, "Must here break off my political remarks, lest I be insensibly carried too far for the company of a letter. But could easily write a large pamphlet on the subject."

When it came to his fourteen-year-old daughter, Lydia, Dana saw no point in policing himself. He drew the lines sharply between his public (and to him distasteful) interactions with the military and his family's social world. He reassured Edmund in August 1769 that he planned to take every precaution to ensure that Lydia would have no opportunity to socialize with military men. "You need not have reminded me of your Sister. Have had too much experience . . . to be off my guard, or taken in by any of 'em. Have the fore taken due care & precaution. Have no familiarity with any of 'em nor shall any in my family. Nor do any of 'em come under my roof, but when bro't by a civil officer to answer for some offence. They know me too well to expect any freedom with me or mine. I seldom suffer your sister to be out in an event — save at a next door neighbor — & this but rarely. This is a standing ordinance of my house." This Son of Liberty clearly thought it better to put his own daughter under house arrest than allow her to socialize with soldiers.

The *Boston Evening-Post,* unable to physically confine young women to their homes, turned to editorials to try to keep Boston's women from flirting with soldiers. As the winter social season of assemblies, concerts, and plays picked up steam in 1769, "the Young Ladies of Boston" were treated to dire warnings about the "many thousands of your sex [who] have been gradually betray'd by innocent amusements to ruin and infamy." Even in this particular anonymous screed, intended to terrify eligible young women away from flirtations, the author, using the pen name "Homosum," had to acknowledge that "a mutual intercourse of both sexes may in many cases be allowable, in some perfectly innocent." The only problem with these innocent amusements, Homosum admitted, was the soldiers. While reassuring his audience that New England women so far had an unblemished reputation, he admonished, "But still, when we have among us a number of the other sex . . . who (if you will believe their account) are as famous for their exploits in the warfare of Venus, as that of Mars, a word of caution may not be unnecessary." A liaison with a soldier could ruin a woman's body and character at once.

Like Caesar's wife, Homosum urged, Boston's young women must be above the suspicion of dallying with the enemy. Only by publicly and visibly rejecting courtship with soldiers could nubile young women "convince the world that the daughters of America are friends to that cause [of liberty]." Even an innocent romance could have dire political implications. It would be better for Boston's women not to flirt at all than to seem to condone the presence of soldiers.

Initially, perhaps, this public relations campaign may have worked. The *Journal of the Times* claimed that army officers had tried to organize a dance to celebrate the anniversary of George II's coronation a few weeks after the regiments' arrival, "but the ladies of the town could not be persuaded into the propriety of indulging themselves in musick and dancing with those gentlemen who have been sent hither in order to dragoon us into measures, which appear calculated to enslave and ruin us." In precisely the same language that Homosum would adopt a few months later, the *Journal* gloated that political considerations compelled Boston's liberty-loving women to reject their would-be suitors. Their reward, the *Journal* assured the young women, would be fame that would last long after they had become old. They may have lost an opportunity for courtship, but they had gained a role in a worthwhile cause:

> For this when Beauties blooming Charms are past,
> Your Praise, fair Nymphs, to latest Times shall last.

In a doggerel competition, the *Journal*'s moralizing rhyme might win against the saucier "Boston's Beauties." But the newspaper's verses and editorials were not ultimately persuasive: the grumpy Sons of Liberty did not long stand a chance against the Boston women's desire for partners.

During the social season of 1768–69, members of the liberty party organized a "Liberty Assembly" in "opposition," as one observer noted, to the official Boston Dancing Assembly. Claiming that the organizers of the Boston Dancing Assembly could produce only ten or twelve unmarried women, even after beating the bushes for miles around, the *Journal* scoffed that there were so few women relative to the number of men that the evening could hardly be dignified with the term "mixt dancing."

News accounts in the *Journal* tended to exaggerate for satiric effect. Ann Hulton claimed that some sixty couples attended the assembly that year. When Selectman John Rowe went for the first time that season in January, he disparaged the evening, not because the attendance was too small but because there was "too much confusion." As the season wore on, however, Rowe came to enjoy the assemblies, commenting on different evenings that they were "very brilliant," "very large," or that there was "very good dancing."

Exhortations in the newspapers may have been among the few controls that parents or Bostonians aligned with the liberty party had for reining in their children's dalliances. Determined liberty partisans like Dana may have forbidden their daughters to enjoy the company of soldiers, but very few women seemed to heed their advice.

In fact, some did much more than flirt. Soldiers and civilians attending glittering balls and writing arch poems about each other may suggest a society in which young women peeped over fans and correct young men bestowed a single kiss on a fingertip. Eighteenth-century courtship could, however, also be quite sexual. Christian Barnes's young friend Polly Murray giggled in a letter to her cousin that their mutual friends Anny and Prudence went to church one Sunday with no cloaks "in hopes to captivate the adorable Mr. Brideoake whose charms Prudence, who is to be the bearer of this, will not fail to give you the full description." Anny and Prudence clearly hoped to snag the attention of this handsome young officer by revealing a little flesh. Fortunately for young women who were better judges of appearance than character, Ensign Brideoake was not in Boston long. He lasted fewer than six months in the army before he was forced to resign his commission, having been "accused of theft, cowardice, and almost every other crime." His commanding officer wrote to General Gage, "No young man has ever I believe been more totally abandoned." The regiment paid for his passage back to England to get rid of him as soon as possible.

It seems unlikely that a dalliance with young women got Brideoake into hot water. But it was different for Ensign William Fitzpatrick of the Sixty-Fourth Regiment, who, in the summer of 1769, tried to seduce, and then threatened to rape, Susannah Dalton, the wife of one of the wealthiest men in Boston. When he first met her in the street, Fitzpatrick, in the language of a newspaper report, "made up to her and after using a great deal of fulsome language and attempting some indecencies," he was rebuffed; Susannah managed to escape into her house. When Fitzpatrick returned, Susannah's husband, Peter Roe Dalton, was in the room. In a curious combination of passion and violence, Fitzpatrick shouted up to Dalton that he wanted "that Angel at the window." When that angel's husband reminded Fitzpatrick that he was talking about Dalton's wife, the unhinged Fitzpatrick yelled back, "I don't care whose wife she is, for by G—d I'll have her in spite of all the men in the country; if you are her husband, by G—d you won't keep her long, and if you don't put your head into the window immediately, I'll be d—d if I don't blow your brains out."

Yet even violent public demands to sleep with a married woman did little to damage a soldier's reputation. Dalton immediately went to Justice Dana to swear out a complaint against Fitzpatrick. When Fitzpatrick went to trial, he pleaded no contest to the charges. Or rather, he instructed his lawyer, the Son of Liberty Josiah Quincy, to plead on his behalf. He was let off with a fine that his lawyer immediately appealed. Rather than expressing horror at his conduct, Fitzpatrick's commanding officers promoted him to lieutenant before he left Boston.

Violence and profligate sexual behavior were hardly limited to officers. In August 1770, a Boston woman named Thomasin Charlton crossed the street from the almshouse, where she had been living since February. At the Court of General Sessions she confessed to having had sex with Corporal Archibald Browning of the Fourteenth Regiment the previous summer. The result was a healthy baby boy, born in early May. The court seemed less concerned with Browning's behavior than with Charlton's. When Charlton confessed that this was her second child out of wedlock, the court ordered that she be punished with ten lashes on her bare back. No charges were brought against Browning.

That premarital sex was part of courtship for less elite men and women—privates and poorer women—sometimes seems less surprising to modern readers. But even for middling and elite New Englanders, going to bed with an intended before marriage was quite unexceptional. Unlike in seventeenth-century Puritan New England, in the latter eighteenth century, premarital sex alone almost never resulted in legal charges for fornication before a public court. If the affair resulted in a pregnancy but did not end in marriage, the implications, at least for poorer women, were often quite difficult. Someone would have to help support the child, and if the woman's father could not afford to keep her and her child at home, she would be forced to turn to the public almshouse for shelter.

In truth, Boston officials had some cause to be concerned. As a fornication complaint against one private explained, the child of a soldier was "likely to be born a bastard and chargeable to Boston." It was nearly impossible to force a soldier, who might be gone tomorrow, to pay a bond committing to future child support. Two months after Elizabeth Thomas gave birth to a daughter in the almshouse in August 1771, she claimed that Private John Wooll of the Fourteenth Regiment was the father of the baby. Her sister and another woman came forward to support her claim. The court fined the mother for fornication and threatened her with jail until she paid. No record exists as to whether the county tried to compel Wooll to pay for child support. Instead, in May 1772, the overseers of the almshouse took in "Lydia Wool a Child of Eliz. Thomas." The town of Boston, rather than John Wooll, ended up footing the bill for the child's upkeep.

Abandoned and pregnant in the almshouse, Elizabeth Thomas had plenty of company. Two years earlier, in August 1769, Mary Saunders and John Morris of the Fourteenth had an affair that resulted in a child. In May 1770, Saunders's daughter was born in the almshouse. Like Thomas, whose daughter Lydia returned to the almshouse at nine months, Saunders too moved in and out of that institution with her infant, leaving when the baby was five months old, possibly to work for the merchant Jolley Allens, and returning again when the child was two. We cannot know whether Morris had several strings to his bow. He might never have meant to take a permanent place in Saunders's life. But on the other hand, the relationship between Saunders and Morris might, like many others, be better characterized as a failed courtship than as a successful seduction.

Not all sex between unmarried adults ended up in the courts; the legal system became involved only when the town needed to look for child support. Sometimes sex between a soldier and a Boston woman was simply part of a successful relationship. When the Bostonian Hannah Osborn married the twenty-seven-year-old William

Dundass, a corporal in the Fourteenth Regiment, on Halloween in 1769, she was six months pregnant; William Jr. was born at the beginning of February. Likewise another corporal, Alexander McGregory, married the Bostonian Margaret Sullivan in mid-April 1770; little Margaret appeared a scant eight months later. These married couples might well have been the examples to which Mary Saunders and John Morris, and other pairs like them, aspired.

Marriage

When Mary Nowell married William Clark in the fall of 1769, she may have enjoyed annoying her parents. She may have felt that, at twenty, with fewer men than women in Boston, her chances of marriage were decreasing. Perhaps a romantic appreciation of Clark's uniform swayed her, or it may have been that she wished to escape from a household where her grandfather ruled the roost. It does not appear that she was pregnant. Two and a half centuries later, her personal motives for marriage have been lost. The broader meanings of marriage in occupied Boston, however, may still be discernible. For the most part, imperial politics was not central to the decision to get married. That choice may have excited the concern of families and neighbors, and it had definite implications for property and social standing, but it rarely seemed to have actual political ramifications.

Seeking permission to marry was not William Clark's style. He certainly had not asked Mary's father. Neither, apparently, had he asked his commanding officer. Despite the claim by military pundits that women in the regiment would undermine discipline, the army did not forbid privates from marrying. The actual benefits that women's work could bring to the regiment outweighed the potential disadvantages. Nonetheless, the army was supposed to monitor privates' marriage intentions carefully, as privates were, one authority wrote, "too likely to fix their affections" on women who were sexually promiscuous and unaccustomed to work. Handbooks on army discipline recommended that officers not allow privates to marry without their permission. Acceptable women had to prove themselves "honest [and] laborious." If, upon inquiry, a commanding or noncommissioned officer found that a private was involved with a woman known to be "infamous," he should do his best to discourage the marriage. On the other hand, the same handbooks cautiously admitted that "honest, industrious women are rather good for the company." Women attached to the regiments, as we have seen, could do laundry and nurse the sick. Yet what army life could offer to women was never laid out in an officers' handbook.

Political activists too had ideas about marriage to soldiers. In January 1770, for example, the conservative government-supporter John Mein published a satirical piece in the *Boston Chronicle,* mocking the merchants' nonimportation agreements (which he had refused to sign) and proposing facetiously that Bostonians boycott marriage, as well as imported goods, until the taxes imposed by the 1767 Revenue Acts were repealed. Like the taxed goods listed in the Revenue Acts, the author suggested, women should be locked up in warehouses. "Were the Women thus confined for the sake of Liberty," he wrote sarcastically, "there can be but little doubt, that the troops, at least, would soon leave us." The idea that women are merely marketable commodities is a very old trope, but in parodies like this one, marriage becomes not just an economic exchange, but a political tool.

Boston friends of liberty again turned to doggerel to make their argument that Boston women's liaisons with soldiers were unacceptable. In 1771 the *Massachusetts Spy* republished a 1745 poem by the British poet Robert Dodsley titled "An Epistle from a Society of Young Ladies," which mocked the single life of a bachelor and urged young men to marry. One reader at least seemed to take the poem as a personal attack. "A Bachelor" responded the next week with a bit of rhyming invective that excoriated local women for their interest in soldiers. The only choice now left for young men, the poet claimed, was to decide "is it worse / To marry red coats leavings, or a —!!!? [whore] / Read this, and trouble bachelors no more." Women who had done nothing more than flirt with soldiers, who had become "red coats leavings," were nothing more than prostitutes, unworthy of marriage to the male readers of the *Massachusetts Spy*.

Despite these attacks, some forty local women married soldiers between 1768 and 1772. Naturally, not every eligible woman did so. Three times as many women married civilian men during the same period. Nonetheless, the number of civilian-military marriages in Boston far outnumbered those in Halifax over the previous four years, when the Twenty-Ninth and Fourteenth Regiments were stationed in Nova Scotia. For those years, Halifax records reveal only a single marriage between a private and a civilian woman.

Susannah Sloper was exactly the kind of woman those officers' handbooks warned against. She had given birth to a daughter in the almshouse in 1767, a clear sign that she had little financial support from either her family or from her child's father. Throughout the late 1760s and early 1770s, both of Susannah's sisters had likewise spent some time in the almshouse. Her sister Lydia, who served as a godparent to Susannah's illegitimate child, had several illegitimate children of her own. And then, in 1769, when she was twenty-one years old, Susannah married Private John Brand of the Fourteenth Regiment.

In fact, all kinds of women married across the civilian-military divide. Many of them were not pregnant when they married, nor supporting an out-of-wedlock child. For every Susannah Sloper, there were two or three like Anne Belcher, who married John Wright of the Fourteenth Regiment and still retained her share of her father's tavern in central Boston. Or Mary Welch, who married her soldier in January 1770 and had no child until the following autumn.

Nor does any pattern appear to distinguish privates from commissioned officers. Notwithstanding the disdain Lieutenant Stanton showed for the daughters of local elites, Captain Ponsonby Molesworth of the Twenty-Ninth Regiment eloped with one of those "Boston Beauties" defended in the newspaper poem, the fifteen-year-old daughter of a customs official, Susannah Sheaffe, in April 1769. Although the couple married in New Hampshire, they returned to Boston to baptize their first child ten months later. Certainly, Susannah Sheaffe's father was deeply unpopular among Boston's Sons of Liberty, given his role as enforcer of British taxation, but it seems unlikely that fifteen-year-old Susannah married a soldier because she feared she would never otherwise find a husband.

Perhaps most surprising of all, even after they married soldiers, some of these women continued to be part of Boston's social world. Eight months after Margaret Sullivan married Corporal Alexander McGregory of the Fourteenth Regiment, she was publicly embraced by the Congregational community of New North Church upon testifying to her religious convictions. Even more striking, some women who married soldiers between 1768 and 1772 later remarried, to Boston men, in the 1770s. These couples simply "self-divorced" and then married again. Far from becoming outcasts, women like Hannah Osborn Dundass and Elizabeth Hillman Lindley were welcomed back and would even become supporters of the independence movement after 1775.

For most women, marriage meant throwing their lot in with their husband. For some soldiers' wives, the emotional price of shifting one's community from family to army was overwhelming. While Isabella Graham's life as a regimental wife never brought her to Boston, surely the shape of her experiences was shared by many women married to soldiers who were. Graham married into the Sixtieth Regiment, which was deployed to North America at the same time as the Twenty-Ninth and Fourteenth Regiments. When she left Scotland in the spring of 1767 with her husband of two years, Graham left behind their first child, still an infant, as well as her husband's two sons from his first marriage. As she settled into their first posting, in Quebec, she confessed her homesickness in a letter to her mother: "Had I my dear parents near me, our dear boys, and a few other friends, I might be reconciled to this country; but no place or company, however agreeable, can compensate for their absence."

Graham's husband's regiment was eventually reassigned to Fort Niagara, and four years into their tour of duty, she was no longer homesick, but she continued to long for her mother's presence. Describing her daily round to her mother, she concluded cheerfully, "In short, my ever dear parents, my life is easy and pleasant. The Lord my God make it pious and useful. Could I place myself and family in the same circumstances, and every thing go on in the same manner, within a few miles of you, I should be happy for life; and were it not for this hope, which my heart is set upon, I could not be so, with all I have told you."

Isabella Graham eventually did forge close friendships with other officers' wives, especially those in her husband's regiment. Yet these connections did not compensate for the loss of her family in Scotland. The apprehension of her mother's death hung over all of her letters. In response to a letter from her mother, informing her of the death of her first child, still in her mother's care, she confessed that she had never suspected bad news concerning her child, "for my fears were entirely for you." The distance between Graham and her mother exacerbated her anxiety. In 1773 she wrote desperately, "My ever dear Mother, I have not received one line from you for eight months; judge if my mind can be easy." As it happened, her mother had indeed died, news that devastated Graham. As she tried to comfort her father, she could not contain her own grief at being so far from her family, scribbling through her tears, "I am distressed that I can scarcely write . . . My dearest father, I cannot tell you how much I feel for you; my tears will not allow me, they flow so fast that I cannot write; what would I give to be with you."

As the educated wife of an officer, Graham was able to sustain her relationship with her family to the extent that letters between the backwoods of New York and central Scotland could carry news. Nonetheless, her decision to marry a military man meant that she never saw her mother or son again. When Graham's husband died in 1773, she returned to Scotland and her father as quickly as she could. Her husband's fellow officers paid for her return, and she remained close to some of them and especially their wives for the rest of her life. But her connections with the regiment never rivaled those with her original community.

For Isabella Graham, marriage meant the end of personal relationships as she had known them. But it would change other women's lives even more radically. As was true at this time for all women under British law, marriage made an enormous difference in their legal status. Most obviously, a married woman was usually subsumed under her husband's standing as a person under the law, based on a construct known as coverture. For soldiers' wives, who were likely to move away from home, coverture meant that as married women they lost their legal claim to poor relief from the district in which they had been born. Instead, married women had to claim a husband's birth community. In theory, by marrying into that community, a woman both lost her old connections and made new ones. But it did not always turn out that way.

Mary Welch married Lawrence Northam of the Fourteenth Regiment in January 1770, and gave birth to a son in November. The very next month, however, after Lawrence was moved from his barracks in Boston to Castle Island, a representative from the town's selectmen warned Mary that she had lost the right to claim poor relief in Boston: as the wife of a soldier, she could no longer rely on the town to support her. Jane Crothers, who had married Joseph Whitehouse of the Fourteenth Regiment in that same year, was given the same warning. As locals, Jane and Mary may not have been surprised to find themselves now considered ineligible for public funds. The news was nonetheless a stark reminder of the choice they had made by marrying a soldier.

On occasion, the legal implications of these marriages seemed to be somewhat uncertain in Bostonians' minds. Town and church officials were apparently unsure about how to categorize soldiers. Fewer than four months after the soldiers first came ashore, Annis Parcill married Private Walter Jack of the Fourteenth Regiment. The town clerk's record of their intention to marry did not note that Jack was a soldier. Yet at other times, the clerks of both the town and the churches did note the regiment of a bridegroom. Both Trinity Church and the civil authorities noted that Katherine Skillings married "George Simpson a soldier in the 14th Regt" in April 1769, just a few months after the wedding of Parcill and Jack. Although the recording of the regiment in such cases was no doubt random, the very casualness of the record-keeping itself hints at the ambiguity of the men's place in Boston. Should they be thought of as invading soldiers or as sons-in-law?

A still clearer sign of the confusion surrounding these marriages is preserved in the few records that identify soldiers as "of Boston," sometimes while also recording their regiments. The term "of Boston" indicated a precise legal status. In 1761, John Adams had pondered the specific meaning of the term in his diary. He began with a straightforward definition of what it meant to be legally identified as "of Boston." He reminded himself, "Now it has been adjudged, that, when a Man is called of such a Town, the meaning is that he is an Inhabitant of that Town, a legal Inhabitant of that Town, entituled to all the Priviledges, and compellible to bear all the Burdens of that Town." The legal home of a Boston woman who married a man "of Boston" did not change.

But simply to live in a place is not to be of it. Adams clarified that there was a significant difference between the status "of Boston" and "resident in Boston," and he took as his example officers in the British army who spent winters in Boston during the Seven Years' War: "they are never styled of Boston, but only resident in Boston." Military men passing through without living continuously in the town were not inhabitants, but merely visitors who could not "gain a settlement in any Town." Finally, Adams crowned his argument about the significant difference between residency and habitation with a consideration of the marriageable status of the provincial soldiers who lived in Castle William. These men, Adams asserted, were "all considered as Inhabitants of Boston, so that No Minister will marry a Castle Man, till a Certificate is produced that he has been published in Boston." Like Adams, Bostonians sometimes assumed that members of the Fourteenth and Twenty-Ninth Regiments were legal inhabitants of Boston.

Perhaps this designation made sense for a man who had left his regiment and made his way back to Boston. Twenty-two-year-old Elizabeth Betterly did not hide her new husband's military affiliation when she married Private William Carson of the Twenty-Ninth Regiment in December 1771. Although the regiment had left Boston more than a year and a half earlier, and then had departed for St. Augustine in October 1771, the Trinity Church records clearly identify Carson as a member of that regiment. If he was still a member of the regiment, he was most certainly not one in good standing. Even if the label was intended to do no more than distinguish him from Elizabeth's younger brother (who was, coincidentally, named William Carson Betterly; Elizabeth's mother's maiden name was Carson), it was a striking choice. By referring to her new husband in both the marriage intentions and the church register as "of the 29th Regt.," Betterly identified her marriage as a military one, even as the registers also indicated that both man and woman were "of Boston."

Long before the Twenty-Ninth Regiment had redeployed from Boston to St. Augustine, however, some women were marrying soldiers with the legal claim to be "of Boston." Not only were some of these men unlikely to "bear all the Burdens of that Town," but many of them had no particular love for the place. In July 1770, after the Fourteenth Regiment was supposed to have been moved from Boston proper into the barracks in Castle William, Jesse Lindley married Elizabeth Hillman in King's Chapel, doing so, to all appearances, as a full member of the community. In fact, the church record notes that Lindley and Hillman were "both of Boston." Yet only nine months earlier, while on guard duty, Lindley and another man in his company had been attacked by "a number of Inhabitants" who were angry at being forced to pass through a checkpoint. A month after his wedding, Lindley gave a deposition in which he recalled that the townspeople had said that "the damn'd Sentry had no business there, and that they would soon drive them and all the Rest of the Damn'd Vilians belonging to the King out of Town." These men, at least, did not seem to believe that Lindley was entitled to the privileges of residency that his designation as a Boston inhabitant at his marriage might have implied. Nonetheless, through 1771 and 1772, soldiers continued to be, in Adams's words, "styled of Boston."

Despite the clear hostility between some soldiers and some townspeople, these military men were far from foreigners. By marrying them, Boston women did not reject their families or their town. They did, however, extend their familial bonds into the larger empire. By marrying a soldier, a woman shifted her legal and personal commitments from a father settled in a community to a man whose profession was both peripatetic and unpredictable.

The clearest indication of this shift was the town's system of "warning out." By the middle of the eighteenth century, Massachusetts law assumed that one's legal residence—and the community obligated to give poor relief, as we have seen—was the town into which one was born. A woman could acquire a new legal settlement by marrying into a new community, in which case she would take on the legal residence of her husband.

Not only did these marriages create new ties to an individual, a family, and a military society. They also formed new and more robust links to the empire that sustained this army. Of course, some of these relationships fared better than others; not all marriages lasted long, and some former military wives chose to remarry. But marriages were the first step in making an imperial family, one that the birth of children and the influence of godparents tended to reinforce.

Baptism

When John Morgan brought his daughter, Sarah, to King's Chapel for baptism in the summer of 1770, he was already thirty-five years old. He and his wife, Elizabeth, carried their infant daughter to the baptismal font, and the Reverend Henry Caner invited three others to join them: baby Sarah's godparents. John had enlisted in the Fourteenth Regiment when he was twenty, and he knew the others in his company well. All three godparents had been part of that company with him for years. But the people John and Elizabeth had asked to become fictive kin to their child were more than just mates with a shared past. Future connections mattered as well.

In the eighteenth-century Anglican Church, parents routinely asked three or four other adults to serve as godparents. These god-parents served as links in networks of honor, obligation, and com-mitment. Sometimes they were aspirational connections—a private might ask his sergeant or his sergeant's wife to be a godparent as a sign of respect. Other godparents were friends, or those with whom the parents hoped to forge a relationship.

Because the Morgans were baptizing a daughter, they chose one man, John Morris, and two women, Mary Yeats and Elizabeth Lind-ley. The same John Morris who had had an affair with Mary Saunders in 1769 must have been a particularly charismatic man, as Morgan was not the only member of the Fourteenth who asked him to stand as a godfather. When Morris stepped into the cool granite church, it had been only three weeks since his former lover had confessed in court to fornication. The two women were both regimental spouses: Mary was married to Sergeant Thomas Yeats, and Elizabeth Lindley to Jesse Lindley. All three godparents, as well as the father, came from the company of Lieutenant Colonel William Dalrymple.

It is not particularly remarkable that all three of little Sarah Mor-gan's godparents were tied to her father's military company. More surprising, perhaps, is that Elizabeth Lindley, the third godparent, had not long been affiliated with the company. Jesse Lindley and Elizabeth Hillman had been married barely a month before, and in the same church where Sarah's baptism was now taking place. Taken together, her godparents offered a remarkable array of civilian and military connections. Her parents first chose the sergeant's wife as a gesture of respect within the company; second, a soldier who had had an affair with a local woman; and third, a local woman who had just married into the regiment. Two years after troops had come to Boston, the majority of these new ties to the Fourteenth Regiment were overwhelmingly routed through Boston's local community.

Sarah Morgan's baptism is not the only example of extensive social and emotional networks among soldiers and civilians in Boston. Katherine Skillings married George Simpson of the Fourteenth Regiment in April 1769, and the following March they baptized their first child, named for his father. For godparents they chose two men and one woman. Like the Morgans, they looked to the army for godparents, ones who would strengthen the connection between Boston's military and civilian worlds.

The first was Thomas Wilson, a friend from the same company but not a superior. Although apparently unmarried, he obviously had close friends in Massachusetts, perhaps even closer than those in his regiment, for he deserted the following December, melting successfully into the surrounding community. The second godparent was Joseph Whitehouse, a member of a different company; the fact that he too would marry a local woman less than two weeks after the baptism may have cemented the bond between Whitehouse and Simpson. The third sponsor, Elizabeth Hartley, was married to a soldier. Yet Elizabeth's husband, John, was not from the same company as either Simpson or Whitehouse, and Elizabeth herself was an Englishwoman who had traveled to Boston with her husband. Why the Simpsons asked Elizabeth to be the godmother to their first child is unknown, but we can glimpse a friendship between the two wives. The next year, Elizabeth asked Katherine to be the godmother to her daughter Hannah. Despite the fact that Elizabeth Hartley was not a local woman, she and Katherine had made a bond that seemed to supersede even ties of home or military unit. These two women—one who had traveled with the army for years, the other a Bostonian who had just begun to be a part of the army — had become godmothers to each other's children and, one trusts, friends.

In the years 1768 to 1772, more than a hundred soldiers brought their babies into Boston's churches to be baptized. The baptismal records preserve connections that parents made for their children, radiating outward from the nuclear family. They reveal links that townspeople formed with military families, as well as friendships between women. Perhaps even more than sex or marriage, the role of godparent allowed women and men to publicize their ties to a community.

Hannah Dundass, who was pregnant when she married a soldier from the Fourteenth Regiment and then remarried a few years after her husband's regiment left Boston, used her child's baptism to strengthen her ties to her fellow Bostonians. When her first child was born in February 1770, only one godparent, a fellow corporal from another company, came from the army. The other two godparents were Bostonians and possibly members of the same Congregational church — Old South — in which Dundass herself had grown up. Those two godparents had not rejected their longtime family friend when she married a soldier. Instead, they joined with a noncommissioned officer to sponsor the child of a soldier.

Even parents who had both come to Boston with the army might choose as their children's godparents people with strong ties to civilian communities. Joseph Brocklesby was the son of a soldier from the Fourteenth Regiment and his English-born wife; when he was baptized, his godparents included his father's sergeant, who had himself married a local woman the year before, and a Bostonian, Frances Sheldon, who three months later would marry a man from the same company. The choice of godparents reflected a family's interest in strengthening their bonds with the wider community, and the godparents themselves in agreeing to serve showed a similar desire. Before Frances Sheldon married into the army, she used the social setting of baptism to make yet another tie to the world of her future husband.

Bearing a child in Boston did not compel an army couple to make connections with locals outside the army, and thousands of Bostonians baptized their children without reliance on military godparents. Even so, the recurrence in the historical record of these arrangements speaks to the ease with which civilians and soldiers relied on one another for public support and affirmation.

Agreeing to sponsor a soldier's child did not inspire the same anxiety among Boston's Whigs that marrying a soldier did. No one wrote poems about the depravity of godparents. Baptism was public but not political. Yet sponsoring a child and marrying a soldier performed similar sorts of cultural work. Marriage and sponsorship were affectionate and even loving acts that also had public meanings. When godparents stood with parents at the baptismal font, they made visible the familial connections between civilians and the army in occupied Boston.

When women chose to marry soldiers, or when fathers tried to keep soldiers from becoming their sons-in-law, the imperial power that the British army represented reached into homes, bedrooms, and cribs. It brought together people who otherwise might never have met—and it had the power to pull them apart. For some who wanted these relationships to be more than transient, they had to take matters into their own hands. They had to leave the army.

6

Absent Without Leave, 1768–70

Corporal John Moies had certainly seen his share of punishment since he joined the Fourteenth Regiment in 1765. After all, he had been present at the notorious flogging that his captain, Brabazon O'Hara, had overseen in England. How could it be any worse in Boston? Unlike Moies's former sergeant back in Salisbury, who had died after the vicious flogging ordered by O'Hara, at least most soldiers managed to survive the experience. Yet within the first two weeks of the army's arrival in Boston, rumors were buzzing about the cruelty that the British army dealt out to its own men. The punishment of Private Daniel Rogers was a topic of conversation everywhere. From private letters to newspapers, the lashing of Private Rogers seemed to erase the lines between the army and the town.

On a bright Friday in October 1768, less than two weeks after the Fourteenth and Twenty-Ninth Regiments had arrived from Halifax, Daniel Rogers was tied to stakes in the middle of the Boston Common. A court-martial had decreed that he was to receive a thousand lashes with the cat-o'-nine-tails. He endured 170 before he fainted and the soldiers cut off the bonds that tied him to the halberds. Now he lay on his stomach, waiting to recover sufficiently so they could tie him up and finish the punishment. He wished he could die.

This public flogging might not have seemed worse to Moies than the one he had seen three years earlier. That time, two civilians accidentally stumbled upon the flogging, ordered by O'Hara up on Twyford Downs, and were rooted to the spot in horror. One of them was "so shocked at the cruelty of the whipping" that he thought he might pass out. That witness was no stranger to such proceedings; he himself was a member of the local militia and told the court that he had seen "many men whipped, but no one like this." The Bostonians who observed the flogging of Private Rogers had their own point of comparison. A newspaper reported that more than one man who had held an officer's commission in the army during the Seven Years' War thought that "only 40 of the 170 lashes received by Rogers, at this time, was equal in punishment to 500, they had seen given in other regiments."

In fact, Boston officers with commissions and Boston privates who had enlisted in the British army during the Seven Years' War had extensive experience in observing military punishments; one Massachusetts private recorded observing seventy-one floggings (and six executions) over a seven-month period in 1757, and it seems likely that most soldiers — and the women who traveled with them — would have either seen or heard about a similar number. But, in the eyes of the local people of Boston, as horrific as the whipping itself was the reason for it. Private Rogers had not fallen asleep on guard, gotten drunk while on duty, or even spoken insolently to an officer. He had simply wanted to visit his family.

· · ·

Daniel Rogers grew up in Marshfield, a short distance from Boston, and during the Seven Years' War he had joined the Twenty-Seventh Regiment in its expedition to Canada. But when his original regiment packed up for England in 1767, Rogers transferred to the Twenty-Ninth in order to stay in America. He had been in Halifax with his new regiment for a year before its move to Massachusetts. His family still lived in Marshfield, and for Rogers the move was a homecoming.

The army did not see it that way. Early in October 1768, Rogers was still living in a tent on the Boston Common. Amid the disarray of the army's temporary housing, he had hoped to slip out unnoticed to see his friends. Unfortunately for him, however, someone did notice his absence and labeled him a deserter. As a result, the colonel of the Twenty-Ninth Regiment decided to make a public spectacle of Rogers and several others in his position.

Massachusetts women were particularly shocked at Rogers's punishment. His sisters came to see him after the flogging and were so horrified at his condition that they both fainted. But it was not just members of the Rogers family who were aghast. The Massachusetts courts never handed down more than thirty-nine lashes as corporal punishment. The daughter of one of Governor Bernard's strongest supporters, Dorothy (Dolly) Murray, was alarmed by the spectacle of this kind of military discipline in Boston. Although she herself had been eager to see her fiancé join the army, she did not sugarcoat its potential for violence. Dolly urged her younger sister to remain in the countryside, far from the awful sights of occupation, "for here is poor wretches whipt almost to death, a man that belonged to Marshfield run away to see his friends was sentenced to receive a thousand lashes . . . a miserable object with his back as raw as a piece of Beef."

Nor, she suggested, was Rogers's case an anomaly. Please, she begged, no matter how attractive the idea of handsome young men in red coats might be, stay far away from this town filled with British regulars. In case her graphic description of Rogers's back was not strong enough, she concluded, "now after hearing of many cruelties of this kind which happen almost every day if you don't think you are much happier . . . than in Boston, I am mistaken." Dolly Murray was no radical, but even for her, the cost of having troops in Boston seemed too high.

In the end, a committee of Bostonians petitioned Lieutenant Colonel Carr to spare Rogers any further punishment. The officer, in a gesture directed far more at the town than at the unfortunate soldier, graciously acceded to the committee's request to forgo the rest of the whipping, adding, "He is very glad he has it in his power to oblige the people of Boston." Daniel Rogers's punishment, both in its harshness and its eventual leniency, seemed to supersede the politics that had compelled the governor to request the troops in the first place.

If Rogers had been looking for some home comforts, Corporal Moies certainly could not blame him. For a long month after he arrived in Boston, Moies and the rest of the Fourteenth Regiment slept on the drafty floor of Faneuil Hall; neither the hall nor the Town-House provided luxurious living. Moies's own captain, Brabazon O'Hara, had managed to rent a house from John Rowe within a week. Moies had been in O'Hara's company for three and a half years now, ever since he had joined up back in England. He could not have been surprised that O'Hara was more interested in looking out for his own bodily comfort than that of his men.

But while the captain settled into life in Boston, socializing regularly with John Rowe and other Bostonians, the rank and file of the army started to slip away. John Moore was the first to leave, disappearing just three days after his regiment had landed. After Moore made it out successfully, colleagues from the Twenty-Ninth Regiment started following his example. Four left on October 5, three more on the ninth, and then seven on the tenth. At least thirty soldiers had deserted by the end of the first month.

John Moies knew that the army would not look kindly on desertion. He had been forced to listen to the lecture on the punishment for desertion before he and his mates left Halifax. For that matter, he had heard it before they got to Halifax too. But hardly anyone wanted to desert while they were in Halifax. The entire two years the Fourteenth Regiment had been in Canada, only eight men deserted, all in the summer before they left for Boston.

Even so, this posting to Massachusetts was unlike any that Moies had experienced. Even while they were still living in temporary housing, the soldiers found themselves surrounded by civilians. They were, after all, in the center of Boston. For men like Moies, this fact offered countless possibilities. He just had to find the best way to make the most of them. And he had to avoid being caught.

Back in England, when Moies first joined the army, he and his company were far from the eyes of civilians, for the most part. But not here. In Boston, every act of the army, its officers, and, indeed, many of its soldiers was in plain sight. Nothing drove home to a man like Moies — and to the civilians who surrounded him — the connections between civilians and soldiers as much as the public punishment of deserters.

Desertion hampers every army. Desertion in Boston, however,

was both greater than and different from the usual problems faced elsewhere in the British Empire. Historians estimate that during the Seven Years' War, the British army in North America lost about 3 percent of its force each year to desertion. The Connecticut provincial regiments lost nearly twice as large a percentage of men annually: from 4 to 6 percent. Yet those numbers were minuscule compared to the flood of men absconding from the ranks in Boston. In their first seventeen months in the town, eighty-nine men deserted from the Twenty-Ninth Regiment alone. For that single regiment, the annual rate of desertion was a full 10 percent. Something about the posting to Boston had changed the usual pattern. In addition to the typical motives for desertion — disliking an officer or feeling disgusted with army life in general — soldiers in Boston deserted for reasons that had everything to do with their new friends, families, and other connections.

At first, the commanding officers aggressively searched out deserters. When nearly twenty men had disappeared by October 12, 1768, the officers decided to act. Captain Charles Fordyce of the Fourteenth Regiment sent a sergeant and three men to look for deserters. They headed west on foot, dressed in civilian clothes to avoid attracting attention. The next day, rather tired and thirsty, they stopped at a tavern along the main road in Framingham for a drink. A veteran of the Seven Years' War, Colonel Joseph Buckminster, owned the establishment, but he offered no leads about the deserters. But an enslaved woman who was working in the tavern that day mentioned information that proved useful.

Giving the impression that they themselves were deserters looking for work, the regulars asked the woman if she could help. Oblig-ingly, she told them that just a mile away lived a farmer who had hired a deserter a few days earlier. She went so far as to point out the farmhouse through the open door. One of the soldiers asked the name of the farmer who lived there. "Eames," she told them. As it turned out, Richard Eames was the name of one of the deserters for whom they were searching. Without revealing that, they asked the woman whether she might be confused. No, she answered. She knew that Eames was the name of the farmer "and that the Regular was his namesake."

The other residents of Framingham were just as unsuspecting and helpful. Two of the privates, continuing to pretend to be deserters, approached the farmer to ask if he knew the man for whom they were searching. The farmer took them into his field, where they found the deserter Richard Eames harvesting corn. When Eames saw them, he agreed willingly to a quick break for a drink. And so, continued one of the privates, "they, the prisoner [private Eames], and farmer Eames, went to the house of the farmer, where they drank some cider together." After their drink, the two soldiers pulled out pistols and told the deserter that he was under arrest. He made no protest and got up to leave with them. Pleased with their success but worried that Farmer Eames or his friends might come after them, the army men left Framingham immediately with their prisoner and were in Boston by the next day.

When the search party brought Eames back to Boston, Lieutenant Colonel Dalrymple decided to make a spectacle of the deserter. After a full general court-martial, over which Dalrymple presided, Eames was sentenced to death by a firing squad made up of his own company. Dalrymple was charged with finding a "proper spot on the common near the water side for the Execution."

As a deterrent, Eames's death would be effective only if it was very public. And so General Gage ordered every soldier in Boston to be present at the execution. Before dawn on the morning of October 31, the soldiers stood in formation, waiting for Richard Eames's end. John Moies, standing on the dark Boston Common, had plenty of time to wonder about this execution.

Bostonians were shocked by the spectacle of the first (and, it turned out, the last) execution for desertion on the Boston Common. A number of women had petitioned the lieutenant colonel to show clemency to the first-time deserter but, unlike Carr, who granted an appeal to reduce the number of lashes for Daniel Rogers, Dalrymple turned down their request. Letter writers, from middle-aged men to teenage girls, noted the execution in their correspondence. John Rowe recorded it without comment; he was at a loss for words.

In his panic, and without legal counsel, Eames had offered an extraordinarily weak defense of his actions. With the eyes of twelve army captains, including Brabazon O'Hara, upon him, Eames stammered through excuses that the court-martial easily disproved. First, he said that he was angry at his captain because the officer owed him back pay. But the witness that he called in his own defense testified that his accounts were up to date. And then Eames said that he had deserted because he feared that his captain would hit him for making mistakes when on parade. But another of his own witnesses testified that he made no more mistakes than anyone else.

The fact that Eames had obviously deserted his regiment no doubt counted more heavily against him than any defense he might have made. No one seemed particularly interested in the offhand remark of the enslaved Framingham woman, that Eames was the "namesake" of Farmer Eames, although there was indeed a large extended family of Eameses in Framingham. Whether he really had been angry over his pay or whether, like Daniel Rogers the week before, he had been looking for his family was irrelevant. Now, dressed in white, with a regimental chaplain by his side, he appeared remorseful yet resigned. At 7 a.m. the firing squad shot Richard Eames. Marching around the dead body, Moies must have wondered whether the firing squad was the only way to escape the army.

Both British officers and local proponents of the liberty party might have understood the impact of bringing troops to Boston better if they had paid more attention to the fact that Richard Eames had been found at a farm belonging to the Eames family. Instead, almost every person with a pen interpreted this and other desertions as somehow politically rather than personally motivated. In fact, both Crown and opposition politicians tried to appropriate the unusual uptick in desertions for their own political arguments. The men who deserted, however, and the colonists who helped them performed their own calculus. Desertion, far from solely an army problem, was the result of military-civilian relationships.

Still, observers saw what they wanted to see. Friends of liberty, for example, chortled with pleasure as they watched the ranks thin. By October 18, the Congregational minister Andrew Eliot could write to his English correspondent, "The Soldiers begin to desert, no one will betray them, — about forty are gone already." Commenting on the scarce numbers left in Boston at the end of the fall, the *Journal of the*

Times sniffed that the "thin appearance" of the muster of the troops in honor of the queen's birthday in January 1769 was clear evidence that "their being quartered in this town was a measure as impolitick as it was illegal." The liberty party gleefully interpreted these desertions as one of the best possible attacks on the British garrison.

Even moderates saw deserters as a judgment on the British ministry. The speaker of the Massachusetts Assembly, Thomas Cushing, keeping a close eye on the troops during their first winter in Boston, wrote smugly to the province's agent, Dennys De Berdt, "Our people behave with the greatest caution and prudence, so that I am persuaded the commanders of the troops and men-of-war are not a little surprised at the errand they were sent upon . . . The soldiers are continually deserting. They like the country, and it is so wide and extensive that it will be very difficult to recover those that desert." The idea of officers befuddled by their assignment to Boston, then lost in the countryside, trying to find deserters and wasting the empire's time and treasure, clearly gave Cushing great pleasure. Soldiers' desertions became the Crown's comeuppance.

That same winter the writers of the *Journal of the Times* could declare, "We will not pretend [claim] to say whether this disposition to desert, is owing to a disrelish to the service, or a great liking the troops had taken to the country. They [the soldiers] observe, that the winter is very moderate, the common people cheerful, hearty, and well-clad, and such variety and delicacies in the markets in this town, as lead them to conclude that they are now got into Canaan, a land not indeed abounding with silver and gold, but a land flowing with milk and honey." Writers were convinced that the natural, even divine appeal of Massachusetts was irresistible to soldiers. Thomas

Jarvis, writing to his brother-in-law in Charleston, South Carolina, stated more simply but just as confidently that although "the sogers [soldiers] are thick in the Streats . . . and Sentres placed att Sundreys places," nonetheless "a grat many of them [soldiers] are Goan into the Cuntrey and dont desire to Return."

Adherents to the liberty party believed that even the most faithful soldiers could be tempted by the delights of the Massachusetts countryside. They published fictitious letters in the newspapers that celebrated the joys of the province, at least from a (stereotypical) soldier's perspective. One claimed to be "an Extract of a Letter from a Soldier in Boston, in New-England, to his Brother in London, Dec 12, 1768"; the soldier expressed his longing for his sweetheart to join him before he made the switch from campaigning to farming. The purported soldier wrote that having been extracted from the wilds of Nova Scotia, "there is no danger of us losing our scalps at present . . . We are now among a very good sort of people, who mean us no harm, but wish us to quit the army and live among them. I am told it is easy for a man to get a little farm in this country, and if Moll was but here, I should certainly do it." The letter spoke to the ambitions of most British men to have a chance to marry and live as a comfortable freeholder. By the calculus of the liberty movement, it was a wonder that any privates remained in the army at all. Their desertion was the perfect tacit argument that life in America was superior to life in the British army, which oppressed both civilians and its own soldiers.

Once soldiers began to disappear from Boston, British army officers, like their civilian opposition, focused on the political implications of desertion. They were as unhappy as the liberty party was jubilant, constantly searching for new ways to stanch the flow of men into the countryside. Commanding officers in Boston wrote reams of letters to General Gage, urging him to approve an array of responses, from capital punishment to pardons and back again. Within the first eight months in Boston, General Alexander Mackay, of the Sixty-Fifth Regiment and commanding officer, found the problem of desertion so pervasive that he wrote to Gage, "I must likewise inform you, that whatever Troops are left in this Town, must in all probability be intirely ruined in the course of a Year; what I mean is, that the Bulk of their Men will be induced to Desert."

The extraordinary rate of desertion seems to have been a common topic of conversation among officers of the Crown throughout the empire. In April 1769, the governor of Nova Scotia, annoyed that Halifax had been left with no regiments, carped peevishly to his patron, Lord Egmont, that he did not "think General Gage a very good friend to this Province by keeping as many of the Troops from us as possible and not even leaving us one last Post altho' the Troops are daly deserting [in Boston]." While "daily desertion" was certainly an exaggeration, the fact that in the month of April a soldier deserted every two and a half days on average evidently had caught the Canadian governor's attention.

Even before the troops came ashore in Boston, Governor Bernard imagined that soldiers' desertion—or more exactly, the way his citizens encouraged soldiers to desert—could become the opposition's tool for resisting his administration. The political fight that the governor and officers had had with the Governor's Council and the selectmen over where to house the troops involved concerns about desertion. The reason Bernard had not wanted to scatter soldiers throughout the city, in taverns and private buildings, was at least in part his fear that soldiers would "intermix with the Town's People" and get into fights with locals. But he worried that this intermixing "would also occasion frequent Desertion, for which no encouragement would be wanting." Bernard could imagine townspeople as both hostile to soldiers and eager to welcome them. It was a contradictory but surprisingly shrewd insight.

Bernard was not wrong about civilians' "encouragement" of desertion. John Croker of the Twenty-Ninth Regiment recalled that during his first two months in Boston, while he was still camping on the Boston Common, a local man invited him to a pub for a drink and offered him help if he wanted to desert: not only money, but clothes too, so he could escape detection. The man even gave him a half-dollar to seal the deal. Croker may have been tempted, but he never did leave his regiment.

Francis Lee of the Fourteenth Regiment was also importuned to leave, but his civilian contact, David Geary of Stoneham, was caught in the act. Lieutenant Colonel Dalrymple, as one of the commanding officers in Boston, swore out a complaint against Geary on the advice of the Boston lawyer Robert Auchmuty Jr., thereby setting in motion a lawsuit against the civilian. In November 1768 Geary appeared before the Superior Court to answer the charge that he did "with force and arms unlawfully encourage counsel and advise the said Francis to desert the said service of the said Lord King." The Boston jury found Geary not guilty, to the evident pleasure of a local newspaper. As for Lee, the time was not yet right for him to leave, but it would come.

In their frustration, officers railed against privates and townspeople alike. Yet for all the military's explicit discussion of desertion as a political tactic, the language officers used to describe it suggests a more intimate affront. For example, as Dalrymple wrote to Gage about the case against the Stoneham resident Geary, "[Boston Sons of Liberty] have exerted themselves to the utmost to debauch our men. Their success has been something, however they have received in their turn a defeat the soldiers having informed against the seducers, two of them are now in gaol." "Debauch," "seducers"—it seems the army had suddenly found itself inside a novel by Samuel Richardson.

The idea of seduction permeates the officers' correspondence. Colonel Pomeroy of the Sixty-Fourth Regiment explained to Gage that Matthew French, a deserter from the Twenty-Ninth, "was seduced . . . by a country man who gave him half a guinea." The next month Gage assured General Mackay that he had confidence that the oppressed commander was doing his best in a difficult posting, where "it is to be expected that every means will be used to seduce the soldiers."

Dalrymple's analysis of the situation in the fall of 1769 drew out the overlap of seduction, inducement, and intimacy when he attributed the high rate of desertion to the relationships between soldiers and locals. In a dispirited letter to Gage, the officer wrote, "It is with the greatest concern I am a spectator of the frequent desertions, but nothing can in my opinion be done effectually to prevent it, the encouragement they receive from the inhabitants, as well as the high wages, are enducements too forcible to be withstood besides their long continuation here has naturally created intimacies with the people." He felt helpless before the twin entrancements of money and close relationships.

In contrast to Dalrymple, Gage reassured himself that "encouragement" and high wages alone would not be enough to keep men in the countryside. He was convinced that the colonists offering blandishments to a soldier would invariably turn out to be duplicitous. The general thought that the deserter, like many a seduced and abandoned heroine, would see the error of his ways and try to return. He comforted Lieutenant Colonel Carr of the Twenty-Ninth Regiment: "I have long since been persuaded that both the town and Country People have encouraged the soldiers to Desert, and I don't wonder that after having been some time with them they should be desirous of returning again to their Duty for they keep them under[,] work them hard, Pay them nothing, and upon any complaint, threaten them with delivering them up to their regiment." But this comforting analysis, like the disingenuous claims of the Boston newspapers that the allure of the countryside was all a soldier needed to jettison the army, ignored the fact that soldiers deserted because someone had helped, supported, or hidden them.

Soldiers' friendships, regular interactions, and chance encounters with Bostonians also had the potential to extend their connections with civilians in and beyond the limits of the town. Accounts of deserters as well as the various methods officers used in their attempts to reduce desertion undermine a view of soldiers as isolated strangers on a foreign continent. Most of all, deserters made lasting ties with single women.

Fragments of stories about deserters suggest the social networks these men forged in their new civilian life. Private Hugh Anderson, for example, found himself in the Boston jail for theft in April 1770. As was the case for many soldiers, the legal records erased his military identity, categorizing him only as one among several of the prisoners jailed for theft. Cooped up with twenty other people, both male and female, all accused of theft, Anderson might well have forged some new connections. Once free, he returned only briefly to his regiment; he deserted the following summer. The Fourteenth Regiment never recaptured Anderson; he remained hidden, possibly in Boston itself, for at least a year. Then, in December 1773, he emerged again in the Boston records, having married Susannah Jordan in Trinity Church.

Francis Lee, the soldier whom David Geary was accused of trying to "entice" to desertion, actually deserted in 1769. He may have used the connections Geary offered. Within four years he had married, settled near the New Hampshire border, and started a family.

Desperate to turn these social networks to their own advantage, officers began advertising in newspapers that they would pay three guineas as a reward to any local who captured a deserter. They also promised a pardon to any deserters who returned within the month. But there was a catch: the advertisement included a substantial list of those who were not eligible for a pardon because their "Crimes are of such a Nature" that the army could not forgive them. Daniel Rogers, the Marshfield man who suffered such a brutal lashing after he was caught the first time, was on the list. No one ever turned him in.

Despite the horrific example of Richard Eames's execution by firing squad in October 1768, nothing seemed to discourage men from leaving the army. Gage and other officers regularly debated the best ways both to prevent desertion and to recover men who had left as an example to those who might consider slipping away. At various moments they tried offering rewards for capturing deserters, providing amnesty to those who had left and might want to return, and sending out more search parties to hunt them down. The first two options apparently had little impact; sending a small posse of soldiers out into the countryside, by contrast, certainly produced an effect. But it was not always the desired one.

In January 1769, for example, Major Furlong of the Fourteenth Regiment decided to send out a search party to look for deserters. Three had escaped from the troops' posting in Nova Scotia and had been recorded missing as of August 27, 1768, well before the Fourteenth's transfer to Boston. Furlong had somehow learned that they had made their way to New Hampshire. In the expedition to capture them, officers learned that both men and women in the country were willing to protect deserters.

Furlong sent three privates on the trip, under the command of Sergeant William Henderson. One morning in Londonderry, New Hampshire, the four men came across one of the deserters, Thomas Sherwood, at work near a building so derelict that the sergeant referred to it as a "hovel." Both Sherwood and his current employer, one Edward Akin, at first appeared to admit defeat when the soldiers accosted Sherwood. Akin paid Sherwood some of his wages and brought out his uniform. As the soldiers began their march back to Boston, Sherwood pointed out the house of another soldier, James Darnby, who had deserted with him. The sergeant and one of the privates rapped at the door and found Darnby sitting with a few women at midday dinner.

Seizing Darnby, the men marched out of the house and began their trip back to Massachusetts. But after the first five or six miles, one member of the search party looked back and saw that they were being followed by a mob of men, fifty or so, by his and the sergeant's count, all of them armed with guns and pistols. Edward Akin was among them. The New Hampshire men urged the deserters to run. One man shot at the military party; the armed crowd then circled them and forcibly liberated the two prisoners. As Sherwood and Darnby melted back into the New Hampshire woods, the rescuers warned the sergeant that he was "never [to] come there again to look after deserters."

The local paper offered quite a different account. It suggested that the two deserters were in fact only strangers minding their own business, and claimed that the search party, men dressed neither as soldiers on official business nor as sailors impressing men for the navy, had no business kidnapping people in broad daylight. "Equitas" (the pen name of the writer of the editorial) did not deny that the men were strangers to Londonderry, who "were travelling into the country, and made Londonderry in their way." He suggested, however, that anyone who attempted to seize "even strangers" was not immune from community disapproval and that "such persons might reasonably expect opposition." The extent to which essayists as well as farmers were willing to go to protect deserters was formidable.

Through the winter and spring, Colonel Pomeroy, then the commanding officer in Boston, and Governor Wentworth of New Hampshire corresponded about the incident. Wentworth made clear to Pomeroy that his sergeant would have to come back to New Hampshire to swear out a complaint against the men and that he should have used civilian authorities to find the deserters. Pomeroy was initially affronted by these checks on his authority, but by April the colonel could report to Gage that Wentworth had "done everything in his power to apprehend those concerned in the rescue of the deserters."

Eventually, Sherwood was recaptured without incident, was put in a New Hampshire jail, and agreed to name names. He was so helpful, in fact, that when Governor Wentworth petitioned for a pardon for the soldier, Pomeroy was willing to give him one.

Pomeroy hoped that he and Wentworth had worked so efficiently to capture deserters that they had given up on New Hampshire and were fleeing to New York instead. He was wrong; New Hampshire remained a sanctuary for men who wanted to make a new life away from the army.

Within a month of Sherwood's return to Boston, Pomeroy was reminded of how friendly New Hampshire could be to deserters. A magistrate in that province, having heard a rumor that a new neighbor was a deserter, called him in for questioning. Although he denied it at first, eventually Private Andrew Trumble was willing to admit to his desertion and to return, with a promise of leniency, to the Twenty-Ninth Regiment.

The magistrate sometimes encountered more resistance from those who aided the deserters than from the men themselves. John Butler had deserted from the Twenty-Ninth Regiment during his first month in Boston and eventually found his way to New Hampshire. When the magistrate promised to try to secure a pardon for Butler, as he had for Trumble, if he would turn himself in, Butler readily complied. The family he lived with, the Bailys, were much less intimidated by the local authorities, however, and they warned the magistrate against trying to take Butler by force. Although the family had wisely disappeared when the magistrate and a posse did come to take Butler, thereby avoiding an armed confrontation, Butler himself was not eager to return to army life. Less than three and a half months after his return from desertion, Butler took off again, never to rejoin his regiment.

When Butler and Trumble returned to Boston, their commanding officers were not convinced that the two should receive much in the way of leniency. They apparently preferred the idea of another spectacle on the Common, but after canvassing the opinion of the regiments' captains, they reluctantly agreed that other potential deserters would not be persuaded by a show of force, for, as they wrote, "the whole country harbors and protects them." In fact, Lieutenant Colonel Dalrymple complained that when he sent out search parties to recapture deserters, "the people of the country in very great numbers surrounded them." Smearing black paint on their faces as a disguise and exhilarated at their success in beating the army, civilians fiercely defended deserters, convincing Dalrymple that it would be a waste of resources to try to seize them in a frontal attack.

In the fall of 1769, Dalrymple thought he might have discovered a way to exploit civilians' casual acceptance of deserters. He found a man willing to ride around the New England countryside and chat up new residents, in the hope of finding former army men. Over the course of two weeks in September, this informer clocked over two hundred miles in Massachusetts and New Hampshire and brought back news of dozens of deserters. According to his notes, all of them had found work, and many had settled into communities. Several continued to wear their uniform while doing both skilled and unskilled work, from cobbling shoes to bringing in the harvest. Their status as deserters was apparently an open secret.

Several had begun to make new families. Just over the New Hampshire border, for example, the informer found a deserter "who calls himself Lochlan," a "likely man" who, having lived there all winter, was now married to Sarah Foster, his landlord's daughter, and starting a family. He was easily recognizable, the informer continued, because "he frequently wears his regimental jacket." John Loughran had been one of the first soldiers to leave Boston, deserting with four others the very first week the troops were in Massachusetts. Dalrymple was unable to force Loughran to give up his new life and return to the army.

Dalrymple did have some successes, however, and with the steady stream of deserters being dragged back to Boston, the public whipping sites on the Boston Common were in regular use. Throughout 1769, Dalrymple continued to hold courts-martial for deserters. By his own lights, the lieutenant colonel was often quite lenient when it came to punishment. "The Deserters under the sentence of the late Courts Martial have received part of their punishments, no one more than two hundred lashes," he informed Gage that winter. The general encouraged such moderation at times too. "You may Occasionally mitigate some of the Punishments," he reassured Dalrymple. Or at least he could do so in the situations "where the Prisoners shall not be able to bear them."

But the army's standard of leniency was not the same as civilians', and locals did not accept the sight and sound of men enduring hundreds of lashes with a cat-o'-nine-tails. In the winter of 1768-69, the Boston Congregational minister Andrew Croswell published a pamphlet in which he inveighed against this practice and reminded his readers that thirty-nine strokes was the biblical maximum. More than that "are a disgrace to the human nature." Moreover, such excessive punishments were often inflicted in anger and ended in death. For his prime example, Croswell pointed to a British officer now comfort-

ably ensconced in one of John Rowe's rented houses: Captain Brabazon O'Hara. The story of the sergeant whom O'Hara had ordered to
be whipped to death in 1765 had followed O'Hara from England to
Halifax and now to Boston.

So popular was the Reverend Croswell's pamphlet on the evils
of military punishment that it went into a second printing within a
week. The second edition also contained a second anonymous essay
("by another hand" than Croswell's) on "military cruelties," which
explained the social, rather than moral, implications of flogging. The
author claimed that Richard Eames's execution after his 1768 desertion from the Fourteenth Regiment and the many military whippings
that had followed had created such sympathy for soldiers among civilians that "although they would by no means encourage diserters
when they happen to meet with any upon the road, they will be so far
from securing them, that they will . . . do all in their power to secrete
them from their bloodthirsty pursuers." In other words, if deserters
managed to escape detection, the army had no one to blame but itself.
Given the well-known consequences for captured deserters, no civilian with any "principles of humanity and compassion" could possibly
turn them in.

The Bostonian Joshua Henshaw's visceral reactions to these military punishments bear out the generalizations of Croswell's essay. In
a letter to his cousin, Henshaw recounted a story of a soldier who
had been discovered in the act of sneaking out of Boston because of
the telltale shape of his regimental hat; he had changed the rest of his
clothes. Still shocked by the execution of Richard Eames, Henshaw
hoped that because this desertion had not been entirely successful, the
man would not be shot. He urged his cousin to close his eyes to any

possible deserters, suggesting that "the safest way is to treat them all kindly & ask no questions for conscience's sake." By suggesting that colonists silently overlook possible deserters, Henshaw helped weave a safety net for men trying to join Massachusetts civilian society. Unlike some members of the liberty coalition, Henshaw did not openly urge soldiers to desert. But his attitude of "see no evil" made it possible for deserters to become a part of a new community once they had decided to leave their old one.

But to take advantage of those civilian networks, a soldier first had to slip away from his regiment, and the means of being found out, such as inadequately hiding one's uniform or unwitting betrayal, were numerous. But at times the extensive friendships some soldiers had made in Boston were enough to help them escape from the army. Corporal John Moies decided to make his attempt through an unusual and rather complex scheme: a feigned theft, close coordination with Bostonians, and, possibly, a sweetheart.

In March 1769, Moies and five companions, all from Captain Brabazon O'Hara's company, helped themselves to an enormous stock of goods from John Carnes's dry goods store. The thieves took more than twenty-six British pounds' worth of goods, including twenty-two pairs of shoes and three dozen pairs of stockings. These were far too many shoes and socks for even a half dozen men; Moies clearly intended to resell them. The soldiers probably pocketed the forty shillings in coin that they also stole and intended to turn the stolen clothing into cash.

Moies managed to connect to the informal economy that prevailed in port cities throughout North America and Great Britain, wherein men of marginal status exchanged goods, which might or might not have been stolen, for drink and cash. The women who tended to run these de facto pawnshops then resold the goods, particularly clothing, to those who had no qualms about their provenance. These economic networks ran surprisingly deep.

Moies was caught in possession of the stolen goods. But because the items belonged to a civilian, the case went to the Massachusetts court, rather than the military. At the trial, several women testified that they had purchased most of the goods from the soldiers in exchange for a few coins and some rum. Not realizing that they were dealing in stolen goods, the women then resold the items. The few items remaining unsold were found in Moies's knapsack. The corporal was convicted of breaking and entering John Carnes's shop.

For his punishment, the court gave Moies a civil sentence that was standard for the time: "twenty stripes on the naked back at the publick whipping post" and triple damages, or three times the value of the theft, to be paid to John Carnes. This last item came to the princely sum of seventy-eight pounds, thirteen shillings, and six pence. Given that a soldier's pay was only six pence per day, out of which had to come all of his food, clothing, and other necessities, it would clearly be impossible for Moies to pay such a fine. Two weeks later, then, Carnes was back in court, making the claim that Moies was "utterly unable" to pay his court-mandated fine. Carnes suggested that the court empower him to sell, or indenture, Moies for an appropriate length of time as a way to recoup the loss. The court, following a Massachusetts law passed in the 1690s, agreed that Moies should be sold for a three-year period.

At this point, the extent of Moies's integration into Boston society became clear. William Dalrymple, as the regimental commander, complained in a frustrated letter to General Mackay, then the commanding officer in Boston, that although the Crown attorney and the justices admitted that it was logically impossible to sell a man to a private individual if the man in question was already bound for life to the army's service, they would not lift a finger to act against the lower court's decision. Mackay sent the letter on to General Gage, who exploded in anger that "such an infamous piece of Tyranny, savours more of the Meridian of Turkey than a British Province." His one practical suggestion was that Moies might try to escape the civil authority and hide behind the army's.

But Moies had no intention of figuring out how to escape his indenture. In fact, Mackay started to suspect that an elaborate farce was unfolding, which amounted to a new mode of desertion. He suggested that Carnes and Moies together had worked out this ruse as "a connivance between them in order to secure him his discharge, or in other words a sort of legal dismission from the regt." Moies was not living in barracks but in a private house, yet although he had not disappeared from Boston, he nonetheless avoided his residence. He took care not to be seen out in the street either. If he did, Mackay threatened, he would be arrested by the military. Instead, Mackay fumed, "he keeps close in the inhabitant's house to whom he is made over [that is, Carnes's house] and if we attempt to take him up, by going into the house for him," the justices of the peace would initiate a lawsuit for kidnapping. Two months later, the regiment had still not figured out how to get Moies back. In July 1769, Mackay admitted to Gage, "John Moise of the 14th is such a Rascall, that I am at a loss how to act." He remained convinced that the entire affair was no more than a clever act of desertion on Moies's part, carried out with the help of friendly locals.

Was General Mackay simply angry that one of his men was so obviously flouting his authority, or was there some basis for his suspicions that the court's sale of Moies was an example of soldiers and civilians working hand in glove? Other parts of the story suggest the latter. John Carnes's shop was in the south end of town, an area in which the army had rented homes for many soldiers. In January 1770, Carnes admitted that he had sold liquor for a while to soldiers, supplying rum "indiscriminately to all customers," but that in May 1769—just as Moies's case went to trial—he had been "convinced of the impropriety of supplying the soldiers with that article." Had he decided, after the robbery, that he did not want to be responsible for drunken soldiers? Or, as Mackay might have suspected, did he decide he would rather work with just a few of them more closely?

Meanwhile, the other men accused of the spring robbery had indeed deserted. Thomas Hibbard fled immediately after the robbery of March 1769, in the company of Francis Lee, who had, perhaps, been given some tips after all by David Geary. When Mackay advertised a pardon for deserters at the end of May, he included Hibbard in a list of men exempted from the amnesty, presumably because he was also wanted for the robbery. Although one soldier stayed with the army (possibly because he was ill), the remaining three involved in the original theft deserted together in April 1769. Perhaps the stolen goods had provided them with an entrance into the local black market and so a way to make a living outside the military.

Mackay never did manage to compel Moies to return to the regiment; his muster status for the next three years, corresponding to the rest of the time the Fourteenth Regiment remained in Boston, listed him as a prisoner, although he was not among those recorded in April

1770 as held in "the Boston Gaol for theft." Captain O'Hara presumably used the designation to indicate that his man was being held as a prisoner through his indenture.

But Moies was clearly not bound and chained. He successfully courted a Dorchester widow, Ruth Davenport, and they married in September 1771, when she was four months pregnant with their first child, John. The Moieses returned to Boston once the Fourteenth Regiment had gone, bringing for baptism at Trinity Church the two children who had been born over the previous year and a half. Although there is no evidence that Moies invented his elaborate subterfuge simply to marry his sweetheart, his social and economic networks certainly made their marriage possible. Moies settled into married life in Boston, baptizing seven children in total, three of whom died in childhood. He himself died in 1789 in Boston at the age of forty-nine, his army years long behind him.

7

A Deadly Riot: March 1770

Lead shot blasted through bodies, tearing through bone, muscle, livers, kidneys, groins. Ripped flesh stuck to clothing. Gore sprinkled the packed snow. A town watchman looked down at part of a blown-off skull as the rest of the body collapsed on his foot. Another, darker man sprawled on the street, blood spurting from his head. In the middle of the street a third body lay still. All three died within moments. Peering out from his doorway, a fourth man felt a musket ball rip through his arm. Another man standing in King Street gasped to his friend, "I am wounded"; a musket ball had gone into his hip and out his side. He lived in agony for ten more days. On March 5, 1770, men bled and died in the snow before the front doors of the Town-House, the home of British royal authority. British soldiers, steel bayonets still fixed to their muskets, stood just a few yards down King Street until Captain Thomas Preston ordered them to march away.

In that wide street, ringed with shops, taverns, homes, and offices, Bostonians and soldiers alike were aghast at the carnage. Less than half a mile away stretched the Long Wharf, a finger pointing straight east over the Atlantic toward Europe, from King Street to the king's palace. Were these deaths the sign that the power of the British Empire had finally come to crush Boston?

Paul Revere certainly thought so. As his poem accompanying his engraving of the massacre tells it, British troops reveled in the slaughter:

While faithless P[resto]n and his savage Bands,
With murd'rous Rancour stretch their bloody Hands;
Like fierce Barbarians grinning o'er their Prey,
Approve the Carnage, and enjoy the Day.

The soldiers are condemned as a group: all bloodthirsty, all equally guilty, and all unnamed. Even their commanding captain, Thomas Preston, is deprived of the dignity of being cited by his full name.

From the moment their guns went off, the spotlight of history has focused its narrow beam on those British soldiers. Uniforms are meant to disguise difference, and in their bright red coats they might well have seemed interchangeable. But each soldier who took part in the massacre was just as much an individual as any of the others who had married a local woman, buried a child, or deserted from the army. To different degrees, each of these men had made connections in Boston. Some had made friends; others had made families. All who had been called out for duty that night would be torn between their collective identity as soldiers and their separate identities as individuals.

Before this moment of bloodshed, the night had seemed no different from any other. Earlier that evening, when Private Hugh White marched from the guardhouse and past the Town-House to the small sentry box in front of the Custom House, fresh snow muffled the footfalls of passersby and horses. Lighted windows and doorways

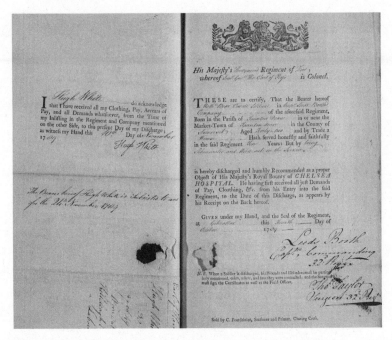

Private Hugh White's signature on his discharge documents.

glimmered on King Street. There were no streetlights — only the dim glow of a quarter moon — and noises and their origins were difficult to identify.

White had joined the Twenty-Ninth Regiment in 1759 from County Down in northern Ireland, just as Matthew Chambers had done. The two had likely been recruited together; both nineteen at the time, they ended up in Captain Pierce Butler's company. Although White was an unskilled laborer, and not an artisan like Chambers, he was literate and could sign his name in a confident, flowing script.

White had also managed to make friends in Boston over the year and a half since he had arrived. A little before nine on the evening of the shooting, one of those friends, Samuel Clark, strolled through the wide plaza of King Street on his way home to the North End. White saw Samuel and called out to him, to pass the time. White asked after his family, and Clark replied politely that everyone was well.

Soon after, however, Jane Crothers heard an unusual amount of noise in the street from her rooms at the head of Royal Exchange Lane. Across the narrow lane, she could see Private White standing sentry duty in front of the Custom House. She crossed the street to ask White whether he knew what was happening, but White told her he had no idea. A few blocks away, on Brattle Street, out of sight but not out of earshot, they could hear shouts. King Street was still quiet.

Jane Crothers may have been a barmaid at the Royal Exchange Tavern. She may have been a recent immigrant; the 1760s and 1770s saw an increase in the number of single women coming into Boston, looking for work or a husband. If she had children, they were not in Boston with her. Before March 1770, Crothers left little trace in the records. Although she did not have enough money to pay taxes, neither did she find herself in the almshouse. In fact, Crothers apparently managed to evade even the vigilant eye of the town warner, whose job it was to warn newcomers to Boston that they would not be eligible for poor relief from the town if they found themselves in need. It is her conversation with Hugh White that first brings Crothers into the historical record.

The Boston streets on which Crothers and White chatted were a web of interconnections between other soldiers and Bostonians. Around the corner, on Royal Exchange Lane, was John Belcher's tavern, where a few months before, Sergeant John White had married the tavern keeper's daughter Anne. Less than a hundred yards from the sentry's box, Captain Edmund Mason chatted with his neighbor, the successful Boston silversmith Nathaniel Hurd.

One of White's mates lived just a few doors down the street, with his new wife. James and Elizabeth Hartigan had rented lodgings with William Hickling, whose children had moved out, leaving a few young adults and a single enslaved worker. But James did not get to spend much of his time at home with his Boston-born wife. That night, he was on duty in the guardhouse with the rest of his company.

One building at the end of King Street dominated the neighborhood. The three-tiered tower of the Town-House was taller even than the cupola of the church behind it. The quarter moon that night meant it was difficult to see the balcony that jutted out from the east side of the building, overlooking the wide street. Flanking the roof were two enormous carvings, a unicorn and a lion representing England and Scotland, joined in the United Kingdom of Great Britain. The rearing animals, made of wood gorgeously painted in several colors, were more impressive than any fluttering Union Jack.

Every year on the king's birthday, the local militia held a parade on King Street, "where they performed many military Manoevres with such Order and Regularity as gave Pleasure to a large Number of Spectators," and then shot off cannons. The past spring, White had been part of the spectacle. All the regiments had mustered on the Common and shot off volleys from their cannons. But even with the regulars in attendance, the local artillery played its part with cannon and parade. As men lit the cannons, women applauded and children played in the street, all taking part in rituals that showed their loyalty to the British Crown.

The building and the area surrounding it were meant to inspire fear as well as celebration. The whipping post remained on King Street even after the new courthouse had opened on Queen Street, just west of the Town-House. For theft or counterfeiting, men and women of Boston might receive up to thirty-nine strokes on the bare back while passersby watched or continued shopping.

No armed guard patrolled the Town-House. Since the troops had arrived, however, three soldiers had stood sentry less than a hundred yards away, across the wide square in front of the Custom House. Of course, when a sentry went off duty, his role might change. He might be a neighbor, a husband, or a man desperately planning to desert. But in their bright red coats and glinting muskets, these sentries stood as symbols of the British Empire.

The hostility sometimes felt between Bostonians and the regiments posted in their town was nothing unusual, nor was it specific to Boston or even to the American colonies. British troops were seldom welcome even in Britain's cities. All around the empire, from Gloucestershire to Halifax, tensions regularly flared between civilians and the regiments stationed among them. Using troops to maintain governmental control in England was the most common role of the peacetime army. So many troops were moved into towns in England and Scotland in the 1760s that the War Office started asking for more regiments just to perform police duty. As the quartermaster general, Lieutenant Colonel Morrison, complained in 1768, "There has most frequently been so many applications for detachments from those regiments for the assisting of His Majesty's officers of the Customs in different parts of the coast and for the quelling of riots in several manufacturing towns etc., that it has hitherto been found, that number has scarcely been sufficient to answer these purposes." In Massachusetts, Governor Bernard was far from alone that same year in asking for troops to support both the work of the customs officials and his own civil authority.

In Boston in 1770, the real power of the British Empire seemed to be its ability to control trade. After all, conflicts with the men sent to oversee imports—the customs commissioners—had led to the request for troops in the first place. As the quartermaster general had noted, most peacetime regiments were deployed to support "His Majesty's Officers of the Customs." But by March 1770, conflicts between soldiers and townspeople had nothing to do with customs officials.

As British officers were well aware, clashes that led to the use of military force were disastrous to the reputations of the officers involved. They could hardly be ignorant of the many riots in England that ended in civilian deaths, especially in the 1760s: in London alone, troops fired on and killed four in 1763, another twelve in 1768, and nine more the next year. In several of those cases, the commanding officer was tried for manslaughter. Only a few months before the Sixty-Fourth and Sixty-Fifth Regiments embarked from Ireland for Boston, an officer and three privates were brought to trial after they had shot and killed several men in London during a riot.

During the four years that the Twenty-Ninth Regiment was in Nova Scotia, soldiers came close to killing civilians more than once. The drunken incident in which four subalterns tried to blow up a tavern with gunpowder was only one of the most colorful; hardly less so was the occasion in November 1765 when Privates Patrick Freeman, William McFall, and John McCollough broke into Elizabeth Murphy's house in Halifax. When they ran into the Murphys' apprentice, Thomas Seanes, McCollough pointed his gun at him and fired. Seanes would have died, had the shot not flashed in the pan of the musket. All three were convicted of assault and fined.

In the quelling of urban tumult, troops were a necessary evil. Eight-

Paul Revere's 1770 engraving succinctly tells the story of innocent people killed by the vicious power of their own rulers.

This anonymous watercolor from the late eighteenth century puts a military family in the middle of a long column of redcoats.

A mid-eighteenth-century embroidery shows Boston Common as a place for both courting couples and army tents.

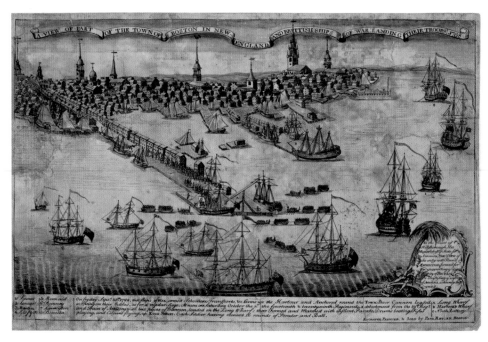

This idealized view of Boston emphasizes the town's many steeples, proclaiming the godliness of its inhabitants.

Troops and civilians share the Boston Common in the first weeks after the army's arrival in 1768.

Soldiers relax near tents in a London park while women do laundry and children and pets play.

Fathers playing with children and women cleaning clothes and nursing babies lend a domestic flavor to army barracks.

Two women flirt with a soldier while washing laundry in a military camp.

eenth-century civil officials in England requested them on occasion, then entreated the War Office to remove them just a few weeks later. Crown officials hoped that the commanding officer would be willing to follow the instructions of the civil authority and resist the urge to use force, but there was no guarantee that troops would not exacerbate the violence that often erupted on city streets. Officers and administrators preferred to believe that a lack of discipline among private soldiers, rather than the officers' own behavior, led to such problems. Following the advice frequently given to officers in England, General Gage told the Earl of Hillsborough in September 1768, "Lieutenant Colonel Dalrymple of His Majesty's 14th regiment of Foot, is appointed to command the Troops who are ordered on this Service, an Officer in whose Prudence, Resolution, and Integrity, I have Reason to confide. I mean to recommend to him very great Circumspection in his Conduct, and the strictest Discipline amongst the Troops." The key to a quiet posting in Boston, Gage hoped, would be caution on the part of the commanding officer and the greatest self-control within the ranks. The incidents in Halifax hinted at what rowdy privates and officers could do in a small town. The potential for a violent clash between soldiers and civilians was not particular to Boston. But when bloodshed did happen there, the outcome was like nothing the British could have imagined.

Troops and the violence they could unleash were never far from the concerns of Boston partisans of liberty, just as riots and their potential violence weighed heavily on the imagination of army officers and the governor. Yet until early 1770 the only death even remotely connected with the military occupation had been caused by a civilian; a local customs officer named Ebenezer Richardson had shot an eleven-year-old boy named Christopher Seider. The boy had taken part in a demonstration against a merchant who had refused to abide by the nonimportation agreement. No soldier had yet fired a gun at a civilian. Through the summer of 1769 and the following winter, General Gage and his supervisors at the War Office had begun to hope that they might yet be able to get out of Boston without incident.

The riots in the spring of 1768, which had so alarmed the governor and the customs officials, now seemed a thing of the past. In June 1769 Gage wrote to the War Office, "I hear of no Riots or Commotions in any of the Colonys, or that any are likely to happen, And I know of no Reasons at present that should induce me to detain the two Regiments [Sixty-Fourth and Sixty-Fifth] above-mentioned any longer in this Country." At his recommendation, the War Office decided in July 1769 that Boston no longer needed four regiments to keep the peace. The Sixty-Fourth Regiment, stationed in Boston, and the Sixty-Fifth, stationed at Castle William, were to be sent to Nova Scotia.

The challenge was to decide who would leave, and how. General Mackay had just overseen the embarkation of the Sixty-Fourth Regiment the previous fall, including the upper limit of women and children, from Ireland to Boston. But there were always more women and children who wanted to travel with the troops than could go; it was a rare officer who was willing to take every family member. This time, however, it seemed to Mackay to be in the army's interest to take along the families as they were able. If the goal was to remove the regiments before relations with Bostonians soured still more, surely removing more people would only help. After all, army wives could create friction with locals as much as their husbands could.

By the end of July 1769, the Sixty-Fourth and the Sixty-Fifth Regiments had left Boston. General Mackay himself sailed for England in

August, his reputation intact. Governor Bernard also left for London that summer. The secretary at war and General Gage even began planning to move the last two regiments to new postings. The general still had several regiments to shift around the empire before there would be room to move the Fourteenth and Twenty-Ninth Regiments out of Boston. As there was no immediate need for the regiments elsewhere, he asked Governor Bernard how long he wished the troops to stay in the town.

Rumors began to spread that all the troops were leaving. As Elizabeth Smith wrote to her niece Dolly Forbes in June 1769, "They say Boston will soon be without troops. We see them sailing every day." The Son of Liberty William Palfrey wrote to his sympathetic correspondent in London, the politician John Wilkes, that he too had just received the "agreeable news" that the "troops are to be remov'd: this seems to be a favorable omen." One hundred and fifty men signed a petition to the selectmen, requesting a town meeting to send a reassurance to the governor that troops were not needed to protect the customs commissioners. But despite the wishes of both town politicians and army officers, Governor Bernard asked Gage to leave two regiments in Boston a little longer. Although Bernard was leaving, his successor, Lieutenant Governor Hutchinson, who was to assume office as acting governor in July 1769, agreed that troops "must remain in the Town."

Governor Bernard continued to hope that the presence of soldiers would tilt the balance of power toward the government. But troops could not provide the stability he craved. The longer the military stayed, the more likely it was that the daily interactions of regiments and civilians would spark an outright clash. Every morning was a roll of the dice: Would this be another day of favors exchanged and drinks shared? Or would this be the day when a comment became a shove or a brawl became a riot?

The Boston watch regularly broke up fights after dark, both between soldiers and between townspeople. Those scuffles involving only soldiers and male Bostonians have been carefully documented. The town watch carefully noted every incident of nighttime rudeness by military officers. Officers reported to Gage several cases in which civilian courts prosecuted soldiers for assault when the officers believed men were doing no more than their assigned sentry duties; conversely, local journalists reported on every rumor of assault against both men and women in the *Journal of the Times*.

Physical violence perpetrated by men captured the imagination of supporters of both the government and the liberty parties. Arguments involving women seemed to carry less political weight and were therefore not publicly reported. They were also less dramatically violent. Their existence, however, points to some of the potential for conflict between soldiers' wives and their new neighbors. In the spring of 1770, the town watch in the North End held overnight two soldiers' wives, whom they accused of creating "several Routs & disorders in the streets." The constable extracted a promise from them to leave Boston at dawn, despite the fact that their husbands were both privates in the Twenty-Ninth Regiment still in Boston, and that at least one of the women had young children. The night watch did not record the nature of the "Routs & disorders" that the women might have perpetrated, but they might have somewhat resembled better-documented ones between men.

Plenty of other conflicts in Boston involved soldiers. Many of these brawls were carefully and deliberately documented at the time, always by parties determined to prove the soldiers' blamelessness. Robert Balfour deposed that he was knocked down by a crowd of inhabitants "without his giving them the least offence," while on separate occasions both William Lake and William Brown testified that they were struck by a Bostonian "without the least provocation." Thomas Smith, Thomas Hault, and John Gregory all swore that a mob attacked them "as they were going peaceably along the street in Boston." Most remarkable, William Holam claimed he was knocked down "without a word passing on either side." As stories of soldiers' complete innocence, they are not particularly believable. But there are enough of these tales to suggest that living together did not necessarily mean getting along.

Conflicts between soldiers and civilians seemed as likely to involve acquaintances as strangers. In a brawl in the marketplace in July 1769, Private John Riley from the Fourteenth Regiment and a Cambridge butcher came to blows. Jonathan Winship, the butcher who provided the Fourteenth Regiment with its fresh meat, had known Riley for some time, and not in a friendly way. Winship asserted that Riley "was a dirty rascal and villain, and would have fallen upon him [Winship] some time ago had he not been prevented." One of Riley's fellow corporals later claimed that when Riley tried to end the fight by offering to make a bet on his innocence in any attempt to attack Winship, the butcher replied that he "would not shake hands with any dirty Rascals like [the soldiers] for fear of Catching the Itch." Crude remarks about soldiers and prostitutes were common, and the butcher presumably knew nothing about Riley's sex life; on the other hand, the rest of Winship's accusation makes it obvious that the two men were not meeting for the first time.

Another altercation, six months later, has caught the attention of historians, who have tended to concentrate only on its partisan aspects. As the troops shivered through their second winter in Boston, there was little army business to keep them occupied. Many looked for work elsewhere. One private in the Fourteenth Regiment worked with a furniture maker and his wife. Private Patrick Doyne, married and with two children, found employment with the popular King Street wigmaker John Piemont. There he became friendly with one of the wigmaker's employees (or "journeymen"), Richard Ward. Doyne and Ward became close enough friends that Ward occasionally dropped by his home after work, as did some of the other apprentices in Piemont's shop.

Hairdressing and woodworking required skill, but men who lacked specialized training could find occasional work at any of the several rope-making factories, known as ropewalks, located in the south and west ends of town. Early in March 1770, one rope maker offered a soldier work requiring no particular skill: cleaning his latrine. The soldier was offended at what he took to be fighting words, and a quarrel escalated over the next several days, as each side brought more friends into the fray. As in other conflicts between soldiers and civilians, both parties later claimed innocence. Private Patrick Walker testified that as he walked past the ropewalk, "he was assaulted, knocked Down, trod under feet, Cut in several places, and Very much bruised, without any Provocation Given." A rope maker likewise claimed that he had been busy at his task when three armed soldiers walked up and said, "You damn'd dogs, don't you deserve to be kill'd? Are you fit to die?" John Gray, the owner of the ropewalk, fired his worker for the original insult to the soldier, while Lieutenant Colonel Dalrymple promised to keep the soldiers under closer watch. Both hoped that this would be the end of the story. It was not.

People on every side said later that trouble had been brewing for a long time. Some became convinced that the conflict over the Townshend duties, which had sparked both the nonimportation agreements and the arrival of the customs commissioners, was linked to the conflicts between civilians and soldiers. Searching for a rational explanation for the clashes, they drew a straight line from Ebenezer Richardson's shooting of the child Christopher Seider to the mass shooting on King Street. Henry Hulton, of the Board of Customs Commissioners, explained in a later account, "Richardson was afterwards taken into custody and remained in Gaol . . . From this time the resentment of the People against the Soldiers, the Commissioners of the Customs, and the Laws of Revenue, continually increased. They sought occasions of quarrelling with the Soldiery . . . 'till the Storm broke forth on the 5 March 1770." Rising tensions and "the People" (by which Hulton meant working-class people) bickering with soldiers were the gathering clouds of the storm. More specifically, if less rationally, another pro-Crown writer suggested that the point of these skirmishes was to allow Bostonians "to drive both [the soldiers] and the commissioners of the customs out of the town" by hiding a full-blown uprising under the guise of the fracas on King Street.

Liberty party Bostonians told a very similar story. In a retrospective part of his 1770 diary, written between March and May 1770, the former Boston selectman Samuel Savage carefully enumerated the same stages of increasing violence through the spring of 1770:

1st. poor Snider [Seider] shot by Richardson . . .

2nd. The attack of the Soldiers at Gray's Rope Walk 2 March . . .

3rd. the party of the main Guard of 29th Regt. Commanded by Capt. [Thomas] Preston firing on the Inhabitants in King Street . . .

But this ropewalk brawl, so central to every version of the story of the Boston Massacre, is in fact a red herring. Rather than explain the shooting that would follow, it focuses attention on only a small group of men. An emphasis on this one set of encounters ignores a much wider and richer catalog of equally aggravating events, ones that show that women as well as men, friends as well as foes, helped heat up the conflict.

In February 1770, the social world shared by soldiers and civilians seemed to continue as it had for over a year. John Rowe and his wife, Hannah, hosted a "genteel" dance for their sixteen-year-old niece, attended by no fewer than seven army officers, including Lieutenant Colonel Dalrymple, Lieutenant Colonel Carr, and Captain O'Hara. Captain Thomas Preston was there too, unaware of how his life was about to change, in just ten days.

That same week, the jeweler John Wilme and his wife, Sarah, hosted a number of soldiers in his North End home. Later, Sarah remembered the evening as less genteel than the Rowes' gathering. She recalled that several of the men had spun out bloodthirsty fantasies about shooting up Boston. One soldier insisted that if a street battle took place in Boston, "he would level his piece [gun] so as not to miss." It would not be long now, he continued with relish, before "blood would soon run in the streets of Boston." Another soldier boasted that "they would soon sweep the streets of Boston."

That kind of violence, one of the soldiers insisted, would have no place for women. If Bostonians fought back, he hypothesized, "the women should be sent to the Castle, or some other place." Eleanor Park, one of the soldiers' wives also at the Wilmes' house that evening, was having none of it. Far from acquiescing to a retreat from Boston, she insisted that she would take part in the violence. She was willing to let others begin the bloodshed, but, she continued, "if there should be any disturbance in the town of Boston, and that if any of the people were wounded, she would take a stone in her handkerchief & beat their brains out, and plunder the rebels."

Eleanor Park was not the only woman contemplating violence in Boston that winter. In early March, two women — a native Bostonian and a soldier's wife — stood on their stoops and exchanged threats. Isabella Montgomery had not found living in Boston easy. When she, her soldier husband, and three children were living near Milk Street in 1769, no fewer than eleven neighbors had complained that she and her husband were loud and disorderly. After they moved to the North End, Montgomery found their new neighbors no easier to get along with, and the feeling was mutual. On the night of March 5, while her husband, Edward, was on duty at the guardhouse next to the Town-House, Montgomery and her neighbor got into a heated argument about Boston itself. Standing on the stoop, Montgomery shouted loudly enough for people in the surrounding houses to hear, "The town was too haughty and too proud and that many of the arses would be laid low before the morning." The Bostonian Susannah Cathcart, tired of both Montgomery and her husband, shot back, "I hope your husband will be killed."

That night, similar angry words could be heard in parts of town besides the North End. Outside one of the barracks on Brattle Street, soldiers may have taunted Bostonians, hollering "Damn you ye Yankey boogers." Bostonians may have been shouting at soldiers "who buys Lobsters." The streets around King Street, Dock Square, and Brattle Street seemed unusually crowded. Some people claimed they were so full that one could not even push through an alleyway. But reports vary as to whether the remarkable number of people in the streets consisted of rampaging soldiers or rioting Bostonians. There were reports of soldiers running around, waving cutlasses, although others claimed that the inhabitants were armed with sticks. Soldiers might have threatened civilians with fire tongs, while inhabitants picked up whatever they could find on the street—ice, shells, and especially hard-packed snowballs—and hurled them at soldiers.

The more than two hundred people who claimed to have seen something happen on the night of March 5 agreed on very little, except that at about nine o'clock, church bells began to ring. Soldiers believed these were a signal to Bostonians to join an uprising in the heart of town, on King Street. Some inhabitants thought that the bells were a fire alarm and came running to put out a conflagration.

As Jane Crothers talked with Private White, more people came into King Street. Was it thirty people, strolling through the main thoroughfare, trying to figure out the source of the disturbance? Or did two hundred people, armed with clubs, pour in from the surrounding streets? Perhaps there were crowds of sailors, led by a tall mixed-race man later identified as Crispus Attucks. Or possibly there were just a few teenagers strutting down the middle of King Street (and a few older men watching them). We know for sure only that White thought he needed reinforcements.

When he called for them, he expected that the soldiers on duty in the main guardhouse — just on the far side of the Town-House — would come to his aid. As the additional soldiers marched up the street, led by Captain Thomas Preston, King Street did not seem big enough for both civilians and soldiers. The soldiers' bayonets poked one man in the back, while another man managed to weave directly through the middle of the column. As people jostled for positions — to stand close to a friend, or to see better, or to get out of the way — the one word that everyone agreed they could hear was "fire." Perhaps it was a warning to the residents of a city of wooden buildings? Or a command to soldiers standing shoulder to shoulder in the dark? Was it a fragment of a taunt — "you dare not fire" — made by a civilian, secure in the knowledge that he, unlike the soldiers, was under no one's command? No one knew then, and no one knows now.

As members of the Twenty-Ninth Regiment — Captain Preston, Corporal William Wemms (sometimes spelled Wemys), and Privates James Hartigan, Matthew Kilroy, William McAuly, Edward Montgomery, and William Warren — joined White and Crothers, the sentry pushed Crothers away from the group of armed men. Crothers seemed comfortable in their presence, but White told her the situation was dangerous; she should go home or risk being killed. Crothers did not return to the Royal Exchange Tavern. She worked her way back a few steps, through the press of people, to the corner of the

Custom House, several feet from where the soldiers had fanned out in a semicircle. From this vantage point, she could see the street, the soldiers, and the Custom House.

Lawyers and historians have been trying, for centuries, to piece together what someone like Jane Crothers actually saw. Her own story was vivid: as she stood on the corner, many more people flooded into King Street. She saw these newcomers threaten to kill White, shouting, "The bloody back Rascall, let's go kill him." As they threw snow, wood, and ice at him, she claimed, he retreated from the open sentry box to the steps of the Custom House itself, better to protect his back. When another seven soldiers came to his support, led by Captain Preston, Crothers moved closer to the soldiers. She could hear a civilian ask Preston if he meant to order the men to fire on the townspeople, and she was close enough to catch Preston's reply: "Sir by no means, by no means." It was at this point that White pushed Crothers away from the soldiers.

Crothers described a chaotic scene of terrified soldiers being pelted with chunks of wood and ice. The man closest to her and to Royal Exchange Lane was hit by a piece of wood, she said, and fell onto his face, dropping his gun. A couple of minutes after that, shots rang out.

Crothers's testimony indicated not only that White, Hartigan, and the other soldiers faced an angry mob, but that Captain Preston had nothing to do with the deadly violence that followed. Under oath the following October, she testified about a mysterious man dressed in a dark coat who stood behind the soldiers, "encouraging them to fire," saying, "Fire, by God, I'll stand by you." As the man spoke, he clapped one of the soldiers on the back, and at that moment, the soldier fired. A minute later, another of the soldiers did the same. Crothers's final testimony exonerated Captain Preston from the charge of having ordered them to fire: "I am positive the man was not the Captain." Crothers knew her soldiers.

Yet other witnesses at the same location, the corner of Royal Exchange Lane, had a very different impression of the event. Thomas Wilkinson arrived considerably later than Crothers had. He had heard bells and seen the fire engine from his home, so he ran to a central water supply, the town pump, situated across from the northwest corner of the Town-House. He claimed that he saw thirty or forty people there, all prepared to fight fires, not soldiers. Rather than oyster shells, ice, or snowballs, they held only fire buckets. From the pump, Wilkinson could not see White and Crothers, but he noticed Captain Preston marching eight soldiers down King Street. Among them, he recognized his neighbor Edward Montgomery. Wilkinson testified that he started toward Montgomery "to ask what they were going to do." Doubling back, so he could get to the other side of King Street without crossing through the soldiers' column, Wilkinson took up a position on the corner of King Street and Royal Exchange Lane nearly next to Crothers. He stood there, he thought, for a full four minutes, during which time he saw no objects being thrown. Moreover, although Wilkinson too was standing close to the right-hand side of the soldiers' line (a mere two yards away, he thought), he saw no soldier fall over onto his face. Finally, he heard an order given to the soldiers: "Fire, d—n your Bloods fire." And then, Wilkinson said, the soldiers fired, calmly and deliberately. It was an orderly volley. The shots rang out, Wilkinson thought, with the regularity of a clock striking.

The Bostonian James Bailey said he had spent five or six minutes standing with Private White that evening. He explained, "I went up

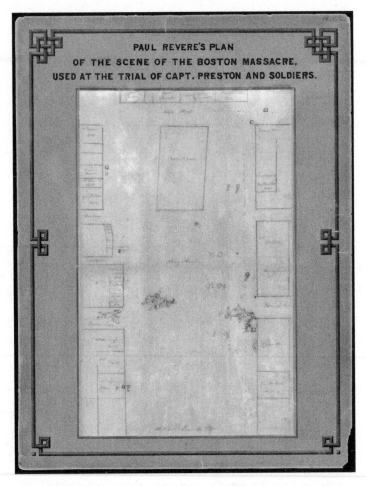

This sketch shows the bodies of the four men killed on King Street.

to him because I knew him, and to see what was the matter." Later, Bailey recalled that there were "boys . . . heaving Pieces of Ice," "large and hard enough to hurt a man, as big as your fist," at the sentry. When reinforcements came, Bailey was still standing with White in the sentry box. Private John Carroll may have recognized Bailey from Gray's ropewalk. He strode up to Bailey in anger and shoved his bayonet against his chest. White was less interested in replaying the weekend's brawl than shutting down the current crisis. He told Carroll to leave Bailey alone. White was a friend; Carroll was not, and Bailey knew them both.

All of these people had genuine social ties, though on the surface, their stories are indeed contradictory. Jane Crothers saw a hostile, violent mob that pelted soldiers with sharp, heavy objects and threatened to kill them. In her version, both the soldiers and their commanding officer resisted the temptation to shoot townspeople, even when provoked. Not until an unnamed stranger ordered them to shoot did they fire. They had no forethought or intent to harm. Standing on the same street corner, Wilkinson apparently saw an entirely different event. Calm, orderly Bostonians, out in the streets for one reason — to save their town from fire — essentially left the trigger-happy soldiers alone. There were no missiles, no shoving, not even any harassing comments about red-uniformed "Lobsterbacks." Crothers saw the military men as paragons of virtue; Wilkinson saw Bostonians as the same. Yet when Wilkinson, Crothers, and others looked at that formation of soldiers, they did share the perception that they were looking at individuals, not automatons. They saw specific persons that night — men embedded in their communities, family men, not faceless soldiers.

After the shooting, as townspeople gathered beneath the balcony of the Town-House, demanding to hear from Lieutenant Governor Hutchinson, it was not clear that the violence was over. Officers ordered men to stay in their barracks, but they had little control over soldiers living in private homes. Meanwhile, Bostonians claimed that armed soldiers were roaming the streets in large packs, looking for more defenseless civilians. At such a moment, it seems likely that neighborly bonds between civilians and soldiers, even those who had drunk together, run away together, and made families together, might rupture beyond hope of reconciliation.

But, luckily for Edward Crafts, those relationships were not so easily broken. Crafts, a Bostonian, was out urging eyewitnesses to tell Lieutenant Governor Hutchinson that they had heard Captain Preston order his troops to fire on Bostonians. Close to midnight, still on the streets, he passed a detachment of twenty soldiers, who immediately surrounded him. On the command of one of the corporals, they prepared to shoot him, and the corporal struck him with the side of his gun. At the last moment, Crafts recognized the other corporal, who pulled his own sword and heroically (at least in Crafts's recollection) declared, "This is Mr. Crafts, and if any of you offer to touch him again I will blow your brains out." Moreover, the next evening, when Crafts again ran into McCann (the corporal "who saved my life"), he recounted that McCann told him, "You would have been in heaven or hell in an instant if you had not called my name." If anything, the night of the shooting intensified the bond between the two men.

Joseph Allen was not in King Street earlier that evening and had missed the entire fracas. Once he heard about it, however, he armed himself "with a stout cudgel," left his house, and walked to the Town-House on a path that went by one of the barracks. There a group of soldiers surrounded him and his friends, ripped off his coat, and seized his stick. Lieutenant Minchin, observing the scuffle, told the men to stop and then "entered into conversation" with Allen, grumbling about the behavior of Allen's fellow Bostonians. Their conversation continued as Allen defended his townsmen, and Minchin looked for a leader on whom to pin the blame. When their conversation drew to a close, Minchin politely returned Allen's stick to him.

From the balcony of the Town-House, Lieutenant Governor Hutchinson tried to calm the angry crowd. A promise of a full and immediate inquiry satisfied many, but at least a hundred people remained in the street. Hutchinson was as good as his word. He took examinations until three in the morning, when he sent Captain Thomas Preston to jail. The other soldiers who had marched out that night with the guard, including the sentry Hugh White, would join him in the morning.

Now, with the apparent culprits being sent to jail, the crowd dispersed, and the soldiers returned to their beds; escalation of the crisis had been prevented. It seemed that Boston's tense but definite neighborliness between civilians and the military could hold. A few days later, the Bostonian Ephraim Fenno would stop to chat with a doctor from the Fourteenth Regiment who both addressed him as neighbor and told him he wished that more Bostonians had died. It was a conversation much like those reported before the shooting: an everyday interaction between two people with wildly divergent, even hostile things to say.

But the shooting did change everything — only not right away. While conflicts between townspeople and soldiers did not lead inevitably to the Boston Massacre, the shooting would come to redefine those conflicts in new and harsher terms. The unexpected aftermath of the deaths on King Street was a slow estrangement that transformed neighbors into strangers.

8

Gathering Up: March 6, 1770–August 1772

The morning following the shooting, no one in Boston could talk about anything else. People tried to pump anyone and everyone for information. When British navy sailors from the HMS *Rose* entered William Rhoades's tavern on King Street the next morning, he asked them what they had heard about the shooting, and whether any of the other sailors had been carrying guns the night before. The shoemaker David Loring similarly brought up the deaths with Sergeant Whittle of the Fourteenth Regiment. At the inquests that morning, men stood over the bodies of the slain and tried to puzzle out what had happened.

Early on March 6, the town crier went through every street in Boston, announcing a special town meeting, to be held at 11 a.m. that day. As usual, this meeting was open to all Boston residents, not just those who could vote. That meant women, apprentices, and children could attend. Three or four thousand "Freeholders and other Inhabitants" streamed that morning through the Merchants' Market to Faneuil Hall. The town officials' first order of business was to ask Bostonians, then and there, to "give information respecting the Massacre of the last night," so that the town clerk could take down their testimony at once. The blood spilled in the town's central street had shocked the people of Boston. John Rowe sympathetically characterized his neighbors as "greatly enraged and not without reason." Many wanted to talk about what they had seen the night before. They wanted to bear witness.

John Singleton Copley, already renowned as a painter on both sides of the Atlantic, was the first to stand. Like so many other Bostonians, he had not previously recognized two opposing sides, loyalist and patriot, or accepted that he would have to choose between them. In the preceding two years, he had painted portraits of men who would come to be identified with opposing factions: the Son of Liberty Paul Revere and the commander of the British army in North America, General Thomas Gage. Yet on March 6, 1770, Copley was so stunned by the shooting that he was eager to make a public statement accusing the soldiers of deliberate intent to harm Bostonians.

After four more witnesses gave their depositions, it became clear that the number of townsfolk demanding to share their reactions was far too great for the town clerk, William Cooper, to transcribe by himself at that moment. Still, the demand had to be met, and Cooper accordingly appointed a three-member committee to collect testimonials at a later time. These depositions, eventually numbering nearly a hundred, would fundamentally shape the perception of the shooting, from 1770 to the present. No one at the time had any idea how influential those testimonies would turn out to be.

For the moment, however, the Boston Town Meeting turned its attention to the first priority: namely, getting soldiers off the street. This political body had never stopped calling for the removal of the troops. The previous summer a resolution was passed to the effect that "the Residence of a Military Power in the Body of this Metropolis is upon various Considerations, quite disagreeable to the Inhabitants." Regardless of any individual feelings their daughters or wives or they themselves might have had for the military men and women they had met, the members of the town meeting were convinced that the only way to prevent more bloodshed was to remove the troops and their guns permanently from Boston's streets.

The night before, the elected officials in the council chamber had asked Lieutenant Governor Hutchinson, now the acting governor, to order the troops to leave the public square. Hutchinson had refused to do it himself and asked Lieutenant Colonel Carr, the commander of the Twenty-Ninth Regiment, to give the order. As Governor Bernard had done upon the arrival of the troops a year and a half earlier, Hutchinson claimed that he, a civilian officer, could not give orders to the military. And so the town meeting appointed a committee of fifteen of the wealthiest of the town's inhabitants who were most committed to the liberty movement, including John Hancock, Justice of the Peace John Ruddock, Joshua Henshaw, and Samuel Adams, to tell Hutchinson that the troops had to leave immediately. Some of the fifteen were already serving as selectmen; all of them were formally affiliated with the Sons of Liberty; all of them were willing to tell Hutchinson to his face that "the Inhabitants and Soldiery can no longer dwell together in safety." Presumably, all were likewise ready for the long standoff that was likely to ensue; the most that could be hoped for was that the lieutenant governor's "power & influence may be exerted."

As with the argument over the housing of the troops, the impact

of the deliberations over their departure was wider than anyone imagined at the time. The next set of compromises that these men eventually made created a long trail, throughout the British Empire.

Hutchinson himself had not been idle that morning. While the
town meeting strategized, he sent a message to the Governor's Council, as well as to Lieutenant Colonels Dalrymple and Carr, to meet
with him. Before they could gather in his chambers, however, and
even before Hutchinson himself appeared, representatives of the
town meeting arrived. Hutchinson found the selectmen, including several who were part of the town meeting's new committee of
fifteen, waiting for him. They told him that they could not answer
for the conduct of their fellow Bostonians if the troops stayed in the
town. No sooner had Hutchinson predictably responded that it was
"not in his power" to order the troops to withdraw to Castle Island
than the rest of the members of the committee of fifteen knocked at
the door. They too told Hutchinson "in plain terms" that people in
Boston and the neighboring towns would riot if the troops remained.

In response to the demands of the town meeting delegation and the
selectmen to remove all the troops, Lieutenant Governor Hutchinson
stubbornly insisted that he could not order the soldiers to depart, even
in the face of an armed uprising against them. Besides, he added, "an
attack upon the King's Troops would be High Treason." One wonders how Hutchinson was interpreting the previous night's attack: as
the Bostonians' first step toward such high treason?

Even the representatives of the army offered only partial support
for Hutchinson's desire to keep troops in town. Dalrymple, bow-
ing to the acting governor's statement that the most recent conflicts
with civilians had involved the Twenty-Ninth Regiment, offered to

send that regiment to Castle Island. He also promised that he would keep his own Fourteenth Regiment in the barracks at Wheelwright's Wharf. The promise was no guarantee of peace; even if Dalrymple intended to restrict all the privates to the wharf's three warehouses, Bostonians would still have numerous military families and officers thronging their streets.

By the time Dalrymple and Hutchinson finished suggesting their plan to the committee of fifteen, it was well past time for lunch. The town meeting in Faneuil Hall had adjourned for a few hours during this discussion with Hutchinson; when it reconvened in the middle of the afternoon, at least four thousand people were present, far too many for the hall, so the meeting was moved to the Old South Meeting House, the largest indoor public space in Boston. There the committee presented Hutchinson's proposal—that only the Twenty-Ninth Regiment would move to Castle Island. The town meeting soundly rejected the plan.

Half of the original committee of fifteen returned to the Town-House to try once more to persuade Hutchinson to order the removal of all the troops. The Governor's Council supported the committee. But neither Hutchinson nor Dalrymple wanted to take responsibility for such a retreat. Dalrymple insisted that Hutchinson express, in writing, his desire to remove the troops, and Hutchinson, after some vacillation, complied. For his own part, Dalrymple (in a letter written the next day) assured his commanding officer, General Gage, that when asked to remove the troops, "I absolutely refused. After much persuasion I consented to take the liberty of sending the 29th regiment to the castle, until your pleasure should be known." Only after Hutchinson explicitly required him to move both regiments from town did Dalrymple agree. The lieutenant colonel insisted that he was stuck between the rock of his own military assessment of the situation, in which the town would be better off protected by troops, and the hard place of his responsibility as a military commander to submit to civilian authority: "In this delicate situation was I placed, told if I remain contrary to the governor's order all should be at my peril, yet unwilling to leave the place without your consent, I made an effort to procure time tho in vain, not being of a rank sufficient to refuse obedience to the Civil Governors power I was obliged to submit." Dalrymple noted that Hutchinson lacked both support and authority. "He is without friends, and I may add power," Dalrymple caustically concluded.

The delegation from the town meeting returned triumphantly that afternoon to the meeting, where the news of the regiments' departure provided joy as well as satisfaction. To the relief of both the lieutenant governor and some of the more moderate Bostonians, including John Rowe, the crowd dispersed "very peaceably to their Habitations." It may have seemed to some like the end of the story: the shooters in jail awaiting an impartial trial and the chastened lieutenant governor and commanding officer acknowledging that military force could not subdue a community determined to hold on to its rights, as its spirited activists refused to back down. As the minister and liberty party adherent Samuel Cooper stated, "We are now happily deliver'd from that Army, which instead of preserving the Peace among us, has in numerous Instances most audaciously violated it, and instead of Aiding has overaw'd and sometimes even assaulted the civil Magistrates, and Demonstrated how impossible [it] is for Soldiers and Citizens at least in our Circumstances to live together." To Cooper and others, the shooting proved that the town meeting and the selectmen had been right all along: the troops, and not the Bostonians, had been the disturbers of the peace.

In the same letter, Cooper continued, "For these and other reasons we cannot suppose that Troops [will] ever again be quarter'd in the Body of the Town.—I could say much upon this Subject but chose to forbear." Cooper's silence on the subject of troops living in the "Body" of Boston is intriguing. What was he refusing to discuss? Clearly, there was plenty of food for thought on the topic of troops and inhabitants living in close quarters, but none of it was spoken aloud. Marriages, baptisms, and friendships between soldiers and civilians had become a forbidden topic.

It was no easy matter to pack up several thousand men, women, and children. Military families resisted the breakup of their homes, and Dalrymple himself was in no rush to comply with his agreement. If he proceeded slowly enough, he thought, perhaps the townspeople's anger might abate. Or perhaps Gage himself might order him to move the troops out of Castle William and back into the center of the town. In that case, he thought he could try "to reinstate matters when the popular fury has subsided."

Dalrymple's hope was in vain, however, and he found himself forced to start moving troops to the harbor. John Rowe was one of many who kept an eye on the army's progress. By the Friday following the Monday shooting, he was recording in his diary, "Yesterday two Companies of the 29th went to the Castle & four companies more went this day." One week after the shooting, he noted carefully, "The Remainder of the 29th Regiment went to the Castle this day." Three days later the newspaper reported that "all the 29th Regiment and the greatest Part of the 14th, are gone to the Barracks at Castle-William."

The thousands of Bostonians who had thronged Faneuil Hall and the Old South Meeting House had seen the departure of the troops as a step toward calm. With some eight hundred men gone from the peninsula, the town certainly felt emptier. Edward Ireland, the head constable of one of Boston's central wards, noted with great pleasure, in his March monthly report, that "ever since the Soldiers have been gone the streets that used to be full of uproars and confused men now is still, espesely on satterday night and on the Sabetth." Not only were those rowdy soldiers off the streets, but, he added in a direct note to the selectmen, "gentlemen I can't help taking notice of the town inhabitants, how freely they answer the watch ever since the soldiers have been gone." Did Ireland mean that soldiers' cronies, the ones who were up to no good, had melted away also? Or were the towns-people less tense and more willing to acknowledge the authority of the watch? Ireland himself no longer had to compete with military men patrolling the streets and clearly enjoyed asserting his superior ability to maintain calm.

Little as Dalrymple or Hutchinson wanted to move troops out to Castle Island, they too felt an urgent desire to separate the towns-people from the troops. Two weeks after the shooting, Dalrymple wrote to Gage with evident relief, "Nothing can be more effectual to prevent further disputes with the inhabitants than the situation of the 29th [on Castle Island]; their intercourse [with Bostonians] is neces-sarily all at an end, no complaint was made of them after the affair of the 5th, at least no just complaint, and at the Castle no further altercation can happen." Dalrymple thought he had found the silver lining in the retreat.

Hutchinson was heartened as well: no more soldiers living among Bostonians determined to undermine the government, no more conflicts between civil and military authorities, no more squabbles in the streets. Dalrymple complained that the island quarters were far too crowded for both regiments, and Gage proposed sending the regiments to new postings elsewhere, but Hutchinson disagreed with both men. The soldiers were perfectly happy, he wrote to Gage, and any possible problem with the new arrangements was "caused by the multitudes of women and children belonging to the 29th." In Hutchinson's eyes, those families were the "difficulty" in an otherwise excellent arrangement.

Now that the opposition had stopped complaining about the presence of the troops, Hutchinson was not eager to see Gage send them completely out of the province. Though troops barracked on Castle Island might not be as easy to recall to put down riots in the heart of Boston, as Governor Bernard had argued in 1768, when he insisted on their living in town, they still had some use, including the protection of the customs commissioners. Despite Dalrymple's attempts to persuade both Hutchinson and Gage that the situation was far from perfect, Hutchinson was sure that the move would turn out to be a blessing, and not even one in disguise. "The men seem to me to be in better condition since they have been at the castle than when they were in Town," he reported to Gage a week later.

While Hutchinson was putting on his rose-colored glasses, his political supporters and opponents alike were coloring their reputations and spreading their versions of the March 5 shooting. Within days any Bostonian with access to the media—printed, spoken, or artistic—swung into action; by the following Monday, the newspapers had printed varied accounts of the event. The *Boston Gazette* reported that Captain Preston had ordered the soldiers to fire, while the *Boston Chronicle* was willing to go no further than to call it an "unfortunate affair." In protest of the *Chronicle*'s halfhearted condemnation of the shooting, most of its advertisers pulled their support from the paper; it folded less than four months later. The artist Henry Pelham was hard at work on his drawing of the event within a few days of its occurrence; it took Paul Revere only several days more to acquire the cartoon (without Pelham's approval) and use it as the foundation for his own famous engraving. Like the difference between the newspapers' accounts, the two artists' titles speak to the varieties of interpretation immediately following the deaths. Pelham called his work "The Fruits of Arbitrary Power." Revere, of course, called his "The Bloody Massacre."

The horror of the deaths affected thousands. On March 8, John Rowe joined the funeral procession for the slain. He was amazed at the number of people who followed the victims to the gravesite. As he marched solemnly through the narrow streets with others, in rows of six, he wondered if more than half of the town had joined the procession: ten to twelve thousand people, he estimated, were with him, out of a town of sixteen thousand. Others had come from neighboring towns to take part in the somber occasion. The Reverend William Emerson of Concord (grandfather of Ralph Waldo Emerson), fifteen miles away, happened to be visiting his in-laws that day. He watched the "awful & solemn Procession." It was "extremely affecting!" he wrote to his wife. The sounds of the funeral echoed for miles; church bells pealed throughout Boston. Bells from the neighboring towns of Roxbury and Charlestown joined in the tolling.

Anyone who did not know what to think about the deadly event could hear it from the pulpit. On March 11, the first Sunday after the shooting, the Reverend John Lathrop used his sermon in the Second Congregational Church to condemn the soldiers. His parishioners rushed his sermon into print in London, with the title *Innocent Blood Crying to God from the Streets of Boston*.

As a result of Lathrop's sermon and those of equally persuasive ministers, news of the atrocity spread quickly through Massachusetts and beyond. Within a week of the shooting, other towns had taken official action. The town meeting of nearby Medford authorized a committee to send a letter of support to Boston. Medford blamed the shooting on "the detestable machinations of a few wicked & artful men," an unsubtle reference to the British government in London, but lamented as well "the deplorable Condition the Town of Boston has been reduc'd to, by the insolent & savage Behaviour of the Soldiery, quartered among them."

The second week after the shooting, the Boston Town Meeting returned to the issue of taking depositions from witnesses to the shooting. In place of the three men who had formed the original committee, three new men were chosen, all of them powerful, well connected, and far more active members of the Sons of Liberty: James Bowdoin, Joseph Warren, and Samuel Pemberton. Their task was to put together "a particular Account of all proceedings relative to the Massacre in King Street." The original goal was to have the committee collect the affidavits in order to aid the prosecution. The committee's charge now, however, was to shape and spin the affidavits into a narrative that they would send to supporters in London. The town meeting tasked them "to prepare a true state of facts relating to the execrable massacre." Despite the claims to "truth," this narrative framing of the depositions carefully laid out a chronicle of aggressive soldiers, innocent townspeople, and a clear separation between the two.

The committee chose to publish the affidavits, with a long introduction, as *A Short Narrative of the Horrid Massacre in Boston, Perpetrated in the Evening of the Fifth Day of March, 1770, by Soldiers of the XXIX Regiment*. They sent some forty copies abroad to sympathetic members of Parliament, as well as one to the outgoing prime minister, the Duke of Grafton. These were accompanied by a letter, reprinted in the local newspapers, that explained the reason for sending the copies in the first place: "to intreat your Friendship to prevent any ill Impressions from being made upon the Minds of His Majesty's Minesters and others against the Town."

But this was disingenuous; the persuasive nature of the pamphlet lies in what Bostonians themselves had to say about their own experience of the events. The lengthy appendix of first-person testimony, drawn from ninety-six depositions, dwarfs the introduction both in size and in importance. The depositions were collected over a period of nineteen days, as Bostonians told their stories and as Bowdoin, Pemberton, and Warren took notes. At the end of his or her testimony, each deponent signed an affidavit in the presence of two justices of the peace, to swear that the written deposition was accurate. Since the three-man committee welcomed anyone who wanted to testify against the soldiers, it took depositions from people whose

voices were not usually welcome in the town meeting or other political venues: white women, both married and single, and black men,
both free and enslaved. Black women did not testify, but whether
their voices are absent by choice or exclusion, we cannot know.

The depositions were arranged by the committee in roughly
chronological order, intended to show the soldiers in the worst possible light. Many of them dealt not with the night of March 5 itself
but with other points of conflict, such as the fight at the ropewalk on
March 2 and the soldiers' alleged ensuing desire for revenge. Other
depositions spoke to the longstanding hostility between soldiers and
townspeople; still more claimed that soldiers knew in advance that
something momentous would happen on the night of March 5. For
anyone reading the depositions from beginning to end, the cumula-
tive effect is an acceptance of the idea that the firing on the townspeople constituted premeditated murder.

Because the clear aim of the *Short Narrative* was to shape public
opinion against the troops, Bowdoin, Pemberton, and Warren attempted to embargo local distribution of the pamphlet. They were
eager to send their version of events to London but determined not
to distribute it in Boston. The town meeting sanctimoniously but
perceptively voted to lock away any copies not sent to England out
of a concern that "the unhappy Persons now in custody" might see
the pamphlet as "tending to give an undue Byass to the minds of the
Jury" who would try them. The town meeting was likely less concerned that the soldiers might not get a fair trial and more concerned
that the town of Boston might appear to be stacking the deck against
the defendants. Above all, Bostonians wanted to look moderate, fair,
and high-minded.

Various army officers had their own concerns regarding public perceptions. Lieutenant Colonel Dalrymple wrote to his commander, General Gage, that on a ship leaving for England the next day he would "send home copies of the narrative [of this whole affair]; they may prevent opinions being formed prejudicial to truth." Dalrymple's letter crossed in the mail with one from Gage, who advised Dalrymple, "Be so good to Collect the most impartial Accounts of this unhappy affair from the Beginning." Gage understood that the essential question was whether the army, and especially its officers, had acted appropriately. The behavior of individual soldiers was not his concern; rather, he wanted to ensure that the world knew that British officers could control their men. In a postscript to Dalrymple, Gage added, "Enquiry should be made into the Conduct of the Soldiers, previous to the last affair, and if any are found to have Acted in any manner deserving Punishment, they should be Confined."

With the help of Lieutenant Governor Hutchinson and one sympathetic justice of the peace, Dalrymple managed to put twenty-five depositions on the boat to England a full week before the town had finished collecting its stories. Those deposed claimed, as Gage had hoped, that Bostonians had premeditated and precipitated the riot in King Street and that the soldiers had fired only in self-defense. Moreover, Officers Hugh Dixon and David St. Clair, the same men who had assaulted the Halifax magistrate three years before, now claimed that "since they have been in Boston they have been frequently insulted and abused." Titled *A Fair Account of the Late Unhappy Disturbance,* the pro-military pamphlet was an explicit rejoinder to the *Short Narrative of the Horrid Massacre.* Not only was the title less gory than the town's—made even more vivid in the London editions of the

Short Narrative by an accompanying miniature version of Revere's engraving on the frontispiece — but its depositions began at number ninety-seven, as if in continuation of the depositions included in the *Short Narrative*. In the race to frame the narrative, the army seemed to win. But although the depositions in support of the army made it to England first, the pamphlet did not enjoy a wide distribution, and the pro-colonial *Short Narrative* reached England before the pro-imperial depositions were published.

Still, Gage did not give up. He labored over his report to his superiors at home. In April he pleaded with Lieutenant Governor Hutchinson to postpone the soldiers' trials as long as possible, in order to stir up sympathy for the defendants and anger at Bostonians. "In my accounts of the unhappy Transactions of the 5th of March, I have not omitted to state the situation of the Town and temper of the people, the efforts to inflame them to think of revenge, and the endeavours used to overawe the judges," he assured the lieutenant governor. "But my Letters unfortunately go home late," he added, and he worried that the trials might begin before officials in England had time to appreciate how desperately the soldiers might require a royal pardon.

In June 1770, after the first sets of depositions from both sides had left for London, Dalrymple wrote to Gage to suggest that he ask the Twenty-Ninth Regiment to search their recollections of violent encounters with Bostonians: "The 29th regiment having in many cases suffered from the violences of the Magistrates and people, it might be proper that affidavits should be obtained from them, which when sent here will properly find a place in the proposed publication, everything apposite to one purpose shall be collected, and if there is any further attention to be paid to military grievances, it will make our suffering appear extraordinary tho in that hope I am not sanguine."

Given how explicitly Dalrymple urged that evidence be collected in order to show the army's "extraordinary" torment while stationed in Boston, it is clear that most of these stories of brawls between townspeople and soldiers were recorded (although not necessarily invented) by him in order to shape public opinion. Lieutenant Colonel Carr obediently interviewed men from the Twenty-Ninth Regiment, but even before reading the affidavits, Gage was sure he knew what the men would say. "Carr has not yet transmitted them to me," he informed Dalrymple. "I am told they tend to prove the People of Boston, the most Vile sett of Beings in the whole Creation."

Throughout the summer and fall of 1770, the two pamphlets spread through the English-speaking world. Notices of their arrival began to show up in the London literary magazines. In the *Critical Review,* the writer and satirist Tobias Smollett reviewed both publications, as did Ralph Griffiths, the editor of the *Monthly Review.* Smollett was deeply incredulous of the *Short Narrative,* and he particularly abhorred Revere's engraving, which accompanied the London version. The print, he scoffed, is in "every-way dismal." *A Fair Account,* on the other hand, he was sure would completely exculpate the army. By contrast, Griffiths's only complaint about the *Short Narrative* was that it contained nothing that had not already been printed in the English newspapers. He read the *Fair Account* with a more skeptical eye than did Smollett, sardonically noting that the supporting affidavits were given by people "most of whom, however, it will be observed by every attentive reader, are officers in the army." Both sides had disseminated their stories to London readers. Surprisingly, neither side had been able to dominate public opinion.

Given how explicitly each side intended to cast blame on its opponent, it is not difficult to find the biases in each pamphlet. As Smollett noted in his review of the *Short Narrative,* "The design of this narrative . . . is evidently to enflame." "It must be remembered," Smollett continued, "that when people are inflamed to a certain degree, there is no difficulty in procuring evidences who will, even *bona fide,* prove anything conformable to the prevailing disposition of the times." Bostonians and soldiers alike were angry and willing to say anything that fit with the story they were trying to tell — a story of anger, violence, self-defense, and revenge.

As the accounts of the shooting — the town's *Short Narrative* and the army's *Fair Account* — passed from printer to bookseller to reader, the outlines of a new story were becoming clear. Gone, or at least much less prominent, was the narrative of an army closely enmeshed with the citizens of the town; in its place arose a stark portrayal of conflict and separation. The connections between soldiers and civilians were still evident to those who paid careful attention to the pamphlets' appendices, but the story of inexorably growing hostility dominated perceptions. Whether siding with the town or the army, members of the public agreed that only one question needed to be answered: was it the citizens or the soldiers who had placed the final straw on the camel's back?

While these pamphlets provided much fodder for conversation on both sides of the Atlantic, the prize that Crown and town officials alike hoped to capture was the moral high ground. Both sides accordingly framed the pamphlets, the pictures, the letters, and most of all the trials of Captain Preston and the soldiers to answer one basic question: Was the shooting simple murder or an act of self-defense? In other words, who was guilty, the living or the dead? A courtroom, with judges and jury weighing the merits of each side, seemed to be the ideal setting to resolve the question.

Yet precisely because they were trying to shape a story that blamed the other side, the people giving the depositions focused on finger pointing. They may have had reason to color or tilt their testimony toward accusation, but they had no reason to lie about the context in which their conversations took place. Distressed as Boston's inhabitants may have been after the shooting, it did not occur to any of them to hide evidence of civilian-military relationships. While the soldiers accused of deliberately shooting Bostonians sat in jail, everyone else went about their lives as best they could. The story in the pamphlets —of angry and threatening words—was both underpinned and belied by evidence of neighborliness so unexceptional that deponents could not be bothered to remove it from their testimony.

Even members of the Twenty-Ninth Regiment, profoundly affected by the shooting and its aftermath, did not completely sever their relations and interactions with the town following the lieutenant governor's decision to send them to Castle William. Throughout March and April, men slept on Castle Island while many of their wives tried to stay in Boston. The overcrowded fort would be particularly unpleasant for children, and even with only some of the families in the barracks on the island, the cramped quarters were vulnerable to epidemics.

But staying in Boston without their husbands or the presence of the military was hard for wives. Dalrymple was eager to start saving money on rent, now that he was moving so many people out to the free housing on Castle Island. General Gage's first order to him, when he heard about the shooting and the town meeting's pressure to remove the troops, was to "incur as little Expence as possible for the accommodation of the regiments." Within two weeks of the shooting, Dalrymple had emptied many of the larger buildings that the army had rented and was preparing to hand them back to their owners. Women who did not join their husbands on Castle Island found themselves essentially evicted.

Mary Dickson and Margaret Bishop tried to stay in their rented housing after their husbands moved into Castle William. In Boston, they were surrounded by both women and children of their old military community and their new civilian acquaintances. With Mary were her two children: four-year-old John, who had been born in Halifax, and baby William, born and baptized just thirteen months earlier. The military husbands and wives who had acted as William's godparents at Christ Church—Richard and Eleanor Starkey and Dennis and Frances McCormack—also chose to have the women and children in their two families remain in Boston for as long as they could, in that spring of 1770. Eleanor and her three children stayed at the northern foot of Beacon Hill, not far from the Mill Pond. There they rented a house from a free black instrument maker named Daniel Halsey. Frances and her daughter, Mary, stayed in the same neighborhood, sharing a house with Catherine Charloe, the African Jamaican wife of another soldier. All of the women, including Margaret, had been in Halifax together. Margaret and Catherine had both traveled from Ireland on the *Thunderer* five years earlier.

But without barracks or a housing allowance, Mary and Margaret struggled to keep a roof over their heads. It might have been homelessness that led them to squat with their children in an empty warehouse on Bradford's Wharf in the North End. They shared the space with a local couple, the Akeleys. On April 1, the town watch found the four adults. They may have resisted leaving their shelter; the head of the North End watch, Isaac Townshend, described the encounter as "routs and disorders." Certainly, there was no love lost between Townshend and the squatters. When he wrote up his report for the selectmen, Townshend characterized them all as "bad persons." Townshend and Joseph Akeley had clashed the year before, when Townshend had arrested him and a friend for carousing with a local nuisance whom he described as "a drunken Troublesome Noisey fellow." This time, Townshend locked the three women and Akeley in the watch house until morning. Margaret and Mary had to promise Townshend that they would leave town at dawn; the Akeleys merely had to find a new place to live, since Bradford's warehouse was "such an old Building and no fireplace," making any light unsafe. Margaret and Mary, meanwhile, slipped away and out of the historical record.

The warehouses the army had leased as barracks were emptying out, but plenty of people remained in the homes that Bostonians had rented to soldiers and their families. Isabella Montgomery and Elizabeth Hartigan, wives of two of the jailed soldiers, were still in Boston, as were at least a half dozen women from their company alone, including Mary Dickson and Catherine Charloe.

The presence of these women in Boston, and comings and goings of soldiers as well, were apparent to everyone. A committee of Boston's leaders, including Samuel Adams, John Hancock, and the speaker of the Massachusetts Assembly, Thomas Cushing, wrote in July 1770 to Benjamin Franklin, who was in London, that "since their removal the Common Soldiers, have frequently and even daily come up to the Town for necessary provisions, and some of the officers, as well as several of the families of the Soldiers have resided in the Town."

These families worried town officials, who feared that their presence in Boston was permanent rather than temporary. The officials may have managed to force the soldiers to leave, but they had not been quite so successful with the military women and children. If the army was not going to support these families, who would? The Boston selectmen might have had some sympathy with the otherwise unpopular governor of Halifax, who, after the departure of regiments there, wrote angrily to the commanding officer that "as great inconveniences have arisen from numbers of idle, helpless and indigent Women left in this Town by regiments on their departure from this Province, together with a very heavy expense to the inhabitants for their Support and Maintenance, I must therefore intreat that you will be so good as to give such Orders as may prevent an addition of this inconvenience so that the Women which have been brought here by the Troops may be obliged to embark with them."

Officials in Boston knew that they could not force most of these families to leave. Robert Love, a representative from the selectmen tasked with "warning out" strangers, did, however, hunt down more than forty families of soldiers still living in Boston to give them the reminder that, even if they were destitute, the town had no obligation to pay for their relief. The thin legal formality of a warning did not mean that the families had to leave, nor even that they might not receive relief, but it did alert women and their children that the town felt no obligation to them.

And so when Dalrymple began to move troops to Castle Island in the weeks after the shooting, women had to make a choice. Should they try to go to the overcrowded fort? Or should they stay in Boston, thereby increasing the possibility that the commanding officers would leave them behind when they embarked for the next deployment, but allowing them to remain close to recently made friends, and possibly even family?

For the wives of the two married soldiers held in Boston's jail for their part in the shooting on King Street, the choice was clear, at least for now. Both the newlywed Elizabeth Hartigan and the Irishwoman Isabella Montgomery stayed in Boston while their husbands were imprisoned. It took more than ten weeks after the shooting before Robert Love came to visit both women. Montgomery may have been warned of the possibility of this visit by her landlord, a member of the Governor's Council, Royall Tyler. Elizabeth Hartigan, as a Boston resident, might have known about the practice.

Love's visit was not an act of vengeance by the town. He was legally committed to let Montgomery know that, with her husband in jail and the rest of the Twenty-Ninth Regiment departed from Boston, the town was not obliged to give her poor relief in the event that she could not support herself. On the other hand, Love's warning of Montgomery was one of the very few moments when he preserved his political passions on paper. The Irishwoman was on her own, he noted in his report to the selectmen, because her husband "is now under Confinement in our Gaol for the murder of our people the Last

March." It seems not impossible that Love elaborated to Montgomery that if the regiment deserted her here in Boston, a likely possibility if her husband was found guilty and executed, then she and her children, Mary, Esther, and William, were on their own.

Just because the town of Boston was giving warning that it would not support army women did not mean that it would actually leave these families to starve. Edward McCarthy was still living out at Castle William when Love warned his wife, Mary McCarthy, in May 1770 that she and her daughter, Frances Mary, then living in a rented house in the South End, were not entitled to support from the town. Once the regiment left Boston, however, and the army stopped paying a housing allowance, apparently the McCarthys could no longer afford the rent. They were admitted to the poorhouse two months later, where they stayed for some six weeks. Taxes from the province of Massachusetts paid for their stay.

The soldiers had hardly left Boston before rumors began to fly that they were moving back to town. Several people informed town officials that "a number of Soldiers with their Baggage landed . . . at Wheelwright's Wharf." One eyewitness claimed that at least sixty men had disembarked. To keep an eye on the soldiers, the town meeting established a committee to ensure that no more soldiers came from Castle Island "than they think necessary." Boston was no longer a garrison town. But that did not mean that the troops, including their families, were gone. In some ways, life went on as before.

John Rowe had watched with mixed feelings as the regiments moved out to Castle Island. He was deeply shaken by the shooting. When Patrick Carr, after lingering for another week and a half with a shattered hip, died on March 14, Rowe recorded the funeral of the

"unhappy sufferer." He seemed to be playing the role of town official the next day, when Lieutenant Colonel Dalrymple invited him to
visit and shared with him the news that General Gage had approved
the removal of the troops. But when Dalrymple came to Rowe's
house two days later for a midday dinner, it was as a friend rather than
as an army official. Throughout the spring Rowe had kept his social
calendar full of drinks with Sons of Liberty like John Hancock and
dinners with British army officers like Dalrymple. A year and a half
later, he was still enjoying the company of army officers. On a hot day
in August 1771, he spent the day on the ship of the British naval commander, with seven officers among the guests. Rowe thought it was
an excellent evening: "a fine entertainment and the Genteelest supper
I ever saw. Twas a very agreeable and polite affair."

Rowe was not the only Bostonian willing to leave behind any sense
of rancor after the shooting. For all the violence of that night, few
seemed willing to cut all ties between the citizenry and the military.
Flirtatious soldiers continued to draw the eyes of young women. Private Samuel Strain had several of them — and a few town officials
—distressed at the possibility of his leaving town in 1770. After he
had moved to Castle Island in May 1770, he was accused of fathering
a child and was hauled to Justice Dana's house on an arrest warrant.
A young woman named Mary Dean claimed he had gotten her pregnant. Faced with the probability that Strain, now several miles from
the town center, would disappear without paying any child support,
Dana set bail and ordered him to wait in jail until someone paid his
bond. No one did. Two days later, apparently while still imprisoned,
Strain published marriage banns, an official intention to marry a different local woman, Mary Wharf. However, intention is not the same

as fulfillment; as there is no record of their actual marriage, Strain may never have married Wharf either.

Unlike the rakish Samuel Strain, other soldiers and civilians continued to make more conventional ties. In fact, half of the marriages in Boston between civilian women and military men were solemnized between March 5, 1770, and June 1772. These unions are part of the same pattern of intimate connections that developed before the shooting in King Street became the Boston Massacre. Just as the church records documented before March 1770, military families like those of John Spencer and William Mills continued to ask civilians to act as godparents for their children. Most telling of all, local women continued to wed soldiers in the weeks and years after the shooting.

Like the fraught interactions on the night of March 5, these marriages could combine elements of hostility with affection. The Bostonian Elizabeth Hillman married thirty-two-year-old Jesse Lindley from the Fourteenth Regiment in the summer of 1770. After their marriage, Lindley gave a deposition in which he claimed that during the fall of 1769, he and another soldier had an experience much like Hugh White's: the two soldiers were on sentry duty when a cluster of Bostonians began to insult them and hit them with clubs. As he recalled, "The two sentrys were oblig'd to charge their Bayonets in their own Defense." Like White, the sentries had to call on their fellow soldiers from the guardhouse for backup, but help did not arrive until after the crowd had dispersed. It may have been sheer luck that no one was killed that night. Yet when Lindley and Hillman married the following summer, the church record did not mark Lindley as an outsider. Instead, the clerk identified him and Hillman as "both of Boston." For her part, Hillman seemed willing to make a commitment to her new military community. Just a month after her marriage, she stood as godparent to the infant daughter of another man in her new husband's company.

Even the Twenty-Ninth Regiment was not anathema to most Bostonians. Unusually, Simon Bennis decided to join the regiment on March 9, 1770, just four days after the shooting and just one month before his child was born. Although Bennis apparently was not a native of the town, he had been living there since 1769. That year, he married a Boston woman named Margaret Querk, apparently part of a community of immigrants from the Isle of Man. When their child, Susanna, was born in April 1770, her two godmothers were local women with Manx names: Cluckus and Kewen. Even so soon after the shooting in King Street, local women did not reject friends associated with the military.

Neither did local men. John Rowe had enjoyed Captain Preston's company when he first came to Boston. Preston was among the first officers Rowe had met socially in the month after the troops came in 1768, and they had stayed friendly. Captain Preston had even been part of the small circle of guests invited to Sukey's ball at the end of February 1770. Even when the captain was in prison, Rowe did not forget his acquaintance. On a fine Friday morning, as four companies of the Twenty-Ninth Regiment were packing to sail to Castle Island, Rowe went to visit Preston in jail.

Eighteenth-century jails tended to be dark and dreary. In 1765, Thomas Hutchinson had described the Boston jail as "dark, damp and pestilential." But the court had been willing to tax all of Suffolk County for the money to build a new prison in 1768, a two-story stone building looming over Queen Street. High-ranking prisoners like Preston could expect a "cleanly apartment," which he might have to himself. Less fortunate men might be "thrust into a tiny apartment," which they would share with four or five others.

Given the physical surroundings, Rowe was surprised to find the officer in good spirits. A half dozen debtors languished, trying to straighten out their financial affairs, while most of the twenty-one other prisoners were awaiting trial for theft. Many of the cells had iron spikes in the doors to discourage escape, and the structure was sturdily built, as some of its residents knew well. Private Bryan Donnelly of the Sixty-Fourth Regiment and his cellmate, the Bostonian Abel Badger, had tried to set it on fire the previous winter. Just to burn through one of the interior doors apparently took hours, and eventually they succeeded in burning much of the jail, including the roof. In their defense, they later claimed that they were just trying to make a hole in the wall sufficient in size to pass a bottle of rum into the next cell for another soldier—which that soldier vigorously denied.

Neither rum nor food was easy to come by in jail. Most prisoners depended on others to bring them what they needed; in some cases the jailer might be willing to provide food, but for a price. Ever since Lieutenant Governor Hutchinson and Lieutenant Colonel Dalrymple had begun negotiating with the selectmen about the removal of the troops from Boston, Captain Preston, Corporal Wemms, and the seven privates who had turned themselves in after the shooting had been confined in the jail. As the Twenty-Ninth Regiment began to pack up for Castle Island, it was not clear who would remember these inmates. Would their Boston friends be willing to help them?

James Hartigan's new wife was still in Boston and might have brought him food, as Isabella Montgomery might have done for her imprisoned husband, Edward. William McAuly's wife, Mary, had come from Ireland with him, crossing the Atlantic on the same voyage of the *Thunderer* that brought Jane Chambers to America, but then Mary disappeared from the historical record. Perhaps she was no longer alive. If their families and friends did not help, the soldiers could find themselves both cold and hungry for a very long time.

Within the jail, debtors and criminals were not separated. In April 1770, when the soldiers took up residence in the prison, twenty-one of its twenty-three inhabitants there on criminal charges had been charged with theft; the other two had been arraigned for "profane swearing." The colorful term covers more than one might think, since one of the two had in fact committed perjury, while the other was in jail for foul language. The justice of the peace charged the second man a set fee for every time he had used such language: "four Shillings for the first of the said oaths, and one shilling for each of the other and four shillings for the first of the said curses and 1 [shilling] for each of the other." When he refused to pay the fine, however, the justice changed the man's punishment to ten days in jail.

The thieves too were a mixed crowd. Four were women, some of whom had had earlier run-ins with the law. Two more were soldiers, one from the Fourteenth Regiment and another named Patrick Freeman from the Twenty-Ninth. Freeman had been in jail since the end of December. Yet another was a private in the Fourteenth Regiment. And in April 1770, the keeper of the jail added a third designation, for prisoners involved in the shooting: "suspicion of murder."

Debtors were allowed out of the jail during the day; they were required only to sleep there at night. However, those designated as criminals were, in the language of the penal system, "close confined."

That spring, when the jail was more crowded than ever, the term must have felt quite literal. Rather than the usual two dozen prisoners, it held at least forty.

To men accustomed to barracks, the lack of space might not have seemed too onerous. Indeed, to a bold soldier like the playwright William Clark, close quarters offered opportunities. He was still unable to pay the fine of forty shillings with which the court slapped him after he had pushed his pistol into his father-in-law's chest. In town, he might not have had much chance to get close to an officer to plead for aid; in the Boston jail, however, he must have found it easy to corner Captain Preston. By the end of July, he managed to talk Preston into sending a petition to Lieutenant Governor Hutchinson on his behalf. On his salary, it was no surprise that Clark found himself, as Preston wrote in the petition, "entirely unable to pay" his fine and court costs. At this rate, Preston noted wryly, Clark had become both "a burthen to the province and a loss to His Majesty's Service." It would be better all around to release Clark and send him back to his regiment. The governor agreed, remitting Clark's fine and sending him on his way.

The Boston jail was where people were held before their trial; incarceration was very rarely used as a punishment. Only a few people, like William Clark, might remain in jail even after trial. Until they could pay their fine, and sometimes their court or incarceration costs, they had to wait in the jail or the workhouse. But most of the prison's inhabitants were anxiously awaiting their day in court.

Jail could be a terrifying experience for poor families. The Bostonian George White, who was imprisoned with the soldiers in April

1770, could do nothing about the impact of his incarceration on his family. The Supreme Court convicted him that month of breaking into and entering the home of John Moffatt. After he had been in jail for over a year, his children could no longer manage without his support. The selectmen ordered them to the almshouse in August 1771. White had completed his punishment by the next spring, but he was still in jail. Presumably, he had yet to pay his bill.

Other family members suffered even more directly from a family member's imprisonment. The Bostonian Richard Smith had been accused of multiple counts of theft — one of them in conjunction with George White — and was remanded to the town jail. While he was in court, making his case before the justices at the end of March 1770, his pregnant wife came to the jail. As she waited for him to return from court, Mrs. Smith agreed to run an errand for a prisoner who was "close confined." Richard Smith claimed that when his wife got back to the jail, the keeper (whom the imprisoned Smith, tellingly, referred to as the "owner" of the jail) knocked her down "all in the mud and dirt and afterwards used her in a Barborous Manner inhuman like." The pregnant woman feared that the jailer's beating would kill both her and her unborn child.

No fewer than sixteen prisoners observed the assault on Mrs. Smith. Three weeks after they were jailed, four of the soldiers — Wemms, Warren, Hartigan, and White — signed a petition in support of their fellow prisoner Smith. Besides these four, several other soldiers who were in jail for theft testified to seeing the assault too, as did Ebenezer Richardson, still awaiting trial for the murder of Christopher Seider. The prisoners must have been horrified by the abuse, asserting that if the judges wanted to question them concerning it, they would be "willing and more" to help. Despite the accounts of violent hostilities between soldiers and civilians that officers and selectmen were collecting in the weeks immediately following the shooting, the soldiers in Boston's jail continued to treat Bostonians once again like neighbors, rather than strangers.

Still, after the evidence of the jailer's maltreatment of Smith's wife, the spirits of the imprisoned soldiers must have sunk rapidly. Nor were they alone in their concern. Ebenezer Richardson, waiting to be arraigned after shooting Christopher Seider from his window in February, looked to his future with trepidation. Barring a last-minute pardon from the king himself, chances were good that a jury would demand his life in return for Seider's. Richardson spent some of his time reading an Anglican catechism as he prepared himself for an adult baptism, unusual for the era but well suited to his circumstance. It seemed like an appropriate time to pray.

9

From Shooting to Massacre,
October–December 1770

The day following the shooting on King Street was a Tuesday. Early that morning, the commanding officer, Captain Thomas Preston, turned himself in to the justices of the peace. Sitting in the stone prison, Preston realized he would need a lawyer immediately. The officer was sure a Boston court would convict him if his fate were "life left to the mercy of a partial Jury." The only route to saving his life would be a royal pardon, "and God knows if it will come time enough to save me from a shameful end," he wrote to a possible patron in England. But without a lawyer, he certainly had no chance.

How a future president of the United States, John Adams, became the leading lawyer for British soldiers has become the stuff of legend, created in large part by Adams himself through his autobiography. As he explained many years later, he took the cases despite their potential to ruin his reputation as a patriot, "incurring a Clamour and popular Suspicions and prejudices, which are not yet worn out and never will be forgotten as long as History of this Period is read."

Sitting in his office on the day after the shooting, Adams later recalled, he received a visit from a local merchant, James Forrest, who had become friendly with several of the army officers over the previous year and a half. "With tears streaming from his eyes," Forrest choked out, "'I am come with a very solemn Message from a very unfortunate Man, Captain Preston in Prison. He wishes for Council, and can get none.'" In words that are frequently repeated to members of the Massachusetts bar to this day, Adams responded, "Council ought to be the very last thing that an accused Person should want [that is, lack] in a free Country." And so John Adams, in his recollection, took on Preston's case.

By Adams's account, Forrest had gone first to two other lawyers, Josiah Quincy Jr. and Robert Auchmuty, neither of whom would represent Preston until and unless Adams himself agreed to join the legal team. Robert Auchmuty was a strong supporter of the government, and Josiah Quincy Jr. was a young lawyer, committed to the liberty party and younger brother to Samuel Quincy, the Massachusetts solicitor general.

Certainly, Quincy's father was "anxious and distressed" about his twenty-six-year-old son taking on the case. Quincy assured his father that he had taken some time to reflect on whether or not he should help Preston, and decided to do so only after being urged by many Sons of Liberty, including "an Adams, a Hancock, [and] a Molineux." Moreover, in a letter reproduced by Quincy Jr.'s granddaughter fifty years after Josiah Quincy's death, the son reminded his father of "an attorney's oath and duty," a commitment that sounded quite similar to Adams's right to counsel.

In fact, Preston was not the first army officer Quincy had represented. As we have seen, in June 1769, Quincy represented Ensign

William Fitzpatrick after he was accused of attempted assault on Susannah Dalton. In that case, Forrest had put up the hundred-pound bail for Fitzpatrick. Given that they had already worked together once, it must not have taken long for Forrest to think of Quincy as a possible lawyer for Preston.

Meanwhile, the question of the prosecution's legal counsel was also complicated. Every case of murder is prosecuted not by the human victim but by the state. So while the defense would speak for the accused military men, in eighteenth-century Boston, the prosecution would speak for the king. It was a strange position: the prosecution and the defense seemed to change sides. The royal government that had so backhandedly brought the troops to Boston now needed to appoint a lawyer who would try to prove that these troops had acted illegally. In a sense, prosecution lawyers seemed to be prosecuting their own principles.

It was not easy to find a prosecutor. The job would ordinarily have been taken on by the attorney general, John Sewell, but he seemed to have no appetite for the task. The prosecution then fell to the Massachusetts solicitor general, Josiah Quincy's brother Samuel. As a committed member of the liberty party, Samuel's father did not seem to have concerns about his son taking on the prosecution of the soldiers. Yet although Samuel's loyalist leanings had not yet emerged in 1770, by virtue of his appointment as solicitor general, Samuel Quincy was already a government man. He would soon be on the outs with his father.

The Boston Town Meeting was concerned that the Crown, in the person of Samuel Quincy, would not have the stomach to bring an adequate case against its own troops. Feeling it would be best to hire another lawyer to help Quincy and ensure he was trying hard enough, the town meeting "pitched upon" the lawyer Robert Treat Paine. Although he had not been involved in the Boston liberty party, Paine had had a legal practice in Boston until 1761, when he moved to the small town of Taunton, from which he kept up his professional and personal connections to Boston. To their disappointment, the town meeting members were informed by the selectmen that the town of Boston could not bring a criminal prosecution against the soldiers. Paine, as the representative of the deceased's relatives, would have to stand in for Boston.

To help Paine prepare for the case, the merchant William Molineux sent him an early copy of the *Short Narrative*. Paine dutifully worked his way through the depositions, coding each one with a few words that revealed the prosecution's line of attack. "Threats," he jotted next to many of the depositions; "first insults" he added to others. The prosecution might be formally representing the Crown, but Paine at least would argue that soldiers had threatened, insulted, and deliberately shot Bostonians.

The town of Boston, even its more determined adherents to the liberty party such as William Molineux, seemed to be taking two tracks at the same time. On the one hand, it hired Paine to ensure that the prosecution of the soldiers would be robust and thorough. On the other, the town was eager to show how law-abiding a community it was. Not only would the case be tried on its merits, but the defendants would get the best possible representation. Hiring counsel had become the opening salvo in the battle for reputation, but it would not be the last.

While the prisoners sat in the jail around the corner from King

Street, the heart of Boston, rumors swirled. There was still no clarification as to what had actually happened on the night of March 5, or who was accountable. Opinions ranged widely. Some Bostonians were sure that Captain Preston bore the main responsibility for the deaths. As one man wrote to his London correspondent, it "seems plain, upon the whole, that the Capt. must have had an intention of firing upon the people, notwithstanding his declaration to the contrary; otherwise, why should he order his men to load with ball?" Embracing a completely different interpretation, one government ally, trying to pick up gossip while confined to his bedroom with gout, reported that he had heard that Preston "endeavoured to prevent the exasperated Soldiers from firing even at the Risque of his own Life." Sixty-six-year-old Reverend David Hall recorded in his diary a week after the shooting that he had heard that the soldiers (who "had been troublesome" the week before) had "fired their pieces. 8 of them. Killed 3 men on the spot. Wounded many 2 of which died." A week later, he noted that the story continued to shift, "not Just as we heard," although "not less affecting."

As the taking of public depositions continued at Faneuil Hall, Bostonians shared their versions of events. Throughout March, people tried and failed to put together a coherent story. One of John Rowe's fishing companions, Gregory Townsend, wrote to his brother in frustration, "We have the most positive asertions directly opposite so that it is almost impossible to come at the truth." One of Captain Preston's strongest advocates, Justice of the Peace James Murray, illustrated Townsend's point perfectly in a letter to his sister: "Five or six witnesses swear that Preston bid his men fire. Others swear that he did not, and say that if the fireing had been by order it would not have been by single muskets." Murray acknowledged that his information was not utterly reliable. "I will not answer for the Authenticity of every article of the above," he admitted in a postscript.

If finding the truth was indeed "almost impossible," what would happen at the soldiers' trial? Lieutenant Governor Hutchinson had promised, on the night of the shooting, that he would ensure that "Justice [be] done on the Guilty." Others were dubious, however, that justice could be done in Boston. The government supporter Gregory Townsend worried that "poor Preston will stand a very bad chance if his trial comes on speedily before the Passions of people are a little Subsided," and the acting governor's friend James Murray too thought "there will be Little Chance for him and his Men with enraged, prejudiced Juries. The King's Mercy must be their only hope."

Ardent supporters of the liberty party were just as skeptical that the judicial process could lead to what they thought would be a just outcome. In his sermon given on Sunday, March 11, the Reverend John Lathrop warned, "If innocent blood is not heard and avenged . . . it will continue to cry, not only against the murderer, but the government and land, which suffers murderers to go unpunished."

Perhaps recognizing that he should not put his faith in blind justice, Captain Thomas Preston tried to put his thumb on the scales. But although Preston had served in the army for fourteen years, he had not developed a sense of political savoir-faire. His first response to his arrest was alarmingly naive: he took out an advertisement in the March 12 issue of the *Boston Gazette,* the newspaper most sympathetic to the Sons of Liberty. Perhaps he thought that the fastest way to end the ordeal would be to throw himself on the mercy of Bostonians, reminding them of his friendship with so many of the town's elites.

After all, as he claimed, even the members of Boston's liberty movement were willing to admit that he was "a sober, honest man & a
good officer." In one rambling sentence, the captain tried to capture
the goodwill of his readers by thanking them for "throwing aside all
party and Prejudice" in order to defend his "injured Innocence." Preston closed by promising that he would "ever have the highest sense
of the *justice* they have done me." Unfortunately for the captain, his
message had to compete for the attention of the *Gazette*'s readers. The
black-bordered page on which it appeared gave an extensive account
of the shooting from the perspective of the citizens, and Preston's
"card," as it came to be known, stood in jarring contrast to the image
of four coffins that appeared with the article directly above.

No one, except Preston himself, thought it was wise to publish the
card. The potential irony of his final phrase, promising that Boston's
justice "will be ever gratefully remembered," pointed at the very least
to a misplaced confidence, if not a willful blindness to the political
consequences of the shooting on King Street. When the advertisement was reprinted in the New York papers, General Gage was particularly distressed by Preston's assurance that Bostonians would put
aside their prejudices. "I wish he may not have been too premature in
that Measure," he lamented to Lieutenant Colonel Dalrymple. Any
judicial irregularities or even illegalities, he noted, "will Justify themselves by his own Words.

Boston readers also mocked Preston's preemptive claim to innocence. A letter to the paper the next week asked the editors of the
Boston Gazette to explain how anyone "can be satisfied of his *injured
innocence,* until he is acquitted of the high Charge laid against him, in a
due Course of Law." Preston had mistaken the mood of his audience;

they were not predisposed to support him. The captain could expect fairness, the writer argued, but not advocacy. Already Preston's attempts to turn to his personal connections with Bostonians had misfired. The day after Preston's advertisement appeared, a grand jury indicted him and his eight subordinates for murder.

Preston's next attempt at self-exculpation went equally awry. During his second week in jail he wrote a long narrative explaining his own motives and actions on the evening of the shooting. The narrative, published under the title "The Case of Captain Thomas Preston," contained the well-worn and tactless statement that Bostonians had fomented ill will toward the soldiers ever since their arrival. Preston blamed Boston's judges and magistrates for emboldening the civilians. Moreover, he defended taking soldiers into the street with him on the grounds that he feared Bostonians were prepared to attack and plunder the Custom House.

In late March, Preston sent a copy of the narrative to Gage, who cringed when he read it. Gage had hoped that Preston might make a more effective case with this narrative than he had with his card, but it was obvious for many reasons that this composition would not have that effect. "It appears too plainly to be wrote by himself," Gage complained to Dalrymple, "and he takes up the Affair from the first arrival of the Troops at Boston, and censures the Conduct of the Magistrates from the beginning." He was even more distraught when he found that Preston had sent his account to the papers in London, thus clearly and unnecessarily exposing Preston's mistaken actions in King Street. Gage's anger with Preston led him to articulate most clearly the legal argument against the captain: "He had no Business to defend the Custom House, unless legaly called upon."

"The Case of Captain Thomas Preston" appeared in the London papers at the end of April, and by June it was reappearing in news-papers in America. Editorials in the American papers made clear just how much Preston had again miscalculated. The *Boston Gazette* repub-lished it in a special supplement to show "how greatly the Conduct of the Town has been *misrepresented*," a sentiment picked up by most other colonial papers.

In July, a committee consisting of Thomas Cushing, Samuel Ad-ams, John Hancock, William Molineux, and others visited Preston in jail to ask how the same person could have written both the March 12 card to the Boston paper, which praised Boston for its sense of justice, and "The Case of Captain Thomas Preston." The committee pointed out that "those papers directly militate with each other." In fact, the *Essex Gazette* had made the same point to its readers a few weeks ear-lier when it published the card directly preceding Preston's "Case."

When Preston tried to explain to the committee of his former neighbors that others had edited his account before it was published in London, they were unconvinced. Their anger was directed less at the shooting itself and more at the ways in which Preston had charac-terized Boston. By speaking ill of the town, he had eroded his support still further.

The miseries of jail did nothing to improve Preston's mood. He wrote in June to Lord Barrington, the secretary at war, saying he feared he would remain "at least six months close confin'd in a loath-some gaol, almost suffocated with Charcoal, and in case of the Gaol's taking fire as it did last year, must certainly be burn'd to Death. My health is much compromised by my long confinement, my debts in-creased by my great expences, my promotion to the Majority stopt if not lost, my life in danger from the Mob threatening to take me out of Gaol & hang me, and lastly the great probability of the Jury finding me guilty in spite of all laws & evidence." He foresaw the end of his career and even his life — he might be lynched before the trial began or found guilty and hanged for murder.

Preston's fear of lynching had some justification. An anonymous letter written to Preston in July 1770 cautioned the captain that even a pardon from the king might not save him from the crowd. Recent history provided a precedent: in 1736, an army captain in Edinburgh named Porteous had shot into a crowd, killing several citizens. The captain had been dragged from the prison and hanged by a mob before his trial could begin. The same thing could happen to Preston, warned the letter writer.

Even as privates kept on marrying Boston women and John Rowe continued to dine with Dalrymple, Thomas Preston became increasingly isolated from the social world of Boston. His regiment had been redeployed to New Jersey in June, leaving only the Fourteenth Regiment in Boston. Preston's shift to seeing himself as the victim of a lynching, rather than a gentleman at ease with his friends, was a realistic foreshadowing of what would happen in Boston by the end of the trials. Just as Preston's own reputation seemed to shift during his time in jail from that of a "benevolent, humane man" to "a military criminal," so that night's events would be transformed from a "shooting" to a "massacre."

By August, Preston's view of his relationship with Bostonians was dark. He wrote to Gage that the general could "have no conception of their wickedness." He had heard hopeful rumors that some patron of his might be able to acquire a royal pardon, but he put less stock in that rumor than in the anonymous letter suggesting he would be lynched before he could face trial. Unless Dalrymple were to bring the Fourteenth Regiment back from Castle Island to spring him from prison, he suggested morosely to Gage, "this [should] be the last letter . . . I shall trouble you with."

Preston may have felt abandoned by Dalrymple, but in fact the long wait in jail was part of the strategy that Dalrymple and Lieutenant Governor Hutchinson had devised. They had hoped that a cooling-off period would render the eventual jurors less emotional and more willing to acquit. The time finally seemed ripe. Preston asked John Adams and Josiah Quincy to bring his case before the courts in September. He knew that Boston's prominent opposition politicians had just received letters from their major supporters in Britain, urging them to ensure a fair trial. Moreover, Adams and the rest of the legal team had suggested to him that if the case went to trial now and the verdict went against him, the soldiers would still have sufficient time to apply for a royal pardon.

As General Gage saw it, the soldiers' argument should be simple self-defense: "that they were grossly insulted and attacked without Provocation . . . as to endanger their Lives." By this theory, there was no difference between the arguments made for the officer and those made for the enlisted men. "Whether the Captain gave Orders to fire or not, seems a Circumstance something Stronger in his particular favour, and nothing more." He continued blithely, "I should imagine [it will be] not difficult for the Lawyers, to make these particulars appear plain to the Court."

Preston must have been relieved, then, when he and the eight soldiers (along with the four men accused of shooting from the Custom

House window) were brought into the courthouse early in September to enter their pleas of not guilty. At last there seemed to be forward motion. And then, to the disappointment of everyone, the judges simply adjourned the county court for another six weeks.

In those six weeks after the arraignment, the eight other soldiers imprisoned with Preston may have had time to further consider their case. It has never been precisely clear whether Samuel Quincy and Robert Treat Paine had intended to try all of the military men together, or to try the officer separately from the enlisted men. Regardless, when the Superior Court reopened on Tuesday, October 23, the justices declared that the next day's case would be *Rex [The King] v. Preston.*

The privates may have learned or suspected that the defense team planned to take a different tack than Gage's straightforward self-defense theory. The implications of separating the officer from enlisted men seemed ominous to some of them. If Preston was found not guilty of ordering them to fire, what would their defense be? On the morning of the first day of Preston's trial, three of the men — the sentry Hugh White, the newlywed James Hartigan, and twenty-two-year-old Matthew Kilroy — wrote a desperate petition to the judges, asking to be tried together with their commanding officer.

> May it please Yr, Honours we poor Distressed Prisoners Beg that ye Would be so good as to lett us have our Trial at the same time with our Captain, for we did our Captains Orders & if we don't Obay is Command [we] should have been Coufine'd & shott for not doing of it — We Humbly pray Yr, Honours that you would take it into yr serious consideration & grant us that favour for we

only desire to Open the truth before our Captains face for it is very hard he being a Gentelman should have more chance for to save his life then we poor men that is Oblidged to Obay his command—we hope that Yr Honours will grant this our petition, & we shall all be in dut[y] Bound ever to pray for Your honours.

The three privates showed as little loyalty to Preston as he had shown to them. They were happy to tell the judges that Preston had ordered them to fire. Their evident acceptance of Preston's guilt seemed to be the only way out. Evoking the horror that Bostonians had felt seeing the execution of the deserter Richard Ames two years earlier, on the Boston Common, they reminded the justices that the punishment for refusing an order was a firing squad. Besides, they added, Preston had had the opportunity to make a free choice when faced with Bostonians that night, whereas they had not.

The justices were unmoved. The eight enlisted men would be tried separately. Meanwhile, they could only wait in jail and hope that whatever defense strategy the lawyers tried in *Rex v. Preston* would not foreclose their own future.

When his trial finally began on October 24, Captain Preston had only to step across the small alley through a "blustering cold" day from the jail to the courthouse. The room was full of observers. Some of them he knew as possible supporters: they were officers like him, or men he had met at John Rowe's house. Others were new to him. Worryingly, lying on the lawyers' table was a copy of the *Short Narrative*. The prosecuting lawyer, Robert Treat Paine, had apparently brought his annotated copy to the courtroom. Even from across the room, the words on the cover, printed in an enormous black font, caught the eye. Largest and darkest of all were two lines: NARRATIVE . . . HORRID MASSACRE IN BOSTON. The prosecution evidently intended to follow the storyline laid out the previous March: not a loss of control or a sad overreaction, but a massacre. Would the jury decide that Preston had ordered it?

Ostensibly, the question on which Preston's fate would turn concerned responsibility. As the commanding officer, had he ordered his men to shoot? Revere had engraved Preston standing safely behind the privates, his sword raised in a gesture of command. The prosecution would want to show that Preston had shouted the order to fire. The defense's job would be to prove that Revere's engraving was wrong.

As it turned out, however, the skill of Preston's legal team trumped proof and logic. Seven months earlier, when James Murray had written to his sister about his fears of "enraged, prejudicial Juries," he had already foreseen the approach Adams would take in Preston's defense. It is unlikely that James Murray and John Adams agreed on much; Murray was a devoted supporter of the acting governor and the royal government; Adams abhorred Thomas Hutchinson. But when it came to the question of the jury, the two were in agreement. Preston's fate would depend on getting a favorable jury.

John Adams used every lawyering tool he had. When he did not receive the list of potential jurors ahead of time, as was customary, Adams convinced the judges that his client should be able to challenge individual jurors on the basis that he had not seen their names on the jury list. He also apparently convinced the judges that only the defense, and not the prosecution, had this right to challenge individual jurors. Through both his lawyer's management and some good luck, Preston eventually faced a sympathetic jury, one that included his close friends Gilbert Deblois and Philip Dumaresq. The latter had even declared in public that he "believed Captain Preston to be as innocent as the child unborn." Since Massachusetts law required a unanimous jury verdict to convict a defendant of murder, Preston's eventual freedom was assured the moment those two men were sworn in.

Modern historians have not been able to understand why Paine, as the lawyer for the Crown (and the liberty party coalition who had hired him), countenanced such a pro-Preston jury. The tilt of the jury was certainly no secret to Bostonians watching the trial; observers such as William Palfrey were shocked at the number of Preston's friends who sat in judgment on him. "I shudder with horror & indignation at the strange perversion of Justice," he fumed to a correspondent. Yet it seems that neither Paine nor anyone else who spoke in the courtroom mentioned these friendships or their likely effect on the outcome of the trial. Perhaps they were too obvious to need mentioning. Perhaps, however, this silence was an intentional part of the strategy of each side. To ignore the connections between civilians and soldiers, to play down the long-established relationships between Preston and his civilian colleagues, allowed prosecution and defense alike to emphasize the separation between what had in fact been two intermingled elements of one society.

The captain sat through five long days of trial. Proceedings began at eight o'clock and went until close to six, and lawyers often spoke for three hours at a stretch. Attorneys called nearly fifty witnesses to testify to innumerable and minuscule points of detail: where people were standing, what each of them heard. Even now, the mass of detail offered by the witnesses is difficult to keep straight, and the long days of unending oral testimony must have challenged the attentiveness of the jurors, none of whom presumably expected such lengthy proceedings. As the lieutenant governor noted at the time, it was the only capital trial in a regular court of common law in Massachusetts that had ever lasted more than a single day.

Even so, the fate of Preston, who observers thought "appear'd perfectly unconcern'd," did not depend on any evidence given in that courtroom. Sons of Liberty like William Palfrey sneered that the entire trial was nothing but "a farce"; in fact, in addition to his knowledge that the jury would not convict, Preston had a second reason for confidence. Lieutenant Colonel Dalrymple had whispered to the army captain that the king had already prepared pardons for him and for the men under his command.

On the third day of the trial, John Adams called to the stand a woman named Jane Whitehouse to speak in Preston's defense. She claimed definitively that the captain had not encouraged the soldiers to shoot. She was sure, she told the court, because she had been talking with the sentry before any crowds had made their way to King Street. She had stayed on the street corner and therefore was in an excellent position to observe what had happened. No record exists of the prosecution asking Whitehouse how she knew the soldiers well enough to be chatting with them as the confrontation began. More significant, they did not — nor did anyone else — inform the judges and jury that at the time of the event Whitehouse had not been the woman's surname.

At the time of the shooting, this woman had been known as Jane

Crothers; she had married Private Joseph Whitehouse of the Fourteenth Regiment three weeks after the incident. Given that the witness was a woman of no social standing who had now become a part of the military community, Paine might have suggested that Whitehouse would therefore be an unreliable and biased witness. Casting doubt on her veracity in his summation would have been the work of mere moments. To explain her connection to the troops, however, would make public the marriage of a Massachusetts woman to a soldier of the British army.

But just as Paine and Samuel Quincy silently allowed two of Preston's friends to stay on his jury, they said nothing about Jane Whitehouse née Crothers. In fact, no lawyer in that courtroom chose to mention the intimate connections that bound Boston women to British soldiers. To do so would have cracked open the pretense to which both sides had tacitly agreed: that an enormous gulf separated soldiers and civilians.

When at last the jury announced his acquittal on the morning of October 30, Preston felt grimly justified. The verdict of not guilty brought "great mortification of every blood thirsty & malicious Bostonian," he told Gage. Freedom was less a relief than it was a pleasure "of the complete victory obtained over the knaves & foolish villains of Boston." The feelings of connection and trust that he had expressed in his initial letter from jail had dissipated completely. As soon as court was adjourned that day, Preston fled to Castle William and stayed there as long as he could, avoiding his former civilian friends in town.

Meanwhile, the other eight soldiers spent another month in Boston's jail. When the court had refused their petition to be tried with

Preston, the privates and the corporal had no choice but to wait and worry. The fears some of them had expressed in their petition to the justices proved prescient. Since Preston was acquitted of ordering the men to fire, logically speaking, it seemed their only chance lay in the argument of self-defense.

Observers inferred from Preston's trial that winning acquittal depended as much on the character of the jury as on the merits of the case. After Preston's case ended, General Gage repeatedly expressed his hope that "the same Jury will try the Soldiers," but it was not to be. With a new case, the lawyers and their clients had to pick a new jury. Once the trial began, on November 27, Lieutenant Governor Hutchinson fretted that "we have not so good a Jury nor was it possible to obtain better."

No one on this second jury was quite so explicit as Philip Dumaresq had been for Preston in vouching, pretrial, for the innocence of the defendants. It seemed unlikely that any of the soldiers would have friends on the jury; every single juror came from outside Boston. Samuel Adams complained later that it was hardly a jury of peers when none of them had had the experience of living in a town with soldiers.

To those assessing this jury through the lens of Preston's acquittal, its composition certainly did not look promising. The foreman, Joseph Mayo of Roxbury, had been involved for years in the movement to resist the military occupation of Boston. In 1769, he had been part of a committee that instructed the Roxbury representative to the Massachusetts legislature to find out "why the King's troops have been quartered in the body of the metropolis of the Province while the barracks provided heretofore have remained in a manner useless."

The week after the shooting, the town of Roxbury had sent a petition to Lieutenant Governor Hutchinson to express "astonishment grief and indignation, at the horrid and barbarous action committed last Monday Evening . . . in the most wanton, cruel, and cowardly manner." Petitions like this one could hardly have given Hutchinson much confidence in the jury.

The other jurors also came from towns that had explicitly expressed concern about troops or had declared their support for the town of Boston. Three jurors came from Hingham. After the shooting, the Hingham Town Meeting sent a letter to the Committee of Merchants in Boston, assuring them that "we heartily sympathize with our Brethren of the Town of Boston, in the late unhappy Destruction of so many of their Inhabitants." In 1769 Braintree, the home of the juror Isaiah Thayer, had sent instructions to its representative in the Massachusetts Assembly to question how the entire province could have been put "in the odious Light of a factious and rebellious People." All these men came from towns that had plenty of anti-soldier feeling.

The soldiers' trial did not initially catch John Rowe's attention. He did not even realize that the proceedings had started until the second day, when the prosecution's evidence was well underway. From this point onward, however, Rowe made the same careful note in his diary: "The Soldiers still on Tryal." Over eighty people gave evidence; it took six days to get through their testimony. There were two reasons why the soldiers' trial took even longer than Preston's. First, the lawyers who were prosecuting the case for the Crown needed to prove that the men on trial were in fact the soldiers who had been in King Street the night of the shooting. Second, the lawyers had agreed

that each side could introduce evidence about brawls and conflicts oc-
curring elsewhere in town that night, something that had not been
allowed in Preston's trial. The prosecution had suggested this expan-
sion of allowable evidence as part of its strategy to show that soldiers
all over town, not just those in King Street, had been spoiling for a
fight. In the end, however, it was the defense that used these stories to
greater advantage.

From a legal standpoint, citing evidence about conflicts that happened out of sight of the Custom House sentry made "technical evidentiary sense." Obviously, brawls in other neighborhoods or alleys,
regardless of whether civilians or soldiers initiated them, could add
little to an argument about the military men's self-defense. But a long
week of testimony pointing to these conflicts all over town would
serve John Adams's ultimate argument. These witnesses would drive
home a picture of civilians and soldiers at odds with each other, im-
placably and absolutely.

But the ploy to show threats and conflicts beyond those on King
Street ended up demonstrating the wealth of connections between
soldiers and townspeople. For example, on the first day, the Crown
called for the prosecution a man named Samuel Clark. When asked
to identify the soldiers he had seen that night, Clark explained that
he knew that Hugh White was the sentry. He went on to say that he
passed a few words with White, and that no one was near him at the
time. According to John Adams's notes, White testified, "He spoke to
me, and asked how we all did? I said pretty well." The single shorthand reporter who took down most of the trial picked up a few more
words: "He spoke to me and asked how we all did at home." Had
White been to Clark's home? Did he know his wife? The lawyers for

the Crown were not interested in how Clark knew White; they used his testimony to show that at the time of the conversation, all was peaceful and White had no reason to worry about a developing riot.

The next day saw a parade of witnesses testifying to their personal knowledge of the soldiers on trial and to the relative quiet of the streets. What mattered to the prosecution was the evidence of calm; they entirely ignored the social ties that Bostonians acknowledged having with the soldiers. The resident John Danbrooke knew two of the defendants, John Carroll and James Hartigan, and he testified that he saw only peaceful activity in the streets: "no Blow given or stick or anything thrown." While not all the witnesses knew the soldiers well enough to swear to recognition, they all claimed that there were no more than twenty or thirty people on King Street that night, "not so many as often seen there." As the prosecution tried to build its case for premeditated and widespread attacks of soldiers on civilians, they called to the stand Samuel Hemmenway, who testified that he knew Matthew Kilroy "particularly well." Hemmenway claimed that he and Kilroy had been visiting together in a kitchen when the soldier told him that "he never *would miss an opportunity of firing upon the Inhabitants.*" In his summary of the evidence, the lawyer for the prosecution, Samuel Quincy, put particular emphasis on Kilroy's supposedly bloodthirsty intentions. He ignored the circumstances that brought Kilroy and Hemmenway together.

Later that day, Thomas Wilkinson came to the stand as a witness on behalf of the prosecution. His testimony bolstered Samuel Quincy's argument that it had been a quiet evening and the guard had nothing to fear. Wilkinson testified that he had been at home when he first heard bells ringing. He walked the very few blocks to the town center, where he saw, he swore under oath, soldiers with swords and townspeople with buckets for firefighting. King Street itself, he recalled, was completely empty.

Three people in the courtroom took down Wilkinson's testimony that day: John Adams, Samuel Quincy, and a court stenographer. Often any testimony recorded by all three note takers is relatively consistent. This time, however, while all the men recorded that Wilkinson identified Edward Montgomery as a neighbor, only the stenographer also recorded that Montgomery had gone to his former neighbor to ask him to explain the situation. Perhaps neither lawyer thought this piece of evidence worth writing down. The detail that a civilian knew one of the soldiers well enough to march up to him while the soldiers were in formation, in order to ask him for an explanation, never was part of the story that Quincy told the jury.

After calling thirty-four witnesses, most of whose testimony differed only in small details about the size and rowdiness of the people in King Street or nearby, Quincy rested his case on the evidence that his witnesses had identified all of the soldiers standing trial and that some combination of the eight of them must have killed the five Bostonians. Furthermore, Quincy suggested that soldiers all over town were so hostile and violent that "the inhabitants had reason to be apprehensive they were in danger of their lives; children and parents, husbands and wives, masters and servants, had reason to tremble for one another." It was a picture of innocent Bostonians drawn together against the imminent threat of a vicious soldiery.

When Samuel's brother Josiah opened the case for the defense, he began by urging the jury to remember that "the reputation of the country depends much on your conduct." These words are a surprising appropriation of the prosecution's argument. It was impossible to deny that soldiers had shot civilians; the defense therefore needed to shift the blame for those deaths from the soldiers onto someone else. If the case for the defense required innocent Bostonians and vicious soldiers, Josiah and his fellow counsel would have to find a way to plead self-defense for the soldiers while saving Boston's reputation. Emphasizing the conflict between the soldiers and civilians was the strategy.

Adams and Quincy called over fifty witnesses for the defense, and their testimony took three days. The first dozen set the stage, describing how they had seen hordes of citizens in the streets, armed with sticks and clubs. Archibald Gould, walking toward Faneuil Hall from the southern end of town on the night of the shooting, saw so many Bostonians with sticks that he was afraid even to make the journey back home. Gould had deliberately chosen a route that would let him circle around the busy heart of the town; other witnesses, however, found multiple brawls in alleys and streets to the north and east of the sentry on King Street.

Once the evidence turned to the shooting itself, witnesses added a bewildering array of detail in describing where they were and what they heard. Most of them noticed teenage boys; many saw the soldiers pelted with missiles ranging from snow and ice to shells and sticks. They heard shouts and hollers. And they saw a crowd that, in their testimony, swelled from sixty people to two hundred, pressing close to the soldiers and taunting them to fire.

Thomas Wilkinson had testified for the prosecution that he had seen neither "Man nor Boy nor Child" in King Street, much less a woman or girl. Jane Whitehouse, née Crothers, seems to have been one of the few women out on the street that night; the only other woman to testify was Catherine Field. She told the court that at least one of the men on the street that night had planned to go out armed. Patrick Carr had been at Field's house when he heard that there was a fight going on with the soldiers. He had immediately slid a sword under his overcoat and started to slip out the door. Only the combined efforts of Field's husband and two of her neighbors had convinced him to leave it inside. Carr was held up by the defense as Irish and spoiling for a fight; he would become the first exhibit for the defense's argument that it was civilians rather than the soldiers who had set out looking for trouble.

A few of the defense witnesses also mentioned a "stout" man. This was Crispus Attucks, one of the victims of the shooting. Only three of fifty-one witnesses mentioned seeing a "molatto," or mixed-race man, before the shooting; one thought he had noticed that Attucks was dressed as a sailor. The same witness also testified that Attucks had handed him a club and then walked down Crooked Lane to the corner of King Street, where he "went on cursing and swearing at the soldiers." A few of the prosecution's witnesses had also spotted Attucks, although most of them did not claim that he was particularly aggressive. One observed him silently resting his weight on a stick; the other affirmed that Attucks neither spoke to the soldiers nor threw anything at them.

Only one witness, James Bailey, who had spoken earlier and not too effectively for the prosecution, gave a different picture of Crispus Attucks. He told the court that he had seen Attucks "at the Head of 25 or 30 sailors," some of whom had clubs. Bailey had already had a verbal confrontation with some soldiers at a ropewalk on the weekend before the shooting in King Street, which might explain why Private Carroll had thrust his bayonet into Bailey's chest as soon as he saw the man standing next to the sentry while they talked on the Custom House steps. Bailey's testimony gave Adams the foundation he needed for his summation.

On Tuesday, December 4, John Rowe finally decided to go see the trial for himself after dinner. He stood with a few dozen others — some locals, many officers of the army and navy — in the courtroom (its gallery had no chairs) as they listened quietly to the closing remarks of the prosecution and the defense. This was the seventh day of the trial, and it was drawing to a close; if Rowe was to hear any of it firsthand, this was his final chance.

Rowe also may have been curious about a report that was circulating about Adams's defense strategy. The day before, Thomas Hutchinson had sent an update to General Gage about a rumor that "one of the Council is not so faithful as he ought to be." The gossip probably came from Adams's former co-counsel Robert Auchmuty, who was still watching the case closely from the sidelines. Gage had worried from the beginning that a local lawyer might damage his client's case for his own political gain. Gage heard from Dalrymple too, who complained that despite his daily nagging "the Lawyers have held back much on the occasion . . . they do their parts but ill."

Hutchinson had a better appreciation for Adams's defense of the soldiers than either Auchmuty or Gage did, however. Hutchinson thought that Adams was wary "of the necessity of entering into the examination of the Conduct of the Townspeople previous to the Action itself, he being a Representative of the Town and a great Partisan

[who] wishes to black the people as little as may be consistent with his Duty to his Clients." Hutchinson understood that Adams was hoping to save his clients without smearing Boston. It would be a difficult needle to thread. To do so would require a virtuoso performance.

On the face of it, an eighteenth-century courtroom — crowded, dark, and filled with the sound of lawyers reading pages of recondite legal philosophy for hours to juries accustomed to lengthy Sunday sermons — seems hardly the place to tell a gripping story. Yet court cases inevitably were and are dramatic narratives. Modern audiences may look for drama on the stage or screen, but eighteenth-century Bostonians found it in oratory.

When Adams began the second half of his speech on December 4, he turned away from legal questions of self-defense and returned to the evidence given by the witnesses over the previous week, reviewing it at great length, and in somewhat confusing detail. As he pulled apart the testimony offered by the prosecution, he lingered on the language of the town watchman, Edward Langford. The watchman had said that he saw some boys, whom he referred to as "young shavers," in King Street that night. Apparently struck by the phrase, Adams went on: "We have been entertained with a great variety of phrases, to avoid calling this sort of people a mob. — Some call them shavers, some call them genius's." Perceptions, not bullets, were at the heart of this controversy.

The time had come to define these young men. "The plain English is gentlemen, most probably a motley rabble of saucy boys, negroes and molattoes, Irish teagues, and out landish jack tars." This is how Adams managed to steer a course between saving the soldiers and saving Boston's reputation. He accused outsiders — apprentices, people of color, alien Irish, and uncouth sailors—of attacking the soldiers. Likewise, soldiers were lonely outsiders, neither aggressors nor friends. Boston, just as much as the soldiers, was an innocent victim of the mob.

Here, then, was the storyline for the four judges and jury to hold on to as they sorted through contradictory and confusing evidence. Adams offered his listeners—and the future readers of the trial transcripts—a convenient shorthand for understanding a complicated event. An unruly crowd, separate from both the town and the soldiers it was taunting, had driven soldiers to think that they needed to defend themselves from Boston's inhabitants.

Members of the jury came from towns that had recently declared that their sentiments were "united" with Boston. Adams would not be able to convince them that the provincial capital was rife with mobs. It would be simply too offensive. Instead, he redefined the genealogy of mobs.

Do not fear, Adams urged the jury, the implications of admitting that there was a mob in Boston. "The sun is not about to stand still or go out, nor the rivers to dry up because there was a mob in *Boston* on the 5th of *March* that attacked a party of soldiers." Far from it; a mob was exactly what one might expect from the presence of troops. "From the nature of things, soldiers quartered in a populous town, will always occasion two mobs, where they prevent one.—They are wretched conservators of the peace!" This mob of outsiders, in other words, did not have its origins in a "mobbish" Boston. The soldiers —or rather, the government that had sent them—had themselves brought it into being.

The men on the jury had heard similar arguments before. Most of their town meetings had penned screeds about the inevitable evils that accompanied the presence of a standing army—a military force —among civilians. They were not predisposed to have sympathy for soldiers; rather, they were part of a political culture that saw soldiers as distinct, different, and disconnected from civilians. Their sympathies lay with Boston. But to acquit Boston, they would have to acquit the soldiers. They had to accept the new picture that Adams had drawn for them: civilians on one side, soldiers on the other, and the middle ground covered with a sudden and shifting mob. This picture looked surprisingly like the one that Paul Revere had engraved, with white gun smoke billowing between the soldiers and the townspeople.

Adams's explanation of this "motley rabble" expanded on the overblown imagery of Revere's "Bloody Massacre" print. Adams's description likewise left little room for soldiers' wives, their neighbors, and their landladies. He too swept away the intimacy of shared doorways and stoops that brought together civilians and soldiers. His was a story of strangers.

In every court case, the prosecution and the defense tell competing stories; the job of the jury is to determine which version they find more compelling. In both of these trials, however, the stories told by the prosecution and the defense were surprisingly similar in one important respect. Naturally, the two sides disagreed on the identities of the villains and the motivation for their actions, but they nonetheless copied each other in using the trials to reinforce the overall account portrayed in the pamphlets, which pitted soldiers and civilians against each other. Despite the fact that the explicit purpose of the trials was to determine blame for the deaths of five Bostonians, the final verdicts

clarified very little about what had happened in King Street the previous March; in fact, they did just the opposite. The true importance
of the Boston Massacre trials is to be found in what they managed to
conceal.

In the end, the defense was almost entirely successful. Wemms,
McAuly, White, and Hartigan were exonerated. Kilroy and Montgomery were found guilty of manslaughter, not murder, and their
punishment was commuted from hanging to branding on the thumb.
Disgusted after their long months in prison, the soldiers wanted nothing more to do with the army. Fearing that they might desert, Dalrymple decided to send them by boat to join their regiment in New
Jersey, thus giving them much less opportunity to slip away. As for
Captain Preston, he did not even wait for his soldiers to embark for
their next posting; he sailed for England the morning after the verdict.

Ten months after the deaths in King Street, the trials had not solved
the question of who was to blame for the shooting. But in creating a
new image of Boston, they did other important work. They showed
Americans that British soldiers stood on one side of a chasm and colonial civilians on the other. By downplaying the plentiful evidence,
given by witnesses on both sides of the case, of longstanding connections between town and Crown, the trials made clear that the concept
of a cross-cultural community no longer had a place in the story of
the Boston Massacre. It easily could be removed from the picture of
life in the British Empire.

With his usual immodesty, John Adams later commented that the
verdicts of the two trials were "exactly right." There is no need to
agree with him; the trials never did settle the question of blame, the

evidence was contradictory, and Adams managed to pick juries that no one then or now would call impartial. In the end, however, even if we had the ability to ascribe responsibility for those deaths 250 years ago, the answer would bring us no closer to understanding how the massacre brought us to the American Revolution. Focusing on the question of responsibility leads us down the wrong path. It conflates the events of March 5, 1770, with the political, legal, and even literary maneuvering that immediately followed. And the ultimate end of that political spin was to erase the shared lives of soldiers and civilians — even, sometimes, in their own memories.

Just three months after the soldiers' trial ended, Boston officials began to commemorate the Boston Massacre with an oration, an event that became an annual celebration. In the second annual oration, held in 1772, Dr. Joseph Warren asked his audience of four thousand Bostonians to remember the threat that the regiments had offered to "our children subjected to the barbarous caprice of the raging soldiery; our beauteous virgins exposed to all the insolence of unbridled passion." Some of those children, of course, were in fact the offspring of soldiers and local women, and some of the "beauteous virgins" had chosen to share their own passion, unbridled or otherwise, with their military husbands. But such friendships and marriages and births and baptisms were rapidly becoming a distant memory. No longer integrated into their homes and families, soldiers seemed to have lived in a world apart.

With the eventual disappearance of these families came the disappearance, more specifically, of all women, both civilian and military, associated with this event. There is hardly a trace of them in witnesses' accounts of the shooting, and this absence was no accident. Lawyers on both sides, to simplify the legal and political elements of the drama, simply wrote out the many intimacies between civilians and the army. The trials' revised version of history smoothed the path to the American Revolution.

Civil War

We inherit the story of the American Revolution from a far wider range of people and a far more complicated set of connections than we ever acknowledge. Those who call the American Revolution a civil war portray the conflict as a clash of citizens, a struggle over the definition of a new country. But it would be no less accurate to call the revolution a sibling war. It played out in the upheaval of innumerable families formed and split by the same military occupation. Every family wrestled with that conflict in its own way, and every family was forced to make choices as difficult as they were inevitable.

War, peacekeeping, and political administration brought together civilians and soldiers, men and women, children and godparents throughout the British Empire. Those same forces buffeted families, and sometimes tore them apart, as they moved around the Atlantic rim. In an eighteenth-century Anglo-American world in which family and government were closely connected notions, the shooting in Boston marked not the beginning of the American Revolution but the breakdown of a family. Prior to 1772, the language of family had long saturated British political discourse, but in the context of military families it took on new and personal meanings. We think of the American Revolution as a political event, but it was much more like a bad divorce. This family history reminds us of the human bonds as well as the political ones that were broken at the beginning of the American Revolution.

While stationed in Boston with the Twenty-Ninth Regiment, Ensign John Melliquet fell in love with a well-connected local woman, Hannah Newman. Her father was a merchant who had died in 1765; her mother, Margaret, continued their mercantile business while raising Hannah and her seven siblings. The family was no stranger to town politics. As a shopkeeper, Hannah's widowed mother had signed John Rowe's 1767 agreement to refrain from buying imported goods, and her uncle was Thomas Cushing, the speaker of the Massachusetts Assembly during much of the later 1760s and early 1770s. John Melliquet wanted to marry Hannah, but in the spring of 1770 it may not have seemed easy for a young woman from such a politically connected family to marry an officer in the occupying force.

After the shooting in March, Melliquet saw that he would have to choose between Hannah and the army. Early in April, he wrote to General Gage to say that he wanted to resign his commission. Gage counseled him not to be hasty: "As to your intention of retiring from the service, I would have you consider well of that matter." As a stopgap Gage offered the ensign a leave of absence to travel to England. But Melliquet seemed in no hurry to return to his home country, and when the rest of his company left for New Jersey that summer, he and Hannah rode to New Hampshire and got married there.

Four months later, Gage wrote again to him in Boston, scolding him sharply: "when I granted you leave of Absence, I concluded that you intended to go to Europe. I must therefore desire that you will join your regt." Melliquet hoped to sell his commission and be put on half-pay; that would give him some funds for settling himself in Massachusetts. But Boston was not an easy place to find a purchaser for a commission in the Twenty-Ninth Regiment. Through the spring and summer of 1771, Gage wrote regularly to Melliquet, reminding him, "You have been a long time absent from your Regiment and it is proper that you should join it, which I must beg you will do as soon as you can after the receipt of this letter." At some point, Gage seemed to think he had found someone to buy Melliquet's commission, but the arrangement fell through. At last, in December 1771, Melliquet headed to London to see if he could arrange an exchange for his ensigncy in person.

After a year and a half away from his regiment, in the company of Hannah and her family, Melliquet had planted himself firmly in Boston's merchant elite and its network. And so, when he arrived on the other side of the Atlantic, he went to visit the most famous colonial in London, Benjamin Franklin.

Hannah's neighbor Jonathan Williams, another successful merchant and Franklin's nephew by marriage, had furnished Melliquet with a letter of introduction. "The Bearer of this is Mr. John Maliquet who was an officer in the 29 But is now Left the Regiment and marred [married] our Neighbour and Friend Daughter; Speaker Cushing Neice, any Civilities Shall be greatfuly acknoledgd By your Dutyfull Nephew and most Oblig'd Humble Servant."

Though Melliquet had indeed left the army, on paper he was still one of its officers. Perhaps with Franklin's help, Melliquet managed eventually to exchange his commission through an arrangement that put him on half-pay as a member of the reserve forces. He returned to Massachusetts and Hannah; within three years they had moved to the town of Waltham, where he supported his family as a tavern keeper. But just as his ties to the army were diminished but still tangible, John's new family also preserved a reminder of his origin in England. John and Hannah Melliquet named two of their five children for John's own parents: Ann Barbara, for his mother, and John Henry, for his father.

In the spring of 1775, even as Thomas Cushing represented Massachusetts in the Continental Congress, some of his niece's former neighbors had not quite forgotten that she had married a British officer. When Hannah went to visit her mother in Boston a month after the battles at Lexington and Concord, the Committee of Safety suspected that she might be collecting information for her husband, "one Mr. Mellicut of Waltham who is an officer in His Majesty's service under half pay." Yet the selectmen in Waltham defended their new neighbor. They attested to his "known integrity, uprightness, and good conduct" and concluded that the rumor of his being a spy was from someone who "suspected him to be our enemy, because he is on the half-pay list." Such an assumption, the selectmen maintained, must have come either from ignorance or "prejudice." Six years earlier, it was easier for a deserter to blend in to his new community than it was for even a former army officer to live openly with his new patriot family.

In 1771, Abraham and Margaret Glossup of the Fourteenth Regiment baptized their second child, Joseph, in King's Chapel in Boston. They gave him a private baptism, a common practice when a child was ill. The child survived but the marriage did not. The next summer, Abraham boarded a transport ship for St. Vincent, in the Caribbean, with the rest of his regiment, leaving behind his wife and their two sons. Margaret could not manage long in Boston without her husband. By November of the same year, she and her children had been committed to the almshouse "on the Province charge." She remained there for nearly two years, finally obtaining a discharge late in the summer of 1774. She stayed out of the almshouse for only four months, and in December she was readmitted. Finally she found a way to provide for at least one of her children, though it cannot have been an easy choice. In 1777, at age six, Joseph was apprenticed to a farmer in Murrayfield (now Chester), Massachusetts, over a hundred miles from Boston. Joseph was indentured to the farmer until he was nineteen. He probably had no memory of his red-coated father.

In 1774, Samuel Quincy and his brother Josiah found that the rest of their families had begun to weigh in on their continued commitment to opposing sides of an argument. When Abigail Adams spent a fall day with the Quincys, she found "a little clashing of parties you may be sure," as she reported to her husband, John. Most striking was that Samuel Quincy's wife vigorously disagreed with his increasingly loyalist politics. Hannah Hill Quincy complained to Abigail Adams that "she thought it was high time for her Husband to turn about" from his government party politics. In fact, she continued, "he had not done half so clever since he left her advice."

Eight months later, Samuel fled to England while Hannah remained in Massachusetts with her brother and her children. Samuel missed his family intensely. In 1777, he wrote to Hannah, "The continuance of our unhappy separation has something in it so unexpected, so unprecedented, so complicated with evil, and misfortune, it has become almost too burdensome for my spirit." He missed his father as well. "It is now more than eighteen months since I parted with him in a manner I regret," he lamented. Yet he refused to return to Massachusetts. Not only had his property been seized by the state, but he could not face the anger of his former friends. Hannah's apparent reassurance to him that he could return without facing the death penalty as a political traitor was outrageous to him. "I have never once harbored such an idea. Sure I am I have never merited from them such a punishment. Difference of opinion I have never known to be a capital offence." Samuel never saw his wife or children again.

As the wife of a wealthy loyalist and the mother of three daughters, Hannah Flucker had within a few short years successfully married off three daughters: Hannah, the eldest, to Lieutenant James Urquhart of the Fourteenth Regiment; Lucy to Henry Knox, a bookseller in King Street; and Sally to another British army officer. Had Hannah lived long enough to read *Pride and Prejudice,* she might have exclaimed with Mrs. Bennet at the novel's end, "Three daughters married! . . . Oh, Lord! What will become of me. I shall go distracted." But distraction had already arrived. By 1775 Lucy's new husband, Henry, was fighting the British army at the Battle of Bunker Hill. When the British army left Boston late in 1776, most of the Flucker family left with them; only Lucy and Henry threw their lot in with the Continental army. The three sisters never saw one another again, and though Lucy repeatedly wrote to her mother, now traveling with the British army to Halifax and then England, she never received a reply.

. . .

As Lucy wrote in 1777 to her sister Hannah, "How horrid is this war, Brother against Brother—and the parent against the child." The struggle between the mother country and her colonies was more than a figure of speech; the metaphor contained a genuine truth. The British Empire of the 1770s was built on friendships and families, and thousands of connections among British soldiers and Boston civilians were a part of what sustained that empire. And when families dissolve—when spouses separate, generations quarrel, and allegiances break down—so do the larger structures they support. The physical intimacy of the occupation of Boston had created these families and friendships, and their destruction is the cornerstone of America's founding.

ACKNOWLEDGMENTS

I feel profoundly fortunate that the decade I spent on this book allowed me to meet so many wonderful people while keeping me grounded in my loving homes.

This project grew out of my first encounter with British soldiers' wives in the Special Collections of Carleton College. Had Kristi Wermager not told me about Carleton's pamphlets from the American Revolution, I might never have learned about Isabella Montgomery and Susannah Cathcart talking trash on their stoops on the night of March 5, 1770. Since that initial discovery, Carleton has generously supported this project in ways large and small. The Dean's Office funded an exploratory trip to Boston; on my first day in the archives, I found a soldier's marriage record and felt sure that I was onto a new story of the Boston Massacre. The Faculty Grants Committee helped me travel to England, Ireland, and Nova Scotia. I am intensely grateful to the talented archivists and library staff at the National Archives in London, the Public Record Office of Northern Ireland in Dublin, and the Public Archives of Nova Scotia in Halifax. Terese Austin and others at the Clements Library in Ann Arbor went far beyond the call of duty to assist me.

As the evidence of military families in Boston piled up, I knew I needed support in sorting out all the connections I was finding. Nikki Lamberty, administrative assistant extraordinaire of Carleton's History Department, found me the amazing undergraduate research assistants without whose meticulous work this project would have been impossible. Special thanks to Becky Canary-King, Lauren Nakamura, and, in particular, Lief Esbenshade: they transcribed thousands of names from muster rolls and church records and painstakingly checked the database of military-civilian connections at the heart of this book.

Historians, teachers, students, and history buffs across the country offered me warm support and helpful feedback in many venues. My thanks to all, though I can list only a few by name. John Sensbach, Margaret Newell, Rick Bell, Dan Richter, Mark Peterson, and Barbara Oberg created welcome opportunities for me to share my findings. Katherine Gerbner, Kirsten Fischer, and Joanne Janke-Wegner make the University of Minnesota Atlantic Workshop the perfect place to try out ideas. Special thanks to Carolyn Eastman, Janet Polasky, and Rosie Zagarri — magnificent friends and gracious hosts.

I am enormously grateful that Nina Dayton, Nat Sheidley, and Kate Haulman read the entire manuscript. They did their best to save me from errors. I am awed by the liberality of scholars who offered me sources from their own research, including Mary Beth Norton, David Niescior, and Don Hagist. Eric Hinderaker's professional and intellectual generosity will forever be an example.

My Carleton colleagues endured many conversations about war, writing, and family. Andrew Fischer, Adeeb Khalid, Amna Khalid, and Jessica Leiman were patient interlocutors. I thank the Carleton College Humanities Center, especially its former director, Susannah Ottaway, who supported Michael McNally and me as we explored the meaning and practice of accessible scholarship through our seminar, "Varieties of Public Humanities." I learned from all my fellow participants, especially Nancy Cho, who first encouraged me to imagine what lay beyond the edges of Paul Revere's engraving. Wei-Hsin Fu patiently taught me and my students ArcGIS in order to create a meticulous map of Boston. Credit for the beautiful map of Boston is due to her.

I wish to express gratitude to the National Endowment for the Humanities and the American Council of Learned Societies, whose fellowships supported the first draft of this book. I enjoyed a wonderful month at the Huntington Library as well as Betty Medearis's writing retreat. I thank Dean Beverly Nagel for the nearly two years away from teaching during these fellowships.

My heartfelt thanks to the Massachusetts Historical Society. Peter Drummey, Elaine Heavey, Anna Clutterbuck-Cook, and their colleagues create a spectacular home for scholars. I especially acknowledge Conrad Wright, who nurtured this project by making it possible for me to spend many summers at the MHS.

With a little help from Ari Kelman, I found my agent, Lisa Adams of the Garamond Agency. Her sharp editorial eye and calm guidance improved my manuscript in many ways. She connected me to Deanne Urmy and her superlative team at Houghton Mifflin Harcourt: editorial assistants Jenny Xu and Mary Cait Milliff, production editor Heather Tamarkin, and the copyeditor of every writer's dreams, Susanna Brougham. After nearly twenty years of Minnesota

Nice, Deanne's directness startled and comforted me. Working with Deanne has been one of the most fulfilling and rigorous intellectual experiences of my life. No one had ever really taught me how to tell a story before. Thank you.

Three other women made it possible for me to write this book. First, Kate Haulman, my kindred spirit in early America; Lori Pearson, without whom I cannot imagine life at Carleton; and Jan Lewis, who died before she could read this book in its entirety, but who made me the historian that I am.

It is fitting that a book about family has so shaped my own. My children, Julian, Leo, and Sebastian, have spent every summer for over ten years in New England while I dug through archives. I cannot thank my parents enough for opening their home to us for months at a time, shuttling my children to camp, and making them lunches. I will always treasure the summers I spent commuting from Alewife with my father. The opportunity to luxuriate in my mother's energy and love was an unexpected gift.

My brilliant husband, Christopher Brunelle, sustained this project in every way imaginable, from living with his in-laws to spending countless hours on language and line-editing. Hardly a word would have been written without the coffee that he lovingly brings me each day. That morning cup is only the smallest (if tastiest) manifestation of his unfailing support.

NOTES

Abbreviations Used in Notes

Boston Marriages, BRCR: A Report of the Record Commissioners of the City of Boston, Containing Boston Marriages from 1752 to 1809 (vol. 30) (Boston: Municipal Printing Office, 1903)

Boston Selectmen's Minutes, BRCR: A Report of the Record Commissioners of the City of Boston: Containing the Selectmen's Minutes from 1764 to 1768 (vol. 20) (Boston: Rockwell and Churchill, 1889) and *A Report of the Record Commissioners of the City of Boston: Containing the Selectmen's Minutes from 1769 through April 1775* (vol. 23) (Boston: Rockwell and Churchill, 1893)

Boston Town Records, BRCR: A Report of the Record Commissioners of the City of Boston Containing the Boston Town Records, 1758–1769 (vol. 16) (Boston: Rockwell and Churchill, 1886) and *A Report of the Record Commissioners of the City of Boston Containing the Boston Town Records, 1770 through 1777* (vol 18) (Boston: Rockwell and Churchill, 1887)

BPL: Boston Public Library

GP: Gage Papers, American Series, William L. Clements Library, University of Michigan, Ann Arbor

MHS: Massachusetts Historical Society

PANS: Public Archives of Nova Scotia

PRONI: Public Record Office of Northern Ireland

SF: Suffolk Files, Massachusetts Supreme Judicial Court Archives, Boston

TNA: The National Archives (UK)

Prologue

page

xi *Bending over:* For an analysis of the Pelham and Revere prints, see American Antiquarian Society, *Paul Revere's Engravings,* rev. ed. (New York: Atheneum, 1969).
Revere: See David Hackett Fischer, *Paul Revere's Ride* (New York and Oxford, UK: Oxford University Press, 1995).

xv *Two hundred and fifty:* The most influential twentieth-century interpretation of the event was written by Hiller B. Zobel: *The Boston Massacre,* 1st ed. (New York: W. W. Norton, 1970). His book is deeply sympathetic to the British government and army. On the Sons of Liberty side, see, most recently, Richard Archer, *As If an Enemy's Country: The British Occupation of Boston and the Origins of Revolution,* Pivotal Moments in American History (New York and Oxford, UK: Oxford University Press, 2010). The most neutral (and convincing) interpretation is Eric Hinderaker, *Boston's Massacre* (Cambridge, MA, and London: Belknap Press of Harvard University Press, 2017).

1. Families of Empire, 1765

1 *Jane Chambers:* ADM 36/6908, TNA. This muster roll contains the names of all the soldiers and the sixty-four women who traveled on the *Thunderer;* the report of their departure is in *Stamford Mercury,* "Ireland, Cork, June 10," June 27, 1765.
The name: Every adult who embarked on a British navy ship—including sol-

diers and soldiers' wives—was recorded on a list known as a "muster." See ADM 36, TNA.

It may seem strange: Influential work considering families, sex, and intimacy in the creation of empires includes Ann Laura Stoler, *Carnal Knowledge and Imperial Power: Race and the Intimate in Colonial Rule* (Berkeley: University of California Press, 2002); Kathleen Wilson, *The Island Race: Englishness, Empire and Gender in the Eighteenth Century* (London and New York: Routledge, 2003).

3 *Women like Jane:* Although historians who study the era of the American Revolution have never considered the importance of women in early modern armies to that conflict, military historians have long noted their presence in the British army. The best recent work on women in the eighteenth-century British army is Jennine Hurl-Eamon, *Marriage and the British Army in the Long Eighteenth Century: "The Girl I Left Behind Me"* (Oxford, UK: Oxford University Press, 2014), which focuses primarily on women who lived apart from their enlisted husbands. A careful collection of data for women in the British army during the Revolutionary War itself can be found in Don N. Hagist, "The Women of the British Army in America," last modified 2002, http://www.revwar75.com/library/hagist/britwomen.htm. There are a few excellent studies of women in the British army in America during the Seven Years' War, in particular, Paul E. Kopperman, "Soldiers' Wives." *Journal of the Society for Army Historical Research* 60, no. 241 (Spring 1982): 14–34; Holly A. Mayer, "From Forts to Families: Following the Army into Western Pennsylvania, 1758–1766," *Pennsylvania Magazine of History & Biography* 130, no. 1 (2006): 5–43; and Sarah Fatherly, "Tending the Army," *Early American Studies: An Interdisciplinary Journal* 10, no. 3 (Fall 2012): 566–99. This newer work effectively refutes an older view, exemplified by Walter Hart Blumenthal, *Women Camp Followers of the American Revolution* (G. S. MacManus Co., 1952), that most women who traveled with armies were prostitutes. Groundbreaking work on European armies, such as Barton C. Hacker, "Women and Military Institutions in Early Modern Europe: A Reconnaissance," *Signs* 6, no. 4 (1981): 643–71, and John A. Lynn II, *Women, Armies, and Warfare in Early Modern Europe* (Cambridge, UK: Cambridge University Press, 2008), focuses largely on the material—and sexual—support that women gave to the army, especially before 1650. The most significant study of women in the Continental army remains Holly A. Mayer, *Belonging to the Army: Camp Followers and Community During the American Revolution* (Columbia University of South Carolina Press, 1996).

4   *"scum of every county"*: Campbell Dalrymple, *A Military Essay. Containing Reflections on the Raising, Arming, Cloathing, and Discipline of the British Infantry and Cavalry; with Proposals for the Improvement of the Same. By Campbell Dalrymple, Esq; Lieutenant Colonel to the King's Own Regiment of Dragoons. Part the First* (London: 1761), 8. For more evidence on the attitudes of officers, see Kopperman, "Soldier's Wives."

The army offered: Peter Way, "'The Scum of Every County, the Refuse of Mankind': Recruiting the British Army in the Eighteenth Century," in *Fighting for a Living: A Comparative Study of Military Labour, 1500–2000* (The Netherlands: Amsterdam University Press, 2013), 291–330; Arthur N. Gilbert, "An Analysis of Some Eighteenth-Century Army Recruiting Records," *Journal of the Society for Army Historical Research* 54, no. 217 (1976): 38–47; Richard Middleton, "The Recruitment of the British Army, 1755–1762," *Journal of the Society for Army Historical Research* 67, no. 272 (1989): 226–38. As a native of Ulster, a predominantly Protestant region, Matthew would have been a particularly welcome Irish recruit, since British officials greatly feared accidentally recruiting Catholics. Stephen Conway, *War, State, and Society in Mid-Eighteenth-Century Britain and Ireland* (Oxford, UK: Oxford University Press, 2006), 209.

"people are so full of bread": Nathaniel Nisbitt, Lifford, to [Earl of Abercorn], August 10, 1759, D623/A/33/108, PRONI.

5   *"Soldiers in most quarters"*: Roger Lamb, *Memoir of His Own Life* (Dublin, UK: J. Jones, 1811), 4.

Matthew Chambers: Chambers's age and birthplace can be found in WO 121/9/284. In the 1760s, nearly half of the enlisted men had been trained in a skilled trade, such as shoemaking, tailoring, or weaving. Another 40 percent had been manual laborers, building roads or chopping wood. See Peter Way, "Rebellion of the Regulars: Working Soldiers and the Mutiny of 1763–1764," *The William and Mary Quarterly* 57, no. 4 (2000): 769. For marriage, see Hurl-Eamon, *Marriage and the British Army in the Long Eighteenth Century*, chapter 3.

"in general so abandoned": Bennett Cuthbertson, *A System for the Compleat Interior Management and Œconomy of a Battalion of Infantry. By Bennet Cuthbertson, Esq; Captain in His Majesty's Fifth Regiment of Foot, And Late Adjutant to the Same* (Dublin: Boulter Grierson, Printer to the King's Most Excellent Majesty, 1768), 194.

6   *"officers should frequently"*: Ibid., 35.

"the service suffers": *General Wolfe's Instructions to Young Officers: Also His Orders*

for a Battalion and an Army. Together with The Orders and Signals Used in Embarking and Debarking an Army by Flat-Bottom'd Boats, &c. And a Placart to the Canadians. To Which Is Prefixed the Resolution of the House of Commons for His Monument; and His Character, and the Dates of All His Commissions. Also The Duty of an Adjutant and Quarter-Master, &c. (London: 1768), 28.

From the perspective: Hurl-Eamon, *Marriage and the British Army in the Long Eighteenth Century.*

7   *"necessary to Wash & mend":* Sir William Johnson to Phineas Lyman, Albany, July 27, 1755, in *The Papers of Sir William Johnson,* ed. James Sullivan (Albany: University of the State of New York, 1921), 1: 783.

"honest, laborious Women": Cuthbertson, *A System for the Compleat Interior Management,* 193. For overall negative impressions of women with the army, see Kopperman, "Soldier's Wives."

the military had promised: Lord Bedford, London, to the Earl of Hillsborough, June 9, 1759. T2915/7/50, PRONI.

French invasion: "Copy of a letter from Bedford, Woburn Abbey, to William Pitt, warning him against taking more infantry from Ireland to secure Senegal," August 29, 1759, T2915/8/10, PRONI.

8   *recruiters were everywhere:* Letter from Nathaniel Nisbitt, Lifford, to [Earl of Abercorn], August 2, 1759, D623/A/33/107, PRONI.

from 35,000 men: Fred Anderson, *Crucible of War: The Seven Years' War and the Fate of Empire in British North America, 1754–1766* (New York: Alfred A. Knopf, 2000), 560.

moved every year: For information about the quarters of the Twenty-Ninth regiment, see July 29, 1763, T3019/4667, PRONI; September 1764 T3019/4907, PRONI; also Hugh Edm. E. Everard, *History of Thos. Farrington's Regiment Subsequently Designated the 29th (Worcestershire) Foot, 1694 to 1891 . . .* (Worcester, UK: Littlebury/Worcester Press, 1891), 55–56.

"the custom of the Army": Cuthbertson, *A System for the Compleat Interior Management,* 92.

Army women: For the uniforms paid for out of men's wages, see Way, "Rebellion of the Regulars," 778. For women's work, see Lynn, *Women, Armies, and Warfare in Early Modern Europe,* 118–26. For nursing, see Fatherly, "Tending the Army," 566–99. For just one example of a woman making soap in the barracks, see the case against Jane Ross, who began a chimney fire in the barracks at Crown Point, NY, in 1773 while preparing ashes for soap. Elizabeth M. Scott, *Those of Little Note: Gender, Race, and Class in Historical Archaeology* (Tuscon: University of Arizona Press, 1994), 119.

9   *"If we could be allowed"*: James Prevost to Lord Loudoun, Gravesend, April 20, 1756, Loudoun Papers, 1065, box 24, Huntington Library, San Marino, CA.

     holding pen: Through a combination of creative accounting and sleight of hand, keeping troops in Ireland allowed England to have a much larger professional army than most Britons realized. The British Parliament did not have to pay for regiments that were stationed in Ireland. Instead, the Irish Parliament — browbeaten by a triumvirate of elites known as the Lords Justice — agreed to fund the cost of these troops. Regiments that were funded by the "Irish establishment" (Irish taxes, raised by the Irish Parliament) were smaller than those in England. An English regiment consisted of seventy-five officers and five hundred soldiers. An Irish regiment, by contrast, had the same number of officers but only about three hundred soldiers. An Irish regiment was less expensive to pay and feed, although it still supported a fair proportion of elite officers. Moreover, those regiments were invisible to English voters. Only when a regiment was preparing to be deployed elsewhere in the British Empire did officers enlist enough privates to make up a full complement of five hundred soldiers. And only once the regiment left Irish soil did the English Parliament have to begin to pay for its upkeep. Alan Guy, *Œconomy and Discipline: Officership and Administration in the British Army, 1714-63* (Manchester, UK: Manchester University Press, 1985), 35–36, and Charles Ivar McGrath, *Ireland and Empire, 1692–1770* (Abingdon, UK: Routledge, 2015). A memorandum from Robert Wilmot, March 22, 1765, indicates that the Irish establishment regiments had on average 76 officers and NCOs and 252 privates, totaling 328 men on the Irish establishment. T3019/4984, PRONI.

     plan for rotating regiments: John W. Shy, *Toward Lexington: The Role of the British Army in the Coming of the American Revolution* (Princeton, NJ: Princeton University Press, 1965), 274.

10   *"there have been a good many"*: Great Britain Parliament House of Lords, *The History and Proceedings of the House of Lords from the Restoration in 1660 to the Present Time: Containing the Most Remarkable Motions, Speeches, Debates, Orders and Resolutions* (London: Printed for Ebenezer Timberland, 1743), vol. 8, 77.

11   *"Dear Sir"*: Thomas Waite to Wilmot, "Dublin Castle, 28 Feb 1765," T3019/4974, PRONI.

     froze to death: Everard, *History of Thos. Farrington's Regiment,* 47–48. The governor of Nova Scotia had complained bitterly about the cold, but he was probably exaggerating, as he intensely disliked Nova Scotia, "a most miserable ruinous place," he called it. Cited in Julian Gwyn, *Frigates and Foremasts:*

The North American Squadron in Nova Scotian Waters, 1745–1815 (Vancouver, BC: UBC Press, 2004), 20.

never learned to sign: Chambers signed his pensioner's discharge with an X in 1790: WO 121/9/306, TNA.

12 *"at the Request of his Wife":* Waite, Dublin Castle, to Wilmot, March 28, 1765, T3019/4992, PRONI.

"I had left behind": Joanna Bethune, ed., *The Unpublished Letters and Correspondence of Mrs. Isabella Graham, from the Year 1767 to 1814: Exhibiting Her Religious Character in the Different Relations of Life* (New York: J. S. Taylor, 1838), 12–13.

13 *"above four hundred boys":* Quoted in Michael Quane, "The Royal Hibernian Military School: Phoenix Park, Dublin: Part I," *Dublin Historical Record* 18, no. 1 (1962): 15. For Rich as president of the board of governors, see *Freeman's Journal,* April 23, 1765.

14 *"take the Case":* Dublin Castle, March 24, 1764, SP 63/423/3805, TNA.

"His Majesty's Pleasure": Earl of Halifax to the Lord Lieutenant of Ireland, April 3, 1764, SP 63/423/3810, TNA.

15 *"Popery, Beggary":* Quane, "Royal Hibernian Military School," 19.

their "respective homes": Richard Caulfield, *The Council Book of the Corporation of the City of Cork from 1609 to 1643 and from 1690 to 1800: Ed. from the Original with Annals and Appendices Compiled from Public and Private Records* (London: J. Billing and Sons, 1876). Concerning money for soldier's wives, see May 10, 1757, 700; May 26, 1762, 761; June 19, 1765, 790.

"very much for the good": Thomas Waite to Colonel Barlow, Dublin Castle, May 18, 1765. The captains were hesitant, however. Captain Hood of the HMS *Thunderer* thought that his ship could take "a few more Women than six to a Company, but not near to the number that will be desirous of embarking." Captain Samuel Hood to Philip Stephens, Cork, May 21, 1765, SP 42/43/163, TNA.

"women and children": Stamford Mercury, June 27, 1765; Leeds Intelligencer, June 25, 1765; Derby Mercury, June 28, 1765; Newcastle Chronicle, June 29, 1765; Georgia Gazette, September 5, 1765. One Irish magazine, *The Gentleman's and London Magazine: Or Monthly Chronologer,* elaborated: "The Government hath indulged the Men with the Company of their Wives and Children; to which Indulgence they were well intitled, from their good Behaviour and cheerful Appeareance to serve his Majesty" (Dublin: 1765), 383.

Robert Rich's: He was, by all accounts, a short-tempered and violent man. Alastair W. Massie, "Rich, Sir Robert, fifth baronet (1717–1785)," *Oxford Dictionary of National Biography* (Oxford, UK: Oxford University Press, 2004).

2. Inseparable Interests, 1766–67

17 *"with 500 Troops":* Everard, *History of Thos. Farrington's Regiment,* 56. News of *Thunderer's* arrival: *Boston News-Letter,* August 8, 1765; *Boston Evening-Post,* August 12, 1765; *Boston Gazette,* August 12, 1765.

Seven Years' War: Fred Anderson, *A People's Army: Massachusetts Soldiers and Society in the Seven Years' War* (Chapel Hill: Published for the Institute of Early American History and Culture, Williamsburg, VA, by the University of North Carolina Press, 1984), 60–61.

"We in America": Boston Gazette, March 21, 1763.

18 *"The true interests":* Ibid.

"Wealth, Power, & Glory": Ibid., October 31, 1720.

19 *some Bostonians mocked:* For a versified parody, see *Boston Evening-Post,* April 4, 1763; for a critique, see *Boston Evening-Post,* March 28, 1763. This latter critic signed himself "rode, caper, vitem," a quote from Ovid, *Fasti* 1.357, meaning "go on, goat, munch that vine." The goat in the passage will end up a sacrifice to the gods as a result of its vine eating; perhaps the author is implying that Otis is a goat who, by his presumptuous claims to a marriage with Great Britain, will end up being devoured by the greater power of the British Empire.

"We love, esteem, and": James Otis, *The rights of the British colonies asserted and proved. By James Otis, Esq.* [four lines in Latin from Virgil] (Boston: Edes and Gill, 1764), 51.

"it will always be": "Britannus-Americanus" (anonymous), *Boston Gazette,* July 23, 1764.

Editorialists hoped: Boston Gazette, December 2, 1765.

Destitute Acadians: Cornelia H. Dayton and Sharon V. Salinger, *Robert Love's Warnings: Searching for Strangers in Colonial Boston* (Philadelphia: University of Pennsylvania Press, 2014), 50.

every Boston newspaper: Boston Evening-Post, March 21, 1763; *Boston Post-Boy,* March 21, 1763; *Boston News-Letter,* March 24, 1763.

"hem them in": quoted in Jeffrey Ostler, *Surviving Genocide: Native Nations and the United States from the American Revolution to Bleeding Kansas* (New Haven, CT: Yale University Press, 2019), 35.

"taken the King": Ibid., 42.

20 *peace dividend:* Anderson, *Crucible of War,* 560–80.

"blood and treasure": Oxenbridge Thacher, *The Sentiments of a British American* (Boston: Edes and Gill, 1764), 3.

a new revenue stream: Pauline Maier, *From Resistance to Revolution: Colonial Rad-*

icals and the Development of American Opposition to Britain, 1765–1776 (New York: Knopf, 1972), 3–112.

This new levy: Edmund S. Morgan and Helen M. Morgan, *The Stamp Act Crisis: Prologue to Revolution* (Chapel Hill: University of North Carolina Press, 1953).

21 *John Rowe:* Rowe apparently purchased a warehouse on the Long Wharf in 1736, at the age of twenty-one. Anne Rowe Cunningham, ed., *Letters and Diary of John Rowe, Boston Merchant* (Boston: W. B. Clarke Company, 1903), 3.

letter of thanks: Boston Town Records, BRCR September 18, 1765, 157.

22 *"warmest sentiments":* "The Declarations of the Stamp Act Congress," October 19, 1765, reprinted in Edmund S. Morgan, *Prologue to Revolution: Sources and Documents on the Stamp Act Crisis, 1764–1766* (Chapel Hill: University of North Carolina Press, 1959), 62–63.

Rowe awoke: John Rowe Diary, August 14, 1765, MHS. Morgan and Morgan, *Stamp Act Crisis,* 128–34.

23 *"controlled rioting":* Tony Hayter, *The Army and the Crowd in Mid-Georgian England* (Totowa, NJ: Rowman and Littlefield, 1978).

"intrepidity": Captain Pierce Butler, Magherafelt, to Waite, July 19, 1763, T3019/4650, PRONI.

"at the head": Lord Lieutenant of Ireland to Lord Rochford, January 12, 1775, in R. A. Roberts and J. Redington, eds., *Calendar of Home Office Papers of the Reign of George III. 1760–1775. Preserved in Her Majesty's Public Record Office.* Ed. J. Redington (London: for Her Majesty's Stationery Office, 1899), 314.

24 *The Massachusetts governor:* Maier, *From Resistance to Revolution,* 92, points out that when Governor Bernard demanded that the militia be called out, he was told that most of the drummers were likely among the crowd. This conflation of the militia and the crowd in turn gave these extra-legal protests a certain added legitimacy.

executed over thirty: Serena R. Zabin, *Dangerous Economies: Status and Commerce in Imperial New York* (Philadelphia: University of Pennsylvania Press, 2009).

"to quell Tumults": Gage to Lord Halifax, August 10, 1765, reprinted in Clarence Edwin Carter, ed., *The Correspondence of General Thomas Gage with the Secretaries of State, 1763–1775* (Hamden, CT: Archon Books, 1969), vol. 1, 64.

The general: John Richard Alden, *General Gage in America: Being Principally a History of His Role in the American Revolution* (Baton Rouge: Louisiana State University Press, 1948), 65.

Gage oversaw: Shy, *Toward Lexington,* 204–31.

Gage did not: Thomas Gage to Cadwallader Colden, July 8, 1765, reprinted in

The Letters and Papers of Cadwallader Colden . . . 1711–[1775] (New York: Printed for the New York Historical Society, 1918), 46.

25 "*It is needless*": Gage to Colden, August 31, 1765, *Letters and Papers of Cadwallader Colden*, 58.

"*extreamly weak*": Bernard to Gage, Castle William, August 27, 1765, reprinted in Colin Nicolson, ed., *The Papers of Francis Bernard: Governor of Colonial Massachusetts, 1760–69,* Publications of the Colonial Society of Massachusetts (Boston: Colonial Society of Massachusetts, 2013), vol. 3, 324.

"*affraid to demand*": Gage to Henry Conway, New York, September 23, 1765, Carter, ed., *Correspondence of General Thomas Gage,* vol. 2, 68.

26 "*Indeed,*" *he warned:* Bernard to Gage, Boston, September 13, 1765, in Nicolson, ed., *The Papers of Francis Bernard,* vol. 3.

"*irritate the people*": Bernard to the Earl of Halifax, Boston, August 31, 1765, ibid.

"*subordination to the Mother*": *Massachusetts Gazette,* Supplement, June 12, 1766.

27 *the* "*behavior and good services*": December 1, 1766, *Town Papers,* 195 ("Mr. Samuel Adams, John Rowe, and John Hancock, Esq.").

"*a very Genteel Entertainment*": John Rowe Diary, December 2, 1766, MHS.

Eighteenth-century toasts: See Richard J. Hooker, "The American Revolution Seen through a Wine Glass," *The William and Mary Quarterly* 11, no. 1 (1954): 52–77.

"*the Lords of Trade*": John Rowe Diary, December 2, 1766, MHS.

28 *regiments circulating:* Shy, *Toward Lexington,* 274.

in Gibraltar: Richard Cannon, *Historical Record of the Fourteenth, or the Buckinghamshire Regiment of Foot: Containing an Account of the Formation of the Regiment in 1685, and of Its Subsequent Services to 1845* (London: Parker, Furnivall, and Parker, 1845), 32.

"*All Gentlemen Volunteers*": *Bath Chronicle and Weekly Gazette,* December 10, 1761.

moving around the country: J. A. Houlding, *Fit for Service: The Training of the British Army, 1715–1795* (Oxford, UK, and New York: Oxford University Press, 1981), 403, table A9.

29 "*to hold themselves*": Secretary-At-War (Barrington) to Mr. Secretary Conway, April 29, 1766, SP 41/25, TNA, and reported in *Derby Mercury,* June 27, 1765.

"*women, servants*": Philip Stephens, May 16, 1766, ADM 354/178/158, Caird Library and Archive, National Maritime Museum, Greenwich, UK.

Spanish invasion of Portugal: A. D. Francis, "The Campaign in Portugal, 1762," *Journal of the Society for Army Historical Research* 59, no. 237 (1981): 43.

His promotion: London Evening-Post, July 2, 1765.

Samuel Marsh: May 20, 1765, St. Mary-the-Virgin Church, Dover, Kent, England. Ancestry.com, *England, Select Marriages, 1538–1973* (online database). Provo, UT: Ancestry.com Operations, 2014. Other marriages include Lott Eagle to Sarah Vianal, January 6, 1766, in Hampshire, England, and Thomas Throop to Hannah Adams on February 22, 1766, at St. Thomas Church, Salisbury. Wiltshire and Swindon History Centre; Chippenham, Wiltshire, England; Reference Number 1900/13. Also in St. Thomas Church, Ann Newlan and John Shelton (February 13, 1766).

the "whole" number: Mackay to Gage, Boston, August 14, 1769, vol. 87, GP.

30 *Halifax newspaper: Halifax Gazette,* February 13, 1766.

a stay of execution: O'Hara's stay of execution is discussed in the *Halifax Gazette* of February 28, 1766, SP 44/88/269–270, TNA. For more on the O'Hara case, see also *Newcastle Chronicle,* October 26, 1765 (case against O'Hara), *Salisbury Journal,* November 4, 1765 (defense of O'Hara), *Bath Chronicle,* March 13, 1766 (O'Hara's acquittal), and *Caledonian Mercury,* November 6, 1765 (trial).

3. Seasons of Discontent, 1766–68

31 *"Mr. Dalrymple":* John Rowe Diary, May 30, 1767, MHS.

"The prospect appeared": John Robinson and Thomas Rispin, *A Journey through Nova Scotia* (York: C. Etherington, 1774), 6.

32 *Not including the soldiers:* 1767 General census, RG 1, vol. 443, no. 1, PANS.

Irish Catholics were not: For the ban on Catholics in the army, see Alan J. Guy, "The Irish Military Establishment, 1660–1776," in Thomas Bartlett and Keith Jeffery, *A Military History of Ireland* (Cambridge, UK: Cambridge University Press, 1997), 219.

33 *"her taste is rather":* Graham and Bethune, *The Unpublished Letters and Correspondence of Mrs. Isabella Graham,* 17.

"a shocking place of itself": Lieut. Col. Leslie to Col. John Pomeroy, May 9, 1770, Halifax, T2954/5/9, PRONI.

"a Rascal, a Scoundrel": T 1/450/45–63, TNA.

34 *"intirely insensible":* T 1/450/45–63, TNA. For the governor's recommendation of a pardon, see Governor Francklin to Secretary of State Shelburne, in George F. O'Halloran and Douglas Brymner, eds., *Report on Canadian Archives* (Ottawa: S. E. Dawson, 1894), 274.

"Regimental disputes": Carr to Gage, Halifax, American Series, vol. 72, September 30, 1767, and November 29, 1767.

"to visit his friends in Virginia": See Gage to Carr, February 15, 1768, vol. 74, GP.

35 *fled to Boston*: For Preston, see *Boston Miscellaneous Records,* October 24, 1765, vol. 29, 272. For Mallows (transcribed as "Hollows," "Capt. in the 29th Regimt & 3 Servts"), see ibid., June 8, 1767, 293. For Molesworth, see ibid., November 4, 1767, 287. For information about wives, see ibid., October 30, 1767, 287, or May 28, 1767, 293.

visited during an earlier posting: Francis Coghlan, "Pierce Butler, 1744–1822, First Senator from South Carolina," *The South Carolina Historical Magazine* 78, no. 2 (1977): 104.

After a winter: Peter Manigault and Maurice A Crouse, "The Letterbook of Peter Manigault, 1763–1773," *The South Carolina Historical Magazine* 70, no. 2 (1969): 79–96.

heiress married: *Georgia Gazette*, April 19, 1769.

unsuccessfully challenged: Pierce Butler to Gage, Charlestown (SC), December 2, 1768, vol. 82, GP; Gage to Carr, April 7, 1769, vol. 84, GP. Pierce resigned his commission in 1773 to move permanently to South Carolina, where he eventually joined the South Carolina militia in fighting the British army, signed the US Constitution, and became a major slaveholder.

"I've been very ill": Lieut. Col. Alexander Leslie, Halifax, to Col. John Pomeroy, Dublin, May 9, 1770, T2954/5/9, PRONI. For eighteenth-century ideas about scurvy, see Erica Michiko Charters, *Disease, War, and the Imperial State: The Health of the British Armed Forces During the Seven Years' War, 1756–63* (Oxford, UK: Oxford University Press, 2007), 21–24.

36 *"no Vegetables"*: Ibid.

"it is no uncommon thing": Captain Hugh Debbieg, 1766. Shelburne Papers, vol. 86, 43, Clements Library, University of Michigan. Cited by http://www.heritage.nf.ca/articles/exploration/garrison-life-18-century-2.php.

Newspapers throughout North America: Boston Evening-Post, January 26, 1767; *Boston Evening-Post,* February 16, 1767, 2.

37 *A rising birthrate:* From a healthy 145 births in 1765 (for a population of just over 3,100 people), the number of births rose in two years to 165, within a population of about the same size. In terms of crude birthrates, these numbers indicate a rise from a rate of 46 births/1,000 people to a rate of 55 births/1,000. By comparison, in those years the crude birthrate in England fell from 35.4 to 33.9. For Halifax numbers, see Reverend Mr. Breynton to the Society for the Propagation of the Gospel, Letters series B, *British Archives Online,* October 11, 1765, and October 23, 1767. For England, see E. A. Wrigley and Roger Scho-

field, *The Population History of England, 1541–1871* (Cambridge, UK: Cambridge University Press, 1989), 534, table A3.3.

William Clinton: St. Paul's Church Records, Halifax, Marriages, PANS 11553.

army discharge: WO 121/142/188, TNA.

Catherine Charloe: December 21, 1766, Jean M. Holder et al., *Baptisms, Marriages, and Burials, 1749–1768: St. Paul's Church, Halifax, Nova Scotia* (Halifax: Genealogical Association of the Royal Nova Scotia Historical Society, 1983), 143.

nine pence per day: Thomas Gage Warrants, box 17, no. 21, December 31, 1767, Gage Papers, William L. Clements Library, The University of Michigan.

38 *"their generous regard":* Journals and Proceedings of the House of Assembly of the Province of Nova Scotia* (Halifax, NS: 1767), Wednesday, July 29, 1767, 42.

"never heard the Gentlemen": Carr to Gage, December 2, 1767, vol. 72, GP.

"You are to consider": Gage to Dalrymple, August 3, 1768, vol. 79, GP.

dying almost instantly: New-York Gazette, or Weekly Post-Boy, February 5, 1767.

tried to leave: See Gage to Dalrymple, October 12, 1767, vol. 71, GP. For information about Stanton and Mason, see ibid.

39 *William Dalrymple:* New-York Gazette, or Weekly Post-Boy, November 5, 1767; Boston Gazette, April 25, 1768.

Dalrymple's arrival: John Rowe Diary, April 16, 1768; May 13, 1768; MHS.

socialize across political hostilities: For an explanation of how sociability trumped politics even in an occupied city, see Judith L. Van Buskirk, *Generous Enemies: Patriots and Loyalists in Revolutionary New York* (Philadelphia: University of Pennsylvania Press, 2002).

Charles Townshend: Dora Mae Clark, "The American Board of Customs, 1767–1783," *The American Historical Review* 45, no. 4 (1940): 777–806. About the dual purpose, see Thomas C. Barrow, *Trade and Empire: The British Customs Service in Colonial America, 1660–1775* (Cambridge, MA: Harvard University Press, 1967).

Rowe got involved: Boston Town Records, BRCR, October 28, 1767, 221.

Rowe and others convinced: "Whereas this province labours under a heavy debt, incurred in the course of the late war: and the inhabitants by this means must be for some time subject to very burthensome taxes . . ." Boston: [s.n.], 1767, AB7.B6578.767w, Houghton Library, Harvard University, Cambridge, MA. The printed agreement and manuscript signatures have been digitized and are available at http://nrs.harvard.edu/urn-3:FHCL.HOUGH:10873406.

Rowe organized: John Rowe Diary, May 2, 1768, MHS.

By putting economic pressure: Craig B. Yirush, "The Imperial Crisis," in Edward

G. Gray and Jane Kamensky, eds., *The Oxford Handbook of the American Revolu-tion* (New York and Oxford, UK: Oxford University Press, 2013), 322–26.

40 *headquarters of the customs service:* For an excellent brief discussion of the decision to put the customs board in Boston, see Neil Longley York, *Henry Hulton and the American Revolution: An Outsider's Inside View,* "Introduction," Publications of the Colonial Society of Massachusetts, vol. 80 (Boston: Colonial Society of Massachusetts, 2010).

"As Gentlemen": Ann Hulton to Elizabeth Lightbody, Castle William, Boston Harbor, June 30, 1768, reproduced in York, *Henry Hulton and the American Rev-olution, 220–21.*

lost his boat: See D. H. Watson, "Joseph Harrison and the Liberty Incident," *The William and Mary Quarterly* 20, no. 4 (1963): 585–95. William Molineux to Harrison, June 15, 1768, Sparks Papers, III, f. 1, University of Georgia, cited in Maier, *From Resistance to Revolution, 125.*

41 *"We soon found":* Ann Hulton to Elizabeth Lightbody, Castle William, Boston Harbor, June 30, 1768, reproduced in York, *Henry Hulton and the American Rev-olution, 220–21.*

"without the advice": Henry Hulton, W. Temple, Wm. Burch, Charles Paxton, John Robinson, Castle William, Boston, to General Gage, June 15, 1768, vol. 78, GP.

alerted Dalrymple: Gage to Dalrymple, June 25, 1768, CO 5/86, TNA.

42 *"private hints":* See Bernard to William Dalrymple, Roxbury, July 3, 1768, in Nicolson, ed., *The Papers of Francis Bernard,* vol. 4, 238. For back-and-forth on the letters, see Zobel, *Boston Massacre,* 80–85.

"give every legal Assistance": Hillsborough to Gage, June 8, 1768, in Nicolson, ed., *The Papers of Francis Bernard,* vol. 4, 373.

43 *"usual allowances":* Earl of Hillsborough to Lords of the Admiralty, Whitehall, July 28, 1768, CO 5/86 /122, TNA.

was careful: In 1769, Colonel Mackay assured Gage that he had "ordered pro-visions only for six [women] and company, so as not to exceed the number allowed by Government." Mackay to Gage, August 14, 1769, vol. 87, GP.

"appear[ed] delightful": Ann Hulton to Elizabeth Lightbody, Castle William, Boston Harbor, June 30, 1768, reproduced in York, *Henry Hulton and the Amer-ican Revolution, 221.*

Even John Rowe: John Rowe Diary, June 20, 1768, MHS.

44 *hit songs: Boston Gazette,* July 18, 1768; advertisement, *Boston Chronicle,* Septem-ber 5, 1768. Colin Wells, *Poetry Wars: Verse and Politics in the American Revolu-*

tion and Early Republic (Philadelphia: University of Pennsylvania Press, 2017), 45–50, offers the most extensive analysis of the songs.

45 *opposition party:* As Jeremy A. Stern notes, terminology for discussing political factions in the pre-independence years is particularly fraught. Following his example, I use the terms "friends of government" (Governor Bernard's favorite term) or "government party" in opposition to the loose coalition of people, male and female, who saw themselves defending the traditional rights and liberties of Britons. I introduce these people as members of a "liberty party" or "liberty movement." Stern, "The Overflowings of Liberty: Massachusetts, the Townshend Crisis, and the Reconception of Freedom, 1766–1770 (PhD diss., Princeton University, 2010), xxxi–xxxii.

"EXCULPATORY letter": Boston Gazette, September 26, 1768.

46 *"left a Blank":* Gage to Bernard, Boston, August 31, 1768, Nicolson, ed., *The Papers of Francis Bernard,* vol. 4, 290–91.

"The Governor told": John Rowe Diary, September 9, 1768, MHS.

there had been rumors: Boston Post-Boy, June 20, 1768.

47 *"if what I hear":* Dalrymple to Gage, Halifax, August 6, 1768, vol. 79, GP.

"They seem better calculated": Ibid.

"As this appears to be a service": Gage to Dalrymple, August 31, 1768, vol. 80, GP.

"Two Regiments": Gage to Barrington, September 18, 1768, Add ms. 73549, Barrington Papers, British Library.

48 *Admiral Samuel Hood:* Samuel Hood to Gage, Halifax, September 15, 1768, vol. 80, GP. The muster rolls for each ship list the names of all the soldiers, but only two women in total: Hester (Esther) Fenwick and Mary Walker, who both sailed on HMS *Mermaid.* For the muster rolls, see ADM 36 series, TNA.

find transport: Thomas Gage Warrants, box 17, no. 72, GP, which lists the leased transports as the sloop *Delight,* Thomas DeLap, owner; brigantine *Sea Flower,* William Reed; sloop *Speedwell,* Joseph Rowe; and sloop *LeHavre,* Edmund Amory.

4. Under One Roof, 1768

49 *fair blue sky:* Captain's log, HMS *St. Lawrence,* September 29 and 30, 1768, ADM 51/3883, TNA.

as the flotilla: See the *Mermaid* captain's log, Tuesday, September 20, 1768, "in Company with his Majesty's Vessels *Glasgow, Launceston, Senegal, Martin, Bonetta, Beaver, St. Lawrence, Hope,* with 4 Sail of Transports," ADM 51/1364,

TNA. The first of the transports began to arrive on October 8 (sloop *Speedwell,* Joseph Rowe; see *Boston News-Letter,* Supplement, October 6, 1768). The army provided enough rations for only one hundred women in total, but these official numbers severely undercount children as well as women. For the official numbers, see Thomas Gage Warrants, box 1, 14th Regiment subsistence folder and 29th Regiment subsistence folder, Gage Papers, William L. Clements Library, The University of Michigan.

seen in the distance: Joseph F. W. Des Barres (Joseph Frederick Wallet), "Boston, seen between Castle Williams and Governor's Island, distant 4 miles," map, 1777, *Norman B. Leventhal Map & Education Center,* https://collections.leventhalmap.org/search/commonwealth:7h149z742, accessed May 7, 2019.

the flotilla sailed: Captain's log, HMS *St. Lawrence,* September 29, 1768, ADM 51/3883, TNA.

rotten wooden structures: Gage to Hillsborough, New York, August 18, 1768, in *Correspondence of General Thomas Gage,* vol. 1, 187–88. About beds made of leaves, see Maurice Carr to Gage, Halifax, March 8, 1768, vol. 75, GP.

50 *had been renovated:* In 1755, the then governor of Massachusetts asked the legislature for enough money to expand the barracks from a four-hundred-man capacity to 1100. Although the legislature balked at granting all the funds requested, it eventually allocated about two-thirds. *Journals of the House of Representatives of Massachusetts,* 1754–1755, vol. 31 (Boston: Massachusetts Historical Society, 1756), 258.

had received the order: Gage to Dalrymple, New York, August 31, 1768, vol. 80, GP.

51 *the governor and his council:* A version of this conflict, which depicts the council as essentially unreasonable, can be found in Zobel, *Boston Massacre,* chapters 8 and 9, and correspondence from Bernard to Gage, September 24, 1768, CO 5/86/423, TNA, and Bernard to Hillsborough, November 1, 1768, both reprinted in Nicolson, ed., *The Papers of Francis Bernard,* vol. 4. Also *The Bowdoin-Temple Papers* (Boston: Massachusetts Historical Society Collections, 1897), vol. 9, 106. For the unusual control that the Massachusetts Governor's Council had over the governor, see Stern, "The Overflowings of Liberty," xxvii–xx, and "Proceedings of the Council," September 19, 1768, reprinted in the *Bowdoin-Temple Papers,* vol. 9, 103.

"hoped he was going": Dalrymple to Hillsborough, Boston, October 1, 1768, in Nicolson, ed., *The Papers of Francis Bernard* (Charlottesville, VA: distributed by the University of Virginia Press, 2015), vol. 5, 63.

52 *desire to punish:* Bostonians had seen other British generals try to punish un-

ruly colonies by seizing military quarters. In 1758, Lord Loudoun, then commander of the British forces in North America, threatened "to march troops into Boston and force the people to acknowledge his right to quarters wherever he chose them." J. Alan Rogers, "Colonial Opposition to the Quartering of Troops During the French and Indian War," *Military Affairs* 34, no. 1 (1970): 9.

"in consequence of": Boston *Evening-Post, Supplement Extraordinary*, September 26, 1768.

an official letter: "Proceedings of the Council," September 19, 1768, reprinted in the *Bowdoin-Temple Papers,* vol. 9, 103, and published in *Boston Chronicle,* September 29, 1768.

The officials based their recommendation: Bernard to Hillsborough, Boston, September 23, 1768, Nicolson, ed., *The Papers of Francis Bernard,* vol. 4, 331. For the Quartering Act, see John Gilbert McCurdy, *Quarters: The Accommodation of the British Army and the Coming of the American Revolution* (Ithaca, NY: Cornell University Press, 2019), and Anderson, *Crucible of War,* 647–51.

"Seven Miles by Land": Correspondence of General Thomas Gage, vol. 1, 201.

"the purposes": Bernard to Gage, Boston, September 24, 1768, Nicolson, ed., *The Papers of Francis Bernard,* vol. 4, 338. About alternatives and compromises, see Dalrymple to Gage, Boston, October 2, 1768, vol. 81, GP.

53 *remained anchored:* HMS *St. Lawrence* captain's log, ADM 51/3883, September 30, 1768. About camping out on Boston Common, see Dalrymple to Gage, Boston, October 2, 1768, vol. 81, GP.

54 *brick and wooden buildings:* Allan Kulikoff, "The Progress of Inequality in Revolutionary Boston," *The William and Mary Quarterly,* Third Series, 28, no. 3 (July 1, 1971): 393.

Long Wharf: Nancy S. Seasholes, *Gaining Ground: A History of Landmaking in Boston* (Cambridge, MA: MIT Press, 2018), chapter 3, especially 31.

set their moorings: Although Revere's engraving labels only eight ships, the captain's log of the HMS *Mermaid* lists ten. Paul Revere, *A View of the Town of Boston in New England and British Ships of War Landing their Troops!* (Boston, 1770, and *Mermaid* captain's log, October 1, 1768, ADM 51/3909, TNA.

55 *two elite companies:* "At noon made the signal for the Troops to embark in the Boats came alongside a Schooner and took in the Grenadier and Light Infantry of the 29th Regt." *Mermaid* captain's log, October 1, 1768. John Rowe Diary, October 1, 1768, MHS. For newspaper reports, see *Boston Evening-Post,* October 3, 1768. My particular thanks to Don Hagist for helping me determine which companies marched through Boston's streets that day.

"gallant appearance": John Tudor, *Deacon Tudor's Diary; or, "Memorandoms from 1709, &c"* (Boston: Press of W. Spooner, 1896), 28.

problem of housing: John Rowe Diary, October 1, 1768, MHS: "Col. Dalrymple Summoned the selectmen[;] they all met and did not think themselves obligd to take Cognisance for their [the troops] being Quartered in Town."

56 *the proprietor, Sarah Bean:* The Massachusetts Gazette, and the Boston Post-Boy and Advertiser, April 23, 1770.

Rebecca Payne: See *Boston News-Letter,* March 1, 1770. Women often tended retail shops stocked with their husband's imports. See Zabin, *Dangerous Economies.*

and gloves: Boston News-Letter, October 31, 1771.

John Piemont: Receipt to "Jean Piemont, a Wig and Year's Dressing," March 20, 1770. *The Diary and Letters of His Excellency Thomas Hutchinson* (Carlisle, MA: Applewood Books, 2010), 76.

choice of wigmakers: Boston *Post-Boy*, October 30, 1769 and *Boston Evening-Post,* August 17, 1772.

57 *"French Indigo":* Boston Evening-Post, June 27, 1768.

auctioneers sold people: Robert E. Desrochers, "Slave-for-Sale Advertisements and Slavery in Massachusetts, 1704–1781," *The William and Mary Quarterly* 59, no. 3 (2002): 627.

a fine Sunday: "A fine morning," John Rowe Diary, October 16, 1768, MHS.

58 *Matthew, pleaded:* "Boston, MA: Church Records, 1630–1895," The Records of the Churches of Boston, CD-ROM, Boston: New England Historic Genealogical Society, 2002. Online database: AmericanAncestors.org, New England Historic Genealogical Society, 2008.

"Daughter of Mr. Matthew Chambers": October 16, 1768, "Records of the West Church," New England Historic Genealogical Society.

The child was kidnapped: Two versions of this kidnapping were reported: on October 31, 1768, in the *New-York Gazette,* and on October 27, 1768, in the *Boston News-Letter.*

59 *"a woman belonging":* New-York Gazette, October 31, 1768.

identified that night in North Square: Townshend Watch report, October 1768, Loose Boston Town Records, BPL.

British Coffee House: John Rowe Diary, October 2, 1768, MHS.

two enslaved servers: Dayton and Salinger, *Robert Love's Warnings,* 214, fn. 39.

60 *"Hah John are you there":* John Rowe Diary, October 2, 1768, MHS.

"in Licker": Ireland Watch Report, November 1768, Loose Boston Town Records, BPL.

61 *John Wilson:* Hinderaker, *Boston's Massacre,* 134–47. "Journal of the Times, October 17," *Boston Evening-Post,* December 19, 1768.

Harbottle Dorr: "Harbottle Dorr, *Boston Evening-Post,* December 19, 1768," in *Annotated Newspapers of Harbottle Dorr, Jr.,* http://masshist.org/dorr/.

"an affair": Joshua Henshaw to [Col.] William Henshaw, Boston, November 2, 1768, "Letters to Col. William Henshaw, 1768–1769," MHS.

62 *Slaveholding crossed:* For example, John Rowe and Francis Bernard both held people in slavery. In 1766, John Rowe recorded that he had sent an enslaved man named Cato to the workhouse to be whipped as a punishment. John Rowe Diary, November 22, 1766, MHS. Bernard also held a man named Cato in slavery and apparently forced him to put his child in the almshouse, October 31, 1768, in Eric G. Nellis and Anne Decker Cecere, eds., *The Eighteenth-Century Records of the Boston Overseers of the Poor,* 1st ed. (Boston and Charlottesville: Colonial Society of Massachusetts, 2001), 193. For slavery in Boston, see Jared Ross Hardesty, *Unfreedom: Slavery and Dependence in Eighteenth-Century Boston,* Early American Places (New York: New York University Press, 2016).

step up their surveillance: For the instructions of the selectmen to "be watchful of the Negros & to take up those of them that may be in gangs at unseasonable hours" and for the complaint, see *Boston Selectmen's Minutes, BRCR,* October 31, 1768, 314. For the depositions, see October 29 and 31, 1768, 313–14.

chase around Boston: Joshua Henshaw to William Henshaw, November 2, 1768, "Letters to Col. William Henshaw, 1768–1769," MHS.

63 *"his excuse was":* Ibid.

"some drunken behavior": John Rowe Diary, Tuesday, November 1, 1768, MHS.

serving as drummers: J. D. Ellis, "Drummers for the Devil?: The Black Soldiers of the 29th (Worcestershire) Regiment of Foot, 1759–1843," *Journal of the Society for Army Historical Research* 80, no. 323 (2002): 186–202.

Even free black men: Selectmen's Minutes, *Boston Town Records, BRCR,* December 16, 1762, 240. "To Scipio and other Free Negros residing in the Town of Boston. You are hereby severally Ordered and Required to perform so many Days work as is here under affixed to your Names, and this at the Time and Place you shall be directed to by Mr. Sweetser appointed an Overseer for this purpose. It being such a proportion of Time as is adjudged to be equivalent to the service of Trainings, Watchings and other duty required of the rest of his Majesty's Subjects, the benefit of which you share." For complaints against some of the men for not doing the road work, see *Selectmen's Minutes, Boston Town Records,* November 6, 1766, vol. 20, 236. Also see Dayton and Salinger, *Robert*

Love's Warnings, 113. For training days, see Richard P. Gildrie, "Defiance, Diversion, and the Exercise of Arms: The Several Meanings of Colonial Training Days in Colonial Massachusetts," *Military Affairs* 52, no. 2 (1988): 53–55.

64 *unlawful imprisonment:* Hardesty, *Unfreedom*, 148–50.

"Quere: whether": Joshua Henshaw to William Henshaw, November 2, 1768. "Letters to Col. William Henshaw, 1768–1769," MHS.

rented houses: John Rowe Diary, Friday, October 7, 1768, MHS.

more permanent housing: Boston Evening-Post, October 10, 1768.

65 *muskets:* Zobel, *Boston Massacre,* 101.

the manufactory house: Archer, *As If an Enemy's Country,* 113–15.

"The present disposition": Andrew Eliot to Thomas Hollis, Boston, September 27, 1768, Andrew Eliot Letters (MS Am 882.5), Houghton Library, Harvard University.

66 *"the uncommonly good":* Dalrymple to Gage, October 6, 1768, Boston, vol. 81, GP.

self-justifying letters: Bernard to Hillsborough, November 1, 1768.

Historians have spilled: For a typical comment on the compromised principles involved in this decision, see Zobel, *Boston Massacre,* 104: "Space on [Wheelwright's Wharf], despite Otis' prediction that no one would ever let property to the army, was furnished at £25 sterling per month by William Molineux himself."

67 *roughly 2,000 men:* These numbers are drawn from muster rolls WO 12/3117, WO 12/4493, WO 12/7312, and WO 12/7377 and extrapolated from multiple other sources, especially the Subsistence Warrants, box 1, Thomas Gage Warrants, Gage Papers, William L. Clements Library, The University of Michigan. In the spring of 1768, a few months before the Fourteenth and Twenty-Ninth Regiments prepared to leave for Boston, the minister at the Halifax church affiliated with the garrison claimed that he ministered to 750 soldiers currently in Halifax from those two regiments and 475 women and children. Reverend Mr. Breynton to the Society for the Propagation of the Gospel, January 16, 1769, SPGFP, Letter no. 135, PANS. An account of those families formally "on the strength" of the army and therefore eligible to live in the barracks was given by Lieutenant Montresor, who estimated that when the Fourteenth Regiment was housed in Castle William in 1772, "14th is now 400 men—70 women & 90 children." "Montresor's Journals," ed. G. D. Scull, *Collections of the New-York Historical Society,* vol. 14 (1881), 410.

luxurious housing: For rental of warehouses, see "Accounts of Expenditures in

Boston," Subsistence Warrants, box 2, Thomas Gage Warrants. For size of barracks in Halifax, see LO 6663, box 93, Loudoun Papers, Huntington Library, and Carr to Gage, Halifax, March 8, 1768, vol. 75, GP. For comparing barrack sizes, see July 27, 1767, "Gage Orderly book, August 25, 1766, to July 1, 1768," New-York Historical Society: "The Barracks in the city of New York are distributed in the following proportions, One room to each Captain one Ditto to two Subns. And one Ditto for fourteen men." For details about sugar houses, see the advertisement for the sale of a sugar house "sixty seven feet and a half long," *Boston Gazette,* May 2, 1763; and the bill of sale of a sugar house to Nathaniel Holmes, "the said sugar house measuring on the easterly end or part thereof twenty two feet six inches and a half in width," MS Am 579/10/29, Houghton Library, Harvard University. My thanks to Jordan Smith for this last reference.

Matthew and Jane Chambers: Boston Selectmen's Minutes, BRCR, August 23, 1769, 31.

"a most Odious Service": Viscount Barrington to Weymouth, April 18, 1768, WO 4/83, 316–17, cited in E. P. Thompson, "The Moral Economy of the English Crowd in the Eighteenth Century," *Past & Present* 50 (February 1, 1971): 121.

"Employing the Troops": "Correspondence and papers relating to the use of troops to quell riots in Leicester, Nottingham, etc., 1756," Add ms. 73631, Barrington Papers, vol. lxxxvi, British Library.

68 *commanding officers in Boston*: About requests for home leave, see Mackay to Gage, Boston, March 6, 1769, vol. 84, GP; Gage to Barrington, New York, July 22, 1769, and Mackay to Gage, July 10, 1769, vol. 86, GP.

brigadier general: Gage to Hillsborough, January 5, 1769, reprinted in Carter, ed., *Correspondence of General Thomas Gage,* vol. 1, 209.

"Boston is now become": William Cooper to Thomas Boylston, November 7, 1768, folder Ms. N-4, "November–December 1768," Boylston Papers, MHS.

Lewis Gray: Complaint in "Pleas before Richard Dana Esq. Beginning January 5, 1768, ending March 8, 1772," vol. 19, "Justice of the Peace Records, Suffolk County January 1768–March 1772," Dana Family Papers, December 5, 1768, MHS.

69 *"many people, who":* Minutes of the Massachusetts Council, December 7, 1768, included in John Pomeroy to Thomas Gage, Boston, December 12, 1768, vol. 83, GP.

Samuel Adams: Boston Gazette, December 5, 1768.

Private John Duxbury: For details of this case, see January 31, 1769, General Sessions, Suffolk County docket book, 1764–68, Judicial Court Archives held at Massachusetts State Archives.

"The matter of the Soldiers": Pomeroy to Gage, Boston, February 2, 1769, vol. 83, GP.

"We are in such a situation here": Thomas H. Peck to Boughen & Son., Boston, January 14, 1769, Peck Letterbook, 1763–1776, Ms. N-681, MHS. For the relationship between liberty and commerce, see Jack P. Greene, "Empire and Identity from the Glorious Revolution to the American Revolution," in P. J. Marshall, ed., *The Oxford History of the British Empire, Volume 2: The Eighteenth Century* (Oxford, UK, and New York: Oxford University Press, 2001).

70 *A map of Boston:* These addresses are derived from the warning out records. For McInnis and Walker, see Suffolk File Papers (SF) 89545, Starkey, SF 89546, Massachusetts State Archives.

71 *"kept an ill govern'd & disorderly":* Complaints from SF 89234, Massachusetts State Archives.

Thomas Wilkinson: Samuel Quincy Massacre Minutes, MHS, in Hiller Zobel and L. Kinvin Wroth, eds., *The Adams Papers: Legal Papers of John Adams* (Cambridge, MA: Belknap Press of Harvard University Press, 1965), vol. 3, 124.

73 *husband would die:* A Short narrative of the horrid massacre in Boston, perpetrated in the evening of the fifth day of March, 1770. By soldiers of the XXIXth Regiment; which with the XIVth Regiment were then quartered there: with some observations on the state of things prior to that catastrophe (Boston: Printed by order of the town of Boston, and sold by Edes and Gill, in Queen-Street, and T. & J. Fleet, in Cornhill, 1770), deposition 9.

"did talk very much against the town": Ibid., depositions 1–3. Concerning Wilme's jewelry shop, see *Boston Gazette,* July 24, 1769.

74 *historians have argued:* For labor conflicts, see especially Stephen Conway, "'The Great Mischief Complain'd of': Reflections on the Misconduct of British Soldiers in the Revolutionary War," *The William and Mary Quarterly* 47, no. 3 (July 1, 1990): 376, and Jesse Lemisch, "Jack Tar in the Streets: Merchant Seamen in the Politics of Revolutionary America," *The William and Mary Quarterly* 25, no. 3 (July 1, 1968): 371–407. In fact, I cannot find any evidence for the oft-repeated claim that soldiers in Boston were offering to work at rates lower than those accepted by colonial laborers. See, for example, Lemisch, "Jack Tar," 400, and Paul A. Gilje, *Rioting in America* (Bloomington: Indiana University Press, 1996), 1. This argument apparently originated in Richard B. Morris, *Government and Labor in Early America* (New York: Columbia Univer-

sity Press, 1946), 190: "Quartered throughout Boston, the soldiers accepted work at very low rates of compensation." This claim has no footnote, nor any other evidence about wages. Certainly, soldiers were employed by Bostonians, but there is no evidence that they did so by undercutting the pay of other Bostonians.

Patrick Doyne: (his name in the *Short Narrative* is given as "Dines"), *Short Narrative,* deposition 1.

Bartholomew Broaders: Ibid., deposition 38.

rumor that smallpox: Boston Selectmen's Minutes, BRCR, June 10, 1769, 19.

75 *August 1769:* August 17–20, 1769, "Elisha Story Account book," vol. 1, 1766–1776, MHS.

Boston's selectmen: Selectmen's Minutes, 1769–1775, August 23, 1769, *Boston Town Records,* vol. 23 (Boston: Rockwell and Churchill, City Printers, 1893), 31–34.

76 *Rainsford Island:* Town of Boston to John Williston, "For moving sundry persons with the Small-pox," June–October, 1769, Loose Boston Town Records, BPL.

"It was brought by the soldiers": Harbottle Dorr, "Annotated Newspapers," July 10, 1769, *Boston Evening-Post,* MHS.

in the regimental hospital: Boston Selectmen's Minutes, BRCR, June 10 and June 12, 1769, 19.

Frances Tyler: Ibid., July 12, 1769, 22.

77 *the Tylers nor the Chamberses:* About the death of Tyler, see *Boston Selectmen's Minutes, BRCR,* July 15, 1768, 23. About Chambers leaving Rainsford Island, see September 2, 1769, 32.

"amiable mind": Boston Weekly News-Letter, July 20, 1769.

"a sholyer's": Of the six burials billed to the selectmen on September 2, 1769, three were for soldiers' children. Loose Boston Town Records, BPL.

5. Love Your Neighbor, 1769–70

79 *The Miser:* Elisha Brown, "Proposals for Printing by Subscription, The Miser: Or The Soldier's Humour. A Comedy of Three Acts, as It Is Acted by His Majesty's Servants" (Boston: Russell, 1768). *Early American Imprints,* no. 41700, and *Boston Gazette,* March 6, 1769. For William Clark's enlistment record, see WO 12/4493/17; WO 12/4493/27, and WO 12/4493/33, TNA.

80 *he threatened:* Superior Court of Judicature docket book, 1769, 252, Massachusetts Judicial Archives.

"by a person who": Boston Evening-Post, July 31, 1769.

a loaded pistol: Superior Court of Judicature docket book, 1770, 29, Massachusetts Judicial Archives. Almost thirty years later, Joseph Nowell had still not completely forgiven his daughter. In his 1796 will, he bequeathed cash to his other daughter and his wife; only after her mother died would Mary inherit a fraction of the remaining estate. "Will of Joseph Nowell, boatbuilder, 1796," in *Suffolk County, MA: Probate File Papers,* online database: AmericanAncestors. org, New England Historic Genealogical Society, 2017–2019.

81 *newspapers sympathetic:* For the *Journal of the Times,* see O. M. Dickerson, *Boston Under Military Rule, 1768–1769: As Revealed in a Journal of the Times* (Westport, CT: Greenwood Press, 1971). For *The Annotated Newspapers of Harbottle Dorr, Jr.,* see masshist.org/dorr/.

82 *"that the most* dear*":* Boston Evening-Post, July 31, 1769. There is a rich and robust debate over the relationship between "expression and emotion"; see Nicole Eustace et al., "AHR Conversation: The Historical Study of Emotions," *The American Historical Review* 117, no. 5 (December 1, 2012): 1487–1531. William Reddy's argument for "emotives" is useful for understanding that the language of affection and distress is not rote or empty, but emotionally meaningful. This is not to suggest that Nicole Eustace's insights into "emotional expression" as a means of exerting power are not relevant here also. In these family formations, individual emotion and imperial politics come together in the acts of sex, marriage, and baptism. William M. Reddy, *The Navigation of Feeling: A Framework for the History of Emotions* (Cambridge, UK, and New York: Cambridge University Press, 2001), and Nicole Eustace, *Passion Is the Gale: Emotion, Power, and the Coming of the American Revolution* (published for the Omohundro Institute of Early American History and Culture, Williamsburg, VA, by the University of North Carolina Press, 2008).

A True and Faithful Narrative: New-York Journal, August 18, 1770.

83 *five to four:* Elaine Forman Crane, *Ebb Tide in New England: Women, Seaports, and Social Change, 1630–1800* (Boston: Northeastern University Press, 1998), 13.

Seizing a quiet: Christian Barnes to Elizabeth Murray Smith, August 7, 1768, Christian Barnes Papers, 1768–1784, Library of Congress Manuscript Division, and Patricia Cleary, *Elizabeth Murray: A Woman's Pursuit of Independence in Eighteenth-Century America* (Amherst: University of Massachusetts Press, 2000), 106–7.

"great raptures": Christian Barnes to Elizabeth Murray Smith, February 20, 1770, Christian Barnes Papers.

84 *"for the party disputes":* Ibid.

"*injoyment of Life*": Ibid.

85 "*a genteel one*": John Rowe Diary, February 21, 1770, MHS.

a "*trimmer*": Benjamin L. Carp, *Defiance of the Patriots: The Boston Tea Party & the Making of America* (New Haven, CT: Yale University Press, 2010), 106.

"*Have Boston's Beauties*": *Boston Gazette,* February 20, 1769. Harbottle Dorr annotated his copy of the poem, filling out the names of all the parties. http://www.masshist.org/dorr/volume/2/sequence/438. For manuscript commentary on dances and dancers, see David S. Shields, *Civil Tongues & Polite Letters in British America* (published for the Institute of Early American History and Culture, Williamsburg, VA, by the University of North Carolina Press, 1997), chapter 5.

86 *temper tantrum*: *Boston Evening-Post,* April 17, 1769.

In Boston, courtship: Richard Godbeer, *Sexual Revolution in Early America* (Baltimore: Johns Hopkins University Press, 2002), 227–98, and Lisa Wilson, *Ye Heart of a Man: The Domestic Life of Men in Colonial New England* (New Haven, CT: Yale University Press, 1999), chapter 2.

87 *Dana fumed*: Pomeroy to Gage, Boston, February 2, 1769, GP. "There is no occasion to trouble you with the particulars [of an assault case against a private], my only reason for mentioning it, is to acquaint you with the behavior of one of the justices on the Bench, his name Dana, a man as I am well informed of notorious character, as I think many expressions in his speech to the jury, of a very inflammatory nature."

"*arbitrary tyrannical principles*": Richard Dana to Edmund Dana, August 9, 1769, Dana Family Papers, box 1, MHS.

"*You need not have*": Ibid.

88 "*many thousands*": "To the Young Ladies of Boston," *Boston Evening-Post,* January 30, 1769.

"*convince the world*": Ibid.

89 "*but the ladies of the town*": John Boyle, "A journal of occurrences in Boston," October 25, 1768, MS Am 1926, Houghton Library, Harvard University, 17.

political considerations: Other references to women rejecting balls attended by military officers can be found in the *Journal of the Times*, December 14 and 23, 1768.

desire for partners: Kate Haulman, *The Politics of Fashion in Eighteenth-Century America* (Chapel Hill: University of North Carolina Press, 2011), explains the ways "the imperial crisis magnified the already contested cultural politics of fashion," 153, in which courtship played a central role.

"*Liberty Assembly*": Ann Hulton, *Letters of a Loyalist Lady: Being the Letters of*

Anne Hulton, Sister of Henry Hulton, Commissioner of Customs at Boston, 1767–1776 (Cambridge, MA: Harvard University Press, 1927).

"mixt dancing": Journal of the Times, December 23, 1768, reprinted in *Boston Evening-Post,* February 13, 1769.

90 *Ann Hulton:* Hulton, *Letters,* 19.

"too much confusion": John Rowe Diary, January 19, 1768; March 29, 1769; April 12, 1769; March 15, 1769; MHS.

"in hopes": Mary Murray to Caty Murray, Boston, April 11, 1772, box 1, folder 4, Murray Robbins Family Papers, MHS. About Ensign Brideoake, see WO 12/3117/190, TNA.

"accused of theft": Dalrymple to Gage, June 2, 1772, vol. III, GP.

91 *"made up to her": Boston Evening-Post,* August 21, 1769.

Dalton immediately: Richard Dana, "Justice of the Peace Records," June 30, 1769, MHS. His plea of no contest is recorded in the General Sessions (Suffolk County, MA) Docket Book, August 1, 1769, Massachusetts Judicial Archives.

92 *commanding officers promoted:* Muster roll for November 10, 1772, WO 12/7312–25, TNA.

Thomasin Charlton: Court of General Sessions of the Peace, Record Book, box # 902789, covering 1/1/1738–12/31/1780, reel 4, August 7, 1770. Charlton was committed to the almshouse on February 10, 1770. Nellis and Cecere, eds., *The Eighteenth-Century Records of the Boston Overseers of the Poor,* 205.

That premarital sex: Thomas A. Foster, *Sex and the Eighteenth-Century Man: Massachusetts and the History of Sexuality in America* (Boston: Beacon Press, 2006), 5.

a fornication complaint: October 1, 1771, Court of General Sessions of the Peace, Record Book, 1738–1780, Massachusetts Judicial Archives. For details of the almshouse, see Nellis and Cecere, eds., *The Eighteenth-Century Records of the Boston Overseers of the Poor,* 219, 227. Elizabeth Thomas entered August 2, 1771; Lydia Wool entered May 4, 1772. About Private John Wooll, see WO 12/3117/122, WO 12/3117/141, WO 12/3117/147A, WO 12/3117/163, WO 12/3117/174, WO 12/3117/183, WO 12/3117/193, TNA.

93 *The court fined the mother:* General Sessions, Suffolk County Docket book, 1764–68, August 7, 1770, Massachusetts Judicial Archives. Suffolk County Presentments, October 1771, SF 90510. About the almshouse birth: Boston Overseers of the Poor records, May 12, 1770, box 9, MHS. About admission to the almshouse on March 17, 1770: Nellis and Cecere, eds., *The Eighteenth-Century Records of the Boston Overseers of the Poor,* 206. About discharge from the almshouse on October 30, 1770, ibid., 212. About return on August 5, 1771, ibid., 219.

"Lydia Wool a Child": Ibid., May 4, 1772.

John Morris: See WO 12/3117-120, WO 12/3117-129, WO 12/3117-144, TNA.

Osborn married: Christ Church records, Boston, MA: *Marriages, 1700–1809* (on-line database: AmericanAncestors.org, New England Historic Genealogical Society, 2006). For the birth of William Jr., see Records of the King's Chapel in Boston, February 4, 1770, Boston Church Records, AmericanAncestors. org.

94 *Alexander McGregory:* April 17, 1770, "List of Marriages, 1742–1778," Andrew Eliot Papers, MHS. Margaret McGregory's baptism appears in "Records of the New North Church," December 16, 1770, Records of the Churches of Boston, AmericanAncestors.org.

fewer men than women: In 1765 Boston, there were 122 adult women for every 100 men. The influx of military men three years later would have gone far in redressing the imbalance—a point that no demographic historian has yet investigated. See Crane, *Ebb Tide in New England,* 13.

political ramifications: Mary Beth Norton, *Liberty's Daughters: The Revolutionary Experience of American Women, 1750–1800* (New York: Little, Brown, 1980), chapter 2.

95 *"too likely":* Cuthbertson, *A System for the Compleat Interior Management,* 193.

"Were the Women": Boston Chronicle, January 18, 1770.

merely marketable: On the political meanings of marriage later, in the United States, see Nancy F. Cott, *Public Vows: A History of Marriage and the Nation* (Cambridge, MA: Harvard University Press, 2000), and Jan Lewis, "The Republican Wife: Virtue and Seduction in the Early Republic," *The William and Mary Quarterly* 44, no. 4 (October 1, 1987): 689–721.

96 *"An Epistle":* Massachusetts Spy, January 7, 1771.

"A Bachelor": Ibid., January 14, 1771.

some forty local women: Boston Church Records, passim, AmericanAncestors. org.

Susannah Sloper: For Sloper's career in the almshouse, see Nellis and Cecere, eds., *The Eighteenth-Century Records of the Boston Overseers of the Poor,* 55 and 64. About her sisters, ibid., 21. About Lydia Sloper specifically, ibid., 98 and 125. About Susannah's illegitimate child, "Henrietta of John Jones & Susanna Sloper," see Records of the King's Chapel in Boston, January 21, 1767, Records of the Churches of Boston, AmericanAncestors.org. For her marriage to Private John Brand, see Christ Church Records, June 22, 1769.

97 *Anne Belcher:* Marriage to John Wright in King's Chapel Records, January 15, 1769.

Mary Welch: For marriage to Lawrence Northam, see Trinity Church Records, January 24, 1770, and *Boston Marriages, BRCR,* 400. They baptized their child, James Northam, on October 28, 1770; see Records of the King's Chapel, AmericanAncestors.org.

Ponsonby Molesworth: Boston Evening-Post, May 1, 1769.

Margaret Sullivan: Records of the New North Church, December 9, 1770, AmericanAncestors.org.

98 *simply "self-divorced":* Divorce was a viable option in eighteenth-century Massachusetts for literate or propertied women, but it required a petition to the General Court. For divorce petitions, see Nancy F. Cott, "Divorce and the Changing Status of Women in Eighteenth-Century Massachusetts," *The William and Mary Quarterly* 33, no. 4 (1976): 586–614. Poorer couples were more likely to choose self-divorce if there was not a question of marital property. See Clare A. Lyons, *Sex Among the Rabble: An Intimate History of Gender and Power in the Age of Revolution, Philadelphia, 1730-1830* (Chapel Hill: Published for the Omohundro Institute of Early American History and Culture, Williamsburg, VA, by the University of North Carolina Press, 2006), chapter 1.

Hannah Osborn Dundass: "John Love & Hanah Dundas," August 13, 1774, *Boston Marriages,* 435.

Elizabeth Hillman Lindley: "William Moarn & Elizabeth Lindley," November 16, 1773, *Boston Marriages, BRCR,* 338.

"Had I my dear parents": Graham and Bethune, *The Unpublished Letters and Correspondence of Mrs. Isabella Graham,* 23.

"In short": Ibid., 50.

99 *her letters:* For an explanation of the epistolary habits that tied together the British families throughout the empire, see Sarah M. S. Pearsall, *Atlantic Families : Lives and Letters in the Later Eighteenth Century* (New York and Oxford, UK: Oxford University Press, 2010).

"my fears": Graham and Bethune, *The Unpublished Letters and Correspondence of Mrs. Isabella Graham,* 27.

"ever dear Mother": Ibid., 89.

"I am distressed": Isabella Graham, Joanna Bethune, and Divie Bethune, *The Power of Faith: Exemplified in the Life and Writings of the Late Mrs. Isabella Graham* (New York: American Tract Society, 1843), 23. Graham eventually returned to New York after the American Revolution, where she opened a school and then an orphanage with her New York friend Elizabeth Schuyler Hamilton. See Amanda B. Moniz, *From Empire to Humanity: The American Revolution and*

the Origins of Humanitarianism (New York: Oxford University Press, 2016), 122–23.

100 *legal status:* Cornelia H. Dayton and Sharon V. Salinger, "Was the Warning of Strangers Unique to Colonial New England?" in Daniel Joseph Hulsebosch and Richard B. Bernstein, eds., *Making Legal History: Essays in Honor of William E. Nelson* (New York: New York University Press, 2013).

lost the right to claim: SF 90077, and "Warning [Out] Book from January 4, 1745 to 1770," December 22, 1770, Boston Overseers of the Poor, reel 1, vol. 1 (XT), in "Boston Overseers of the Poor records, 1733–1925," P-368, MHS.

given the same warning: SF 89546.

101 *Annis Parcill:* January 14, 1769, *Boston Marriages, BRCR,* 428.

"George Simpson a soldier": April 9, 1769, Trinity Church Records, AmericanAncestors.org. The marriage intention listed her as Skillingsby. *Boston Marriages, BRCR,* 400.

"Now it has been adjudged": *Diary of John Adams,* vol. 1, January 2, 1761, in *Founding Families: Digital Editions of the Papers of the Winthrops and the Adamses,* ed. C. James Taylor (Boston: Massachusetts Historical Society, 2007).

102 *William Carson:* Marriage to Elizabeth Betterly, Trinity Church Records, December 19, 1771, AmericanAncestors.org and *Boston Marriages, BRCR,* 429.

103 *Jesse Lindley:* Marriage to Elizabeth Hillman on July 27, 1770. See King's Chapel Records, Register of Marriages, 1718–1841, vol. 41 (XT), MHS.

"the damn'd Sentry": Deposition re October 29, 1769, in CO 5/88/196, TNA.

104 *When John Morgan:* For Morgan's age, see WO 116/7/123, TNA.

105 *to serve as godparents:* David Cressy, *Birth, Marriage, and Death: Ritual, Religion, and the Life-cycle in Tudor and Stuart England* (Oxford, UK: Oxford University Press, 1997), 156–61.

Because the Morgans were baptizing: For the muster rolls of Dalrymple's company, including the records of Morris, Morgan, Yeats, and Lindley, see WO 12/3117-120, WO 12/3117-129, WO 12/3117-140, WO 12/3117-144, WO 12/3117-150, WO 12/3117-155, WO 12/3117-165, WO 12/3117-172, WO 12/3117-181, and WO 12/3117-191, TNA. Morgan disappears from the muster after WO 12/3117-172, taken on June 10, 1771.

Sarah Morgan's godparents: August 31, 1770; see King's Chapel Records Register of Baptisms, 1703–1843, vol. 39 (XT), MHS.

106 *Katherine Skillings:* For the baptism of George Simpson on March 14, 1770, see King's Chapel Records Register of Baptisms (MHS). For the enlistment record of Joseph Whitehouse, see WO 12/3117-126, WO 12/3117-140, WO 12/3117-

146, WO 12/3117-158, WO 12/3117-169, WO 12/3117-178, WO 12/3117-188, and WO 12/3117-198, TNA.

Thomas Wilson: For his enlistment, see WO 12/3117/119, WO 12/3117/138, WO 12/3117/148, and WO 12/3117/154. He deserted on December 29, 1770; see WO 12/3117/176, TNA.

Joseph Whitehouse: For his marriage to Jane Crothers, on March 27, 1770, see Old North Church (Christ Church in the City of Boston) Records, Baptismal Registers, box 18, MHS.

Elizabeth Hartley: For the enlistment record of her husband, John, see WO 12/3117-143, WO 12/3117-151, WO 12/3117-166, WO 12/3117-171, WO 12/3117-180, and WO 12/3117-190, TNA.

her daughter Hannah: Baptized on November 8, 1771. See King's Chapel Records Register of Baptisms, MHS.

107 *more than a hundred:* Again, this is a small fraction of the baptisms in Boston over the same period, which number 1,478. The Records of the Churches of Boston, AmericanAncestors.org.

her child's baptism: For William Dundass Jr.'s baptism, see King's Chapel Records, February 4, 1770, AmericanAncestors.org. His godparents were Corporal Alexander Friendly (WO 12/3117/119, TNA), James Preston, and Martha Powell. Powell was baptized February 17, 1750, in the New South Church. After William Dundass left Boston in 1772, with the Fourteenth Regiment, Hannah Dundass (née Osborn) remarried.

their children's godparents: For Joseph Brocklesby's baptism, Februry 24, 1771, see King's Chapel Records. His godparents were Sergeant John Wright (WO 12/3117/121, TNA); Fanny Sheldon, who later married Sergeant Robert Barton (WO 12/3117/121, TNA) on May 28, 1771, in the Brattle Street (Congregational) Church (Records of the Church in Brattle Square and *Boston Marriages, BRCR,* 330); and Ann Woolhouse, wife of Corporal John Woolhouse (WO 12/3117/158, TNA).

6. Absent Without Leave, 1768–70

109 *Corporal John Moies:* Enlistment, WO 12/3117/111, TNA.

notorious flogging: SP 44/88/0139, TNA, and *Salisbury Journal,* November 4, 1765.

On a bright Friday: John Rowe Diary, October 14, 1768, MHS. The flogging is described in John Boyle, *A journal of occurrences in Boston, New England* (Boston: printed sheets, about 1769), MS Am 1926 (2), Houghton Library, Harvard University.

a thousand lashes: See Dorothy Murray to Betsey Murray, Boston, October 27, 1768, Murray Robbins Family Papers, Ms. N-1157, box 1, folder 1, MHS. The *Journal of the Times* also reported the whipping, as did the *Boston Evening-Post,* December 19, 1768.

110 *"so shocked at": Caledonian Mercury,* November 6, 1765.

"only 40 of the 170": Boston Evening-Post, December 19, 1768.

observing military punishments: Anderson, *A People's Army,* 136–37: "From the soldiers' point of view, corporal punishment was one of the constants of life." Anderson argues that the contrast between the harsh punishments of the British army and the relatively lenient punishment typical of New England and New England provincial forces may have exacerbated the colonists' sense of alienation from Britain and British culture, but it seems more likely that the division is between military and civilian cultures, especially given the reaction to flogging in the O'Hara case of 1765.

111 *Daniel Rogers:* Enlistment record is in WO 12/4493-02, TNA; he transferred from the Twenty-Seventh Regiment on September 2, 1767.

packed up for England: Gage to Barrington, New York, October 9, 1767, reprinted in Carter, *Correspondence of General Thomas Gage,* vol. 1, 437.

"for here is poor wretches": Dorothy Murray to Betsey Murray, Boston, October 27, 1768, Murray Robbins Family Papers, Ms. N-1157, box 1, folder 1, MHS.

112 *"He is very glad":* Ibid.

managed to rent a house: John Rowe Diary, October 7, 1768, MHS.

113 *socializing regularly:* On October 17, O'Hara had both breakfast and dinner with Rowe; after that, he was a regular dining companion. John Rowe Diary, October 17, 1768, and passim, MHS.

started to slip away: Desertions are noted in the muster rolls for WO 12/3117, WO 12/4493, and WO 12/6786, TNA.

Desertion in Boston: Numbers for the Seven Years' War are from Thomas Agostini, "'Deserted His Majesty's Service': Military Runaways, the British-American Press, and the Problem of Desertion During the Seven Years' War," *Journal of Social History* 40, no. 4 (Summer 2007): 960. Desertion from the Twenty-Ninth Regiment can be followed through the muster rolls, WO 12/4493, TNA. There were about five hundred men at a time in the regiment. By contrast, only one man deserted from the Twenty-Ninth Regiment in 1767.

114 *an enslaved woman:* Joshua Henshaw to Col. William Henshaw, Boston, November 2, 1768, "Letters to Col. William Henshaw, 1768–1769," MHS.

115 *"and that the Regular":* "Proceedings of a General Court Martial, held in the

Town of Boston, October 22, 1768 . . . ," WO 71/77/118–123, Testimony of
Thomas West, 120–21, TNA. Although parts of Eames's story are well known,
David Niescior is, to the best of my knowledge, the first person to uncover this
part of the story in the archives. My very grateful thanks to Dr. Will Tatum
and David Niescior for sharing copies of this material with me.

"they, the prisoner": "General Court Martial of Richard Eames," WO 71/77/121,
TNA.

116 *a "proper spot":* General Orders and Instructions, General Thomas Gage, October 29, 1768, Add ms. 21683, British Library.

A number of women: "*Journal of Occurrences,* October 31," in *New-York Journal,*
November 17, 1768.

noted the execution: Joshua Henshaw to Col. William Henshaw, Boston, November 2, 1768. Dorothy Murray to Betsey Murray, Boston, October 27, 1768.
John Rowe Diary, October 31, 1768, MHS.

extraordinarily weak defense: "General Court Martial of Richard Eames," WO
71/77/122–123, TNA.

117 *a large extended family:* Massachusetts: Vital Records, 1620–1850, Framingham,
AmericanAncestors.org, New England Historic Genealogical Society, 2001–
2016.

remorseful yet resigned: Boston News-Letter, November 3, 1768.

"The Soldiers begin to desert": Andrew Eliot to Thomas Hollis, October 18, 1768,
reprinted in *Massachusetts Historical Society Collections,* 4th series, vol. 4 (1858),
432.

118 *"thin appearance": Boston Evening-Post,* March 3, 1769.

"Our people behave": Thomas Cushing to Dennys De Berdt, January 19, 1769,
in *Massachusetts Historical Society Collections,* 4th series, vol. 4 (1858), 352–53. For
Cushing's moderation, see Nathaniel Coffin's "Declaration," February 6, 1769,
reprinted in Nicolson, ed., *The Papers of Francis Bernard,* vol. 5, 171.

"We will not pretend": Journal of the Times, January 17, 1769, reprinted in the
Boston Evening-Post, March 6, 1769.

119 *"the sogers":* Thomas Jarvis to "Loving Brother" [Samuel Badger], Charleston,
March 7, 1769, Samuel Badger Papers, South Carolina Historical Society (call
43/2081). Courtesy of Mary Beth Norton.

"an Extract of a Letter": Boston Evening-Post, April 24, 1769.

120 *"I must likewise inform":* Mackay to Gage, Boston, June 12, 1769, vol. 86, GP.

"think General Gage": William Campbell to 2nd Lord Egmont, Halifax, April
10, 1769, Add ms. 47054A, British Library. Twelve men deserted in April 1769.
See WO 12/3117, WO 12/4493, and WO 12/7312, TNA.

121 *"intermix with the Town's People"*: "Extract of a Letter from Governor Bernard to General Gage, Dated Boston September 24, 1768," CO 5/86/423 ff., TNA.

John Croker: Deposition of July 24, 1770, given in New Jersey, CO 5/88/232, TNA.

"with force and arms": An information against Geary, Superior Court of Judicature docket book, 1767–1768, 370, Massachusetts Judicial Archives. Robert Auchmuty to Hutchinson, "Friday morning 7 October [1768]," misc. mss. Ch. f. 11.7, BPL. For Lee's enlistment record, see WO 12/3117/122, TNA.

a local newspaper: Boston Gazette, November 28, 1768.

122 *"have exerted themselves"*: Dalrymple to Gage, Boston, October 13, 1768, vol. 82, GP.

"was seduced": Pomeroy to Gage, Boston, May 1, 1769, vol. 85, GP.

"it is to be expected": Gage to Mackay, New York, June 25, 1769, vol. 86, GP.

"It is with the greatest concern": Dalrymple to Gage, Boston, September 4, 1769, vol. 87, GP.

123 *"I have long since"*: Gage to Carr, New York, March 13, 1769, vol. 84, GP.

Private Hugh Anderson: SF 89447.

124 *he deserted the following:* WO 12/3117/184, TNA. Anderson's marriage to Susannah Jordan is recorded on December 26, 1773, Trinity Church Records, Records of the Churches of Boston, CD-ROM.

Francis Lee: Francis Lee and Abigail Tucker, married December 3, 1772, Massachusetts Vital Records, 1621–1850, AmericanAncestors.org, New England Historic Genealogical Society, 2001–2016, Town of Pepperell Records, vol. 1, 192. Francis had died by 1785, leaving Abigail widowed with their three children, Francis, Hannah, and Abigail. Massachusetts Vital Records, Town of Townshend Records, vol. 1, 438.

"Crimes are of such a Nature": Boston Evening-Post, May 29, 1769.

125 *the search party:* This account is drawn from the deposition of William Henderson, enclosed in a letter from Pomeroy to Gage, January 12, 1769, vol. 83, GP.

126 *"were travelling into the country": Boston Evening-Post,* February 13, 1769.

Governor Wentworth of New Hampshire corresponded: Pomeroy to Gage, February 2 and March 6, 1769, vol. 83, GP.

"done everything": Pomeroy to Gage, April 3, 1769, vol. 84, GP.

127 *fleeing to New York:* Ibid.

A magistrate: Alexander McMillian to Mackay, May 4, 1769, enclosed in Mackay to Gage, May 4, 1769, vol. 85, GP.

John Butler: Ibid. For Butler's muster history, see WO 12/4493/04 (deserted

10/23/1768) and WO 12/4493/14 (returned from desertion 5/29/1769 and deserted again 9/12/1769), TNA.

128   *"the whole country"*: Mackay to Gage, May 25, 1769, vol. 85, GP.

"people of the country": Dalrymple to Gage, Boston, October 28, 1769, vol. 88, GP.

this informer: Report forwarded from Dalrymple to Gage, September 25, 1769, vol. 87, GP.

129   *"who calls himself Lochlan"*: Ibid.

John Loughran: WO 12/4493-04; he deserted October 5, 1768. His marriage, June 9, 1769, to Sarah Foster, was officiated by Amos Moody, clergy: New Hampshire Marriage Records, database with images, FamilySearch, https://familysearch.org/ark:/61903/1:1:FLPT-MBL 10 March 2018. His son, William Loring, was born February 10, 1772: *New Hampshire Birth Records, Early to 1900*, citing Pelham, Hillsborough, New Hampshire, United States, Bureau of Vital Records and Health Statistics, Concord; Family History Library microfilm 1,001,015.

courts-martial for deserters: Unfortunately, the records themselves appear to be lost. Reference to general courts-martial are scattered throughout the correspondence between General Gage and officers in Boston.

"The Deserters under": Dalrymple to Gage, December 10, 1769, vol. 88, GP.

"You may Occasionally mitigate": Gage to Dalrymple, New York, October 29, 1769, vol. 88, GP.

"are a disgrace": Andrew Croswell (printed anonymously), *Part of an Exposition of Paul's Journey to Damascus, Acts XXVI: In Which the Author Having Cautioned against Shedding Blood, Shews That Giving More than the Forty Stripes Allowed Deuteronomy XXV. Ver. 3. Is Breaking a Moral Law of God*, 10871 (Boston: John Kneeland, printer, 1768). The *Boston Gazette,* December 19, 1768, first advertised Croswell's essay.

130   *"military cruelties"*: Croswell, *Part of an Exposition,* appendix 4.

131   *"the safest way"*: Joshua Henshaw to Col. William Henshaw, Boston, November 2, 1768, Ms. S-437, MHS.

enormous stock of goods: See WO 12/3117/126, TNA.

twenty-six British pounds' worth of goods: May 2, 1769, General Sessions Suffolk County Docket book, 1769–1773, and SF 89002; also see Zobel, *Legal Papers of John Adams,* vol. 2.

the informal economy: See Zabin, *Dangerous Economies,* chapter 3.

132   *Moies was caught:* Founders Online, TNA, last modified June 13, 2018, http://

founders.archives.gov/documents/Adams/05-02-02-0010-0003-0001. Original
source: Wroth and Zobel, eds., *Legal Papers of John Adams*, vol. 2, *Cases 31-62*,
436. Also Mackay to Gage, Boston, June 19, 1769, vol. 86, GP.

"twenty stripes": Ibid.

"utterly unable": SF 89002, May 19, 1769.

133   *"such an infamous piece of Tyranny"*: Gage to Mackay, June 20, 1769, vol. 86, GP.

"a connivance between": Mackay to Gage, July 6, 1769, vol. 86, GP.

"keeps close": Mackay to Gage, June 25, 1769, vol. 86, GP.

"is such a Rascall": Mackay to Gage, July 6, 1769, vol. 86, GP.

134   supplying rum *"indiscriminately"*: Boston Gazette, January 29, 1770.

Thomas Hibbard: Listed as deserted on April 20, 1769. See "Crimes," *Boston Eve-ning-Post,* May 29, 1769. Also see WO 12/3117/126, TNA.

When Mackay advertised: Boston Evening-Post, May 29, 1769.

one soldier: George Reader was reported sick on muster taken April 24, 1769.
The remaining three, Thomas Parsons, Thomas Hall, and Edward Armes, all
deserted on April 20, 1769. See WO 12/3117/126, TNA.

135   *"the Boston Gaol for theft"*: For Moies's designation as prisoner, see WO 12/3117-133 and following. For the jail list, see SF 89447.

He successfully courted: For an extensive discussion of John Moies's involvement
in the Boston community during and after the Revolution, see J. L. Bell,
http://boston1775.blogspot.com/2006/09/john-moies-boston-retailer.html,
accessed 2/17/2012.

7. A Deadly Riot: March 1770

136   *"I am wounded"*: See Boston Gazette and Country Journal, March 12, 1770.

137   *fresh snow:* John Rowe Diary, March 5, 1770, MHS.

138   *no streetlights:* In 1773, the Boston Town Meeting first received a committee
report that the town should purchase street lamps. *Boston Town Records, BRCR,*
March 8, 1773, 115.

White had joined: WO 121/7/293, TNA.

strolled through: Wroth and Zobel, eds., *Legal Papers of John Adams,* vol. 3, 108.

139   *Jane Crothers heard:* Ibid., 75.

may have been a barmaid: From her address "near the head of Royal Exchange
Lane," I infer that she lived in the Royal Exchange Tavern. My thanks to Cor-nelia Dayton for her suggestion that Whitehouse may have worked as well as
lived in the tavern.

the town warner: See Dayton and Salinger, *Robert Love's Warnings.*

John Belcher's tavern: Liquor license granted August 4, 1768. *Boston Selectmen's Minutes, BRCR,* 304.

140 *James and Elizabeth Hartigan:* Their residence is derived from SF 89545, May 4, 1770. For Hickling's household, see "1771 Massachusetts Tax Inventory," http://sites.fas.harvard.edu/~hsb41/masstax/masstax.cgi.

a unicorn and a lion: "Old State House Lion and Unicorn: An Unfolding Story (Part I)," Old State House, http://www.bostonhistory.org/king street/2014/07/old-state-house-lion-and-unicorn.html, accessed December 21, 2017.

"where they performed": Boston Gazette, September 25, 1769.

All the regiments: Boston Evening-Post, June 12, 1769.

141 *For theft or counterfeiting: Boston Post-Boy,* April 25, 1768.

when a sentry: Zobel, *Boston Massacre,* 184.

"frequently been so many applications": Report of Lieutenant Colonel Morrison, enclosed with Barrington to Weymouth, April 18, 1768, WO 4/83/3118-19, TNA, cited in Hayter, *The Army and the Crowd,* 23.

142 *the many riots:* Ibid. For the King's Bench riot, which came to be known as the Massacre at St. George's Fields, see chapter 11.

occasion in November 1765: RG39 "C" [HX], vol. 4, #45 a–k, PANS. Their fines were remitted November 6, 1765.

143 *"Lieutenant Colonel Dalrymple":* Gage to Hillsborough, New York, September 7, 1768, in Carter, ed., *Correspondence of General Thomas Gage,* vol. 1, 191. For English advice, see Hayter, *The Army and the Crowd,* 28–30.

Ebenezer Richardson: Boston Evening-Post, February 26, 1770.

144 *"I hear of no Riots":* Gage to Hillsborough, New York, June 10, 1769, in Carter, ed., *Correspondence of Thomas Gage,* vol. 1, 226.

no longer needed: Gage to Hillsborough, New York, July 22, 1769, in ibid., 228.

it seemed to Mackay: Mackay hired four ships to bring women and children to Canada. "An Account of the Expense of Hiring Vessels, Fitting them to Transport . . . the Women and Regimental Stores of the 64th and 65th Regiments to Halifax . . . The Men having Embarked on board His Majesty's Ships." September 4, 1769, Gage Warrants, Box 21, folder 21, 26–78. Gage Papers, Clements Library, University of Michigan.

145 *Governor Bernard how long:* Gage to Bernard, June 18, 1769, Nicolson, ed., *The Papers of Francis Bernard,* vol. 5, 287.

"They say Boston will": Elizabeth Smith to Dolly Forbes, June 22, 1769, box 1, James Murray Robbins Family Papers, MHS.

"agreeable news": Palfrey to Wilkes, June 13, 1769, *Proceedings of the Massachusetts Historical Society,* vol. 47 (Boston: The Society, 1914), 201.

signed a petition: "The Petition of a Number of Freeholders and other Inhabitants," June 23, 1769, Town Papers, Ms f. Bost. 7 v 7, BPL.

leave two regiments: Bernard to Gage, June 26, 1769, Nicolson, ed., *The Papers of Francis Bernard,* vol. 5, 294.

"must remain in the Town": Bernard to Gage, July 5, 1769, Nicolson, ed., ibid., 303.

146 *The Boston watch:* Uncataloged watch reports in Loose Boston Town Records, BPL.

Officers reported to Gage: Pomeroy to Gage, Boston, February 2, 1769, vol. 83, GP.

Journal of the Times*:* Dickerson, *Boston Under Military Rule.*

two soldiers' wives: Margaret Bishop, wife of John Bishop, Fourteenth Regiment, and Mary Dishon (Dickson), wife of Thomas Dickson, Twenty-Ninth Regiment.

"several Routs": Townshend Returns, April 1770, in Loose Boston Records, BPL.

had young children: Mary Dickson had two children: John, baptized March 9, 1766, in St. Paul's Church, Halifax, Holder et al., *Baptisms, Marriages, and Burials, 1749–1768,* and William, baptized February 19, 1769, in Christ Church Records, AmericanAncestors.org.

147 *"without his giving":* August 25, 1770, CO 5/88/185, TNA. For more examples of soldiers struck "without the least provocation": William Lake, CO 5/88/199; William Brown, CO 5/88/202; Robert Balfour, CO 5/88/203, "without his giving them the least offence, knock'd him down," William Holam (knocked down "without a word passing on either side"), CO 5/88/205; and Thomas Smith, Thomas Hault, and John Gregory, "as they were going peaceably along the street in Boston," CO 5/88/199, TNA.

"was a dirty rascal": August 25, 1770, CO 5/88/185, TNA.

Winship's accusation: Riley and Winship had another fight the next day; Riley was arrested and then escaped from the constable, possibly with the help of some of his officers. See Zobel, *Boston Massacre,* 137. There is some evidence that Winship had been the supplier for the British army's meat as early as 1756; it is likely that he renewed this contract in 1768. Jonathan Winship and his son (of the same name) are credited with the creation of the Brighton meat market, which expanded enormously in 1775, when the Winships contracted to provide meat for the Continental army during the siege of Boston. For the possible creation of the 1756 contract to provision the British army, see Karen J. Friedmann, "Victualling Colonial Boston," *Agricultural History* 47, no. 3 (July 1, 1973): 196, fn. 38.

148 *One private in the Fourteenth Regiment:* John Brelsford, employed by Mary Russell, *Short Narrative,* deposition 90. Mary's husband, Nathaniel, advertised his "household furniture" in the *Massachusetts Spy,* December 17, 1772.

Private Patrick Doyne: For Doyne's enlistment, see WO 12/4493-10, TNA. For Doyne's family, from the warning record of April 26, 1770: "Warning [Out] Book from January 4, 1745 to 1770," Boston Overseers of the Poor, reel 1, vol. 1 (XT), in "Boston Overseers of the Poor Records, 1733–1925," P-368, 15 reels (microfilm), MHS. For his friendships, see Richard Ward, deposition 16, and Bartholomew Broaders, deposition 38, in *Short Narrative.*

occasional work: According to John Bell's analysis of the Box and Austin ropewalk in Boston, after 1760, men were paid by the day. J. L. Bell, "Changing Wages for Ropewalk Workers," http://boston1775.blogspot.com/2007/11/changing-wages-for-ropewalk-workers.html, accessed May 22, 2019.

"he was assaulted": *Short Narrative,* deposition 5.

"You damn'd dogs": Ibid., deposition 10.

149 *"Richardson was afterwards":* York, *Henry Hulton and the American Revolution,* 143. Historians have invariably seen the ropewalk brawl as a "precipitating event for the shooting on March 5." Hinderaker, *Boston's Massacre,* 160. Yet Zobel's claim that the ropewalk brawl was a "fatal error" that the Sons of Liberty could manipulate "in which the town rather than the army would appear as the injured party" in order "to satisfy [the radicals'] most sanguine and sanguinary propaganda expectations" is unpersuasive. Zobel, *Boston Massacre,* 181.

another pro-Crown writer: A Fair Account of the Late Unhappy Disturbance at Boston in New England; Extracted from the Depositions That Have Been Made Concerning It . . . With an Appendix . . . (London: Printed for B. White, 1770), 12. It is unknown who penned the introduction to *A Fair Account.* See Neil Longley York, "Rival Truths, Political Accommodation, and the Boston 'Massacre,'" *Massachusetts Historical Review* 11 (2009): 75.

150 *"1st. poor Snider":* Samuel Savage, "MHS Collections Online: Samuel P. Savage Diary, 1 unnumbered page, February 24–28, 1770, and Summary about Important Events in February and March 1770," http://www.masshist.org/database/3057, accessed December 20, 2017.

a "genteel": John Rowe Diary, February 21, 1770, MHS.

the jeweler John Wilme: Boston Gazette, July 24, 1769.

"he would level his piece": Short Narrative, depositions 1–3.

151 *"the women should be sent":* Ibid., deposition 1.

"if there should be": Ibid. Eleanor Park was probably the wife of John Park of the Fourteenth Regiment. See WO 12/3117-147, TNA.

Montgomery shouted loudly: This conversation was reported by Caleb Swan, who said he could overhear the whole conversation while he was "at Mr. Sample's door, at the north part of town near the north battery." The Sample house was apparently on North Street, between Clarke and Salutation Streets. See Massachusetts Historical Society, *The Inhabitants and Estates of Boston (Thwing Database)*, CD-ROM, reference code 52041, no. 1, 1.

"The town was too haughty:" Short Narrative, deposition 11.

152 *"I hope":* Ibid., deposition 19.

"Damn you ye Yankey boogers": Ibid., deposition 50.

"who buys Lobsters": Zobel and Wroth, eds., *Legal Papers of John Adams,* vol. 3, 70.

reports vary: The next few paragraphs are a compilation of evidence from *Short Narrative, A Fair Account,* and Zobel and Wroth, eds. *Legal Papers of John Adams,* vol. 3.

more people: This reconstruction is drawn from the conflicting testimonies contained in the *Short Narrative* and Zobel and Wroth, eds., *Legal Papers of John Adams,* vol. 3.

153 *the sentry pushed:* Ibid., 75–76.

154 *"The bloody back Rascall":* CO 5/759/365, TNA. The same evidence is also reproduced in Zobel and Wroth, eds., *Legal Papers of John Adams,* vol. 3, 75–76.

"encouraging them to fire": Ibid.

155 *"to ask what they were":* Ibid., 123–126 and 151.

156 *"I went up to him":* Rex v. Wemms, ibid., 116.

158 *"This is Mr. Crafts":* Short Narrative, deposition 66.

"with a stout cudgel": See the depositions of Edmund Mason, in *A Fair Account,* 5, and David Loring, in *Short Narrative,* deposition 92.

159 *Lieutenant Governor Hutchinson:* Zobel, *Boston Massacre,* 203–5.

Ephraim Fenno: Short Narrative, deposition 91.

8. Gathering Up: March 6, 1770–August 1772

160 *Rhoades's tavern:* Boston Selectmen's Minutes, BRCR, March 6, 1770, 304. About the sailors: *A Short Narrative,* deposition 70.

The shoemaker David Loring: Ibid., deposition 92.

At the inquests: William Palfrey to John Wilkes, March 13, 1770, "Palfrey, William, 1741–1781. 5 Letters to John Wilkes; 7–11," bMs Am 1704.4 (89), Houghton Library, Harvard University.

"give information": John Rowe Diary, March 5, 1770, MHS.

161   *John Singleton Copley:* Jane Kamensky, *A Revolution in Color: The World of John Singleton Copley* (New York: W. W. Norton & Company, 2016), especially 139–48 and 168–70. *Boston Town Records, BRCR,* March 6, 1770, 1.

collect testimonials: Over the course of the 1760s, both the town and the governor increasingly turned to deposition gathering as a way of shaping public opinion and preparing for possible trials. Stern, "The Overflowings of Liberty," and Stern, email to author, December 17, 2018.

162   *"the Residence of a Military":* Boston Town Records, BRCR, July 4, 1769, 296.

"the Inhabitants and Soldiery": Ibid., 2.

163   *"not in his power":* Hutchinson to Gage, Boston, March 6, 1770, reproduced in Randolph G. Adams, "New Light on the Boston Massacre," American Antiquarian Society, *Proceedings,* vol. 47 (1937), 259–35, 271.

"an attack": Ibid.

164   *"I absolutely refused":* Dalrymple to Gage, Boston, March 7, 1770, vol. 90, GP.

165   *"In this delicate situation":* Ibid.

"very peaceably": John Rowe Diary, March 6, 1770, MHS.

"We are now happily": Samuel Cooper to Thomas Pownall, March 26, 1770, reprinted in *American Historical Review* 8, no. 2 (January 1903): 317.

166   *"For these and other reasons":* Ibid.

" to reinstate matters": Dalrymple to Gage, Boston, March 8, 1770, vol. 90, GP.

"Yesterday two Companies": John Rowe Diary, March 10 and 12, 1770, MHS.

167   *"all the 29th Regiment:"* Boston News-Letter, March 15, 1770.

"ever since the Soldiers": Loose Boston Town Records, Dock Ward Watch Report, March 26, 1770, BPL. Spelling has been modernized.

"Nothing can be more effectual": Dalrymple to Gage, Boston, March 19, 1770, reprinted in Adams, "New Light on the Boston Massacre," 281.

168   *"caused by the multitudes of women":* Hutchinson to Gage, Boston, April 22, 1770, vol. 91, GP. Dalrymple to Gage, Boston, April 19, 1770, vol. 91, GP: "the situation of the troops at the Castle was such that something immediate must be done for them, else sickness must be expected they being extremely crowded."

"The men seem to me": Hutchinson to Gage, Boston, April 29, 1770, vol. 91, GP. Besides, Hutchinson added cunningly, it was easier for the officers to keep order if the men had less access to alcohol. "The Commanding Officers there assure me they are not suffered to have any Rum from the sutler for the Gar-

rison, and if any person attempts to bring any upon the Island the Officers of the Troops may prevent it."

169 *"unfortunate affair"*: *Boston Chronicle,* March 8, 1770.

most of its advertisers: David A. Copeland, *Debating the News in Colonial Newspapers* (New York: Greenwood Press, 2000), 249.

John Rowe joined: John Rowe Diary, March 8, 1770, MHS; *Boston Evening-Post,* March 12, 1770.

Reverend William Emerson: Amelia Forbes Emerson, ed., *Diaries and Letters of William Emerson, 1743–1776: Minister of the Church in Concord, Chaplain in the Revolutionary Army* (private printing, 1972), 53.

170 *his sermon into print:* John Lathrop, *Innocent Blood Crying to God from the Streets of Boston. A Sermon Occasioned by the Horrid Murder of Messieurs Samuel Gray, Samuel Maverick, James Caldwell, and Crispus Attucks, with Patrick Carr, since Dead, and Christopher Monk, Judged Irrecoverable, and Several Others Badly Wounded, by a Party of Troops under the Command of Captain Preston: On the Fifth of March, 1770. And Preached the Lord's-Day Following: By John Lathrop, A.M., Pastor of the Second Church in Boston.* [Three lines of scripture] (London, 1770). Reprinted by Edes and Gill in Boston, 1771.

"the detestable machinations": "Manuscript address from the Inhabitants of the Town of Medford to the Town of Boston," Medford, Massachusetts, March 14, 1770. Loose Boston Town Records "relating to Massacre, March 1770," BPL.

"a particular Account": Boston Town Records, BRCR, March 26, 1770, 20.

171 *They sent:* York, "Rival Truths," 73–74.

"to intreat": *Boston Gazette,* March 19, 1770.

172 *"the unhappy Persons"*: Boston Town Records, BRCR, March 26, 1770, 20.

173 *"send home copies"*: Dalrymple to Gage, March 12, 1770, reprinted in Adams, "New Light on the Boston Massacre," 281. For an excellent account of the public relations battle on which much of the following few paragraphs relies, see York, "Rival Truths."

"Be so good to Collect": Gage to Dalrymple, March 12, 1770, vol. 90, GP.

"since they have been": *A Fair Account,* 12.

174 *"In my accounts"*: Gage to Hutchinson, New York, April 30, 1770, vol. 91, GP.

"The 29th regiment": Dalrymple to Gage, Boston, June 24, 1770, vol. 93, GP.

175 *"Carr has not yet"*: Gage to Dalrymple, New York, October 8, 1770, vol. 96, GP.

"every-way dismal": Tobias George Smollett, ed., "18. A Fair Account of the

Late Unhappy Disturbance at Boston in New England: Extracted from the Depositions That Ave Been Made Concerning It by Persons of All Parties," *The Critical Review, or, Annals of Literature; London* 30 (July 1770): 75–76; Tobias George Smollett, ed., "17. A Short Narrative of the Horrid Massacre in Boston, Perpetrated in the Evening of the Fifth Day March, 1770," *The Critical Review, or, Annals of Literature; London* 29 (May 1770): 390.

"most of whom": Ralph Griffiths, ed., "Art. 23. A Fair Account of the Late Unhappy Disturbance at Boston in New England," *Monthly Review, or, Literary Journal, 1752–1825* 43 (July 1770): 68–69. Ralph Griffiths, ed., "Art. 34. A Short Narrative of the Horrid Massacre in Boston, Perpetrated in the Evening of the 5th of March, 1770, by the Soldiers of the 29th Regiment, Which, with the 14th Regiment, Were Then Quartered There. With Some Observations on the State of Things prior to That Catastrophe," *Monthly Review, or, Literary Journal, 1752–1825* 42 (May 1770): 415.

176 *"The design of this narrative":* Smollett, ed., "17. A Short Narrative of the Horrid Massacre in Boston," 390.

177 *vulnerable to epidemics:* Dalrymple to Gage, Boston, March 19, 1770, vol. 90, GP.

178 *"incur as little Expence":* Gage to Dalrymple, New York, March 12, 1770, vol. 90, GP.

Dalrymple had emptied: Dalrymple to Gage, Boston, March 19, 1770, vol. 90, GP.

tried to stay: Starkey, SF 89546; McCormack, ibid.

on the Thunderer: ADM 36/6908/149, TNA.

179 *"routs and disorders":* Townshend Return for June 1769, Loose Boston Town Records, BPL.

"such an old Building": Townshend Return for April 1770, Loose Boston Town Records, BPL.

remained in the homes: Warnings for women in Corance's company can be found in "Warning [Out] Book from January 4, 1745 to 1770," Boston Overseers of the Poor, reel 1, vol. 1 (XT) in "Boston Overseers of the Poor records, 1733–1925," P-368, 15 reels (microfilm), MHS; SF 89545; SF 89546; SF 89793.

180 *"since their removal":* "To Benjamin Franklin from a Committee of the Town of Boston, 13 July 1770," Founders Online, TNA, https://founders.archives.gov/documents/Franklin/01-17-02-0106, accessed April 11, 2019. Original source: *The Papers of Benjamin Franklin,* vol. 17, *January 1 through December 31, 1770,* ed. William B. Willcox (New Haven, CT, and London: Yale University Press, 1973), 186–93.

"as great inconveniences": Campbell to Bruce, April 1771, RG 1, 136, PANS. 153 film: 15272, PANS.

Robert Love: Dayton and Salinger, *Robert Love's Warnings.*

181 *"is now under Confinement":* See "Warning [Out] Book from January 4, 1745 to 1770," in "Boston Overseers of the Poor records, 1733–1925," reel 1, vol. 1 (XT), MHS, and SF 89546.

182 *giving warning:* MHS Warning Out Book; SF 89545. About the almshouse, see *Selectmen's Records,* August 8, 1770, indicating that the province rather than the town paid for McCarthy's support. Also see Nellis and Cecere, eds., *The Eighteenth-Century Records of the Boston Overseers of the Poor,* 208; also 212.
"a number of Soldiers": Boston Town Records, BRCR, March 27, 1770, 21.
"they think necessary": ibid.

183 *"unhappy sufferer":* John Rowe Diary, March 17, 1770, MHS.
his social calendar: Ibid. Drinks, for example, on May 11, 1770. Dinners, for example, on March 16, 1770 (with Captain O'Hara), March 20, 1770 (with Lieutenant Colonel Dalrymple), and May 17, 1770 (Captain Leslie).
"a fine entertainment": Ibid., with many officers from the Fourteenth Regiment, August 6, 1771.
accused of fathering: "Justice of the Peace Records," May 19, 1770, Dana Family Papers, MHS.

184 *more conventional ties:* See also the marriages of William Woodward and Anne (printed as Ame) Callaham, April 5, 1770, Christ Church Records, AmericanAncestors.org; Samuel Strain and Mary Wharf, *Boston Marriages, BRCR,* May 21, 1770, 429; William Carson and Elizabeth Betterly, December 19, 1771, Trinity Church Records, AmericanAncestors.org. Baptism of William Mills on July 17, 1770 and Sarah Spencer on August 31, 1770, King's Chapel Records.
"The two sentrys": Testimony of Jesse Lindley, August 25, 1770, CO 5/88/196, TNA.
"both of Boston": King's Chapel Records, July 27, 1770.

185 *he married:* Simon Bennis and Margaret Querk, March 19, 1769, Rev. Samuel Stillman (First Baptist Church), *Boston Marriages,* 45. For Susanna's baptism, see King's Chapel Records, April 5, 1770. Mary Kewen also served as godmother for Jane Wall, daughter of Corporal James Wall, Fourteenth Regiment, January 31, 1770, King's Chapel Records. Simon may have been married before (and self-divorced); see his 1767 marriage to Hester Miller in New York. The Archives of the Reformed Church in America; New Brunswick, New Jersey; *Collegiate Church, Ecclesiastical Records, Baptisms, Members, Marriages, 1639–1774.* Miller (now Hester Bennis) married Anthony Simons in 1772.
Captain Preston's company: John Rowe Diary, November 1, 1768, a party at Cap-

tain McNealy's house with Capt. Preston; February 21, 1770, Sukey's dance; March 9, 1770, a visit to jail, MHS.

"dark, damp": Massachusetts Court of General Sessions of the Peace (Suffolk County), "Charge to the Grand Jury," March 1765, *Extracts from Records: Chiefly of the Court of General Sessions of the Peace Within and for the County of Suffolk, Massachusetts, 1764–1768* (New York: G. H. Moore, 1887), 5.

186   *"cleanly apartment":* *Boston Evening-Post,* October 1, 1770. The article also contains a complaint that Preston refused to share this "cleanly apartment" with an imprisoned debtor.

four or five others: Ibid.

debtors languished: "A List of Criminals now in Boston Gaol for various Crimes taken April 16, 1770," SF 89447.

sturdily built: Boston Chronicle, February 6, 1769. For the description of the jail, see *New-Hampshire Gazette,* February 10, 1769.

187   *come from Ireland:* For women who came from Ireland, see Muster of HMS *Thunderer,* ADM 36/6908, TNA.

debtors and criminals: See the testimony of Charlotte Bourgatte, in *The Trial of William Wemms, James Hartegan, William M'Cauley, Hugh White, Matthew Killroy, William Warren, John Carrol, and Hugh Montgomery: Soldiers in His Majesty's 29th Regiment of Foot, for the Murder of Crispus Attucks, Samuel Gray, Samuel Maverick* (Boston: J. Fleeming, 1770), 212, for evidence of his regular conversation with debtors.

"four Shillings": February 24, 1770, Dana Family Papers, Richard Dana, J. P. Records, 1757–1772, vols. 17–19, MHS.

"suspicion of murder": "Prisoner list," April 16, 1770, SF 89447.

188   *"entirely unable":* "Petition of Thomas Preston," July 1770, Massachusetts Archives Collection, vol. 44, 704.

George White: Convicted of burglary, "Boyle's Journal of Occurences," April 20, 1770, Houghton Library, Harvard University. In "prisoner lists," April 16, 1770, SF 89447, and April 21, 1772, SF 90877, "George White, theft, punish'd." "Received into the House (on province Account) 2. Children of George Whites in Jail Order Joseph Jackson Esqr., Mr. Jona. Mason, Selectmen," August 8, 1771. Almshouse records. "Journal of Occurences," March 20, 1770, vol. 1 (manuscript), Houghton Library, Harvard University.

189   *"close confined":* Petition of Richard Smith. Boston Gaol, March the 28th, 1770: SF 101578. For Smith's legal record, see SF 101578. In 1770, the Superior Court justices were Chief Justice Benjamin Lynde Jr., John Cushing Jr., Peter Oliver, and Edmund Trowbridge.

190 *adult baptism:* April 14, 1770, "Ebenezer Richardson/In Prison/Adult," *Records of the King's Chapel in Boston,* 97.

9. From Shooting to Massacre, October–December 1770

191 *"of a partial Jury":* Thomas Preston to the Earl of Chatham, March 17, 1770, the Chatham Papers, TNA. Cited in York, "Rival Truths."

"incurring a Clamour": John Adams autobiography, part 1, "John Adams," through 1776, sheet 12 of 53, electronic edition, *Adams Family Papers: An Electronic Archive,* MHS, http://www.masshist.org/digitaladams/.

192 *a local merchant:* James Forrest was frequently part of social gatherings with John Rowe and army officers, for example, October 2 and 12, 1768. John Rowe Diary, MHS.

"With tears streaming": "1770," Founders Online, National Archives, accessed April 11, 2019, https://founders.archives.gov/documents/Adams/01-03-02 -0016-0016. Original source: *The Adams Papers,* Diary and Autobiography of John Adams, vol. 3, *Diary, 1782–1804; Autobiography, Part One to October 1776,* ed. L. H. Butterfield (Cambridge, MA: Harvard University Press, 1961), 291– 96.

"anxious and distressed": Josiah Sr. to Josiah Jr., March 22, 1770, in Josiah Quincy, *Memoir of the Life of Josiah Quincy, Junior, of Massachusetts Bay, 1744–1775,* 3d ed., ed. Eliza Susan Quincy (Boston: Little, Brown, 1875), 26–27.

"an Adams": Josiah Jr. to Josiah Sr., March 24, 1770, in ibid., 27–28. Previous historians have assumed that the "Adams" of Quincy's letter was Samuel Adams, but in this scenario it might as easily have been John Adams. Zobel, *Boston Massacre,* 220–21, and Hinderaker, *Boston's Massacre,* 172–73.

"an attorney's oath and duty": Josiah Jr. to Josiah Sr., March 24, 1770, in Quincy, *Memoir,* 27–28. Josiah Quincy Jr., *Portrait of a Patriot: The Major Political and Legal Papers of Josiah Quincy Junior,* eds. Daniel R. Coquillette and Neil Longley York (Boston and Charlottesville: Colonial Society of Massachusetts, 2006), vol. 1, 24–25.

193 *William Fitzpatrick:* Richard Dana, "Justice of the Peace Records," June 30, 1769, MHS.

The prosecution: After Sewell brought the grand jury indictments, he seems to have withdrawn from Boston. "Editorial Note," Wroth and Zobel, eds., *Legal Papers of John Adams,* vol. 3, *Cases 63 and 64: The Boston Massacre Trials,* 1–43.

loyalist leanings: James Henry Stark, *The Loyalists of Massachusetts and the Other Side of the American Revolution* (Boston: W. B. Clarke, 1910), 367–76.

194 *"pitched upon"*: William Molineux to Robert Treat Paine, March 9, 1770, Paine Papers, MHS.

town meeting: Boston Town Records, BRCR, March 13, 1770, 14.

"Threats": Paine's copy of *A Short Narrative* is held by the Massachusetts Historical Society and is available online at http://masshist.org/database/337.

Hiring counsel: Quincy, *Memoir*, 26–28.

195 *"seems plain"*: William Palfrey to John Wilkes, March 13, 1770, reprinted in *Proceedings of the Massachusetts Historical Society*, vol. 6 (Boston: John Wilson and Son, 1862), 482.

"endeavoured to prevent": Andrew Oliver Jr. to Benjamin Lynde, March 6–7, 1770, Oliver Papers, MHS.

"had been troublesome": David Hall Diary, March 11–25, 1770, MHS.

"the most positive asertions": Gregory Townsend to Jonathan Townsend, Boston, March 15, 1770, Townsend Family Papers, MHS.

"Five or six witnesses": James Murray to Elizabeth Murray, Brush Hill (Milton, MA), March 12, 1770, Folder "James M. Robbins, 1760–1770," Murray Robbins Family Papers, MHS.

196 *"Justice [be] done"*: Ibid.

"poor Preston": Gregory Townsend to Jonathan Townsend, March 15, 1770, Townsend Family Papers, MHS.

"there will be Little": James Murray to Elizabeth Murray, Brush Hill (Milton, MA), March 12, 1770.

"If innocent blood": Innocent Blood Crying to God from the Streets of Boston, 17.

served in the army: Commissioned as lieutenant, 1756, Great Britain. *A List of the General and Field-Officers, as They Rank in the Army* (London, 1761), 130. For the description of Preston, see William Palfrey to John Wilkes, March 13, 1770, reprinted in *Proceedings of the Massachusetts Historical Society*, vol. 6, 480.

197 *"a sober, honest"*: "Boston-Gaol, Monday, 12 March 1770," *Boston Gazette*, March 12, 1770.

"I wish": Gage to Dalrymple, New York, March 26, 1770, vol. 90, GP.

"can be satisfied": Boston Gazette, March 19, 1770.

198 *a grand jury*: Zobel, *Boston Massacre*, 217. Along with the nine soldiers, four Bostonians were also indicted on suspicion of having shot at the crowd from the upper windows of the Custom House; all were found not guilty. For an excellent discussion of the value of considering this civilian trial as a part of understanding the larger uncertainty surrounding the trials, see Hinderaker, *Boston's Massacre*, 211–20.

"The Case of Captain Thomas Preston": The article was widely reprinted, for example, in the *Providence Gazette,* June 16, 1770.

"It appears too plainly": Gage to Dalrymple, New York, March 26, 1770, reprinted in Adams, "New Light on the Boston Massacre," 292–93.

"He had no Business": Gage to Dalrymple, New York, April 28, 1770, vol. 91, GP.

199 *"The Case of Captain Thomas Preston" appeared: London Evening Post* (London, England), Saturday April 28, 1770; *Essex Gazette,* June 6 and June 26, 1770.

"how greatly the Conduct": Boston Gazette, supplement, June 25, 1770.

"those papers directly militate": Boston Committee to Preston, Wednesday A.M., July 11, 1770, reprinted in Adams, "New Light on the Boston Massacre," 314–16.

made the same point: Essex Gazette, June 26, 1770.

"at least six months": Preston to Barrington, Boston Gaol, June 25, 1770, in packet labeled "Boston (America) Capt. Thos. Preston & 8 men 29th Regt. Prosecuted by the people of Boston on the charge of causing a riot," WO 40/1, TNA.

200 *fear of lynching:* Anonymous letter to Preston, July 20, 1770, enclosed in a letter from Dalrymple to Gage, July 23, 1770, reprinted in Adams, "New Light on the Boston Massacre," 318.

privates kept on marrying: For example, Jesse Lindley and Elizabeth Hillman, July 27, 1770, "King's Chapel Records," "Boston, MA: Church Records, 1630–1895," The Records of the Churches of Boston, CD-ROM (Boston: New England Historic Genealogical Society, 2002).

Rowe continued: John Rowe Diary, March 20, 1770, MHS.

redeployed to New Jersey: Gage to Barrington, New York, June 1, 1770, in Carter, ed., *Correspondence of General Thomas Gage,* vol. 2, 542–43, and "Abstract of Monies Disbursed in the Quarter Master Generals Department from the District of NY, by Major William Shirreff Deputy Quarter Master General to the Army in North America, Between the 25th Dec 1769 and 24th June 1770," box 25, folder "Warrants, June, 1770," Thomas Gage Warrants, Gage Papers, William L. Clements Library, The University of Michigan.

"benevolent, humane man": Andrew Eliot to Thomas Hollis, June 28, 1770, 4 MHS, *Collections,* 4th ser., 449, 451 (1858).

"a military criminal": Boston Evening-Post, October 1, 1770.

"have no conception": Preston to Gage, Boston Gaol, August 6, 1770, reprinted in Adams, "New Light on the Boston Massacre," 321.

201 *part of the strategy:* Zobel and Wroth, eds., *Legal Papers of John Adams,* vol. 3, 14–15.

opposition politicians: York, "Rival Truths," 84.

Adams and the rest: Dalrymple to Gage, September 24, 1770, reprinted in Adams, "New Light on the Boston Massacre," 333–34.

"that they were grossly insulted": Gage to Dalrymple, New York, August 19, 1770, reprinted in ibid., 327.

202 *judges simply adjourned:* Zobel and Wroth, eds., *Legal Papers of John Adams,* vol. 3, 15.

Superior Court reopened: John Rowe Diary, October 23, 1770, MHS.

"May it please": Ch.P.24, mss., BPL, reprinted in Neil Longley York, *The Boston Massacre: A History with Documents* (Abingdon, UK: Taylor & Francis, 2010), 175.

203 *"blustering cold":* John Rowe Diary, MHS, October 24, 1770.

lying on the lawyers' table: Zobel, *Boston Massacre,* 246.

204 *"enraged, prejudicial Juries":* James Murray to Elizabeth Murray, Brush Hill (Milton, MA), March 12, 1770.

Adams abhorred: See Bernard Bailyn, *The Ordeal of Thomas Hutchinson* (Cambridge, MA: Harvard University Press, 1974), 2.

205 *faced a sympathetic jury:* The careful work on Preston's jury is central to Zobel's argument. See *Boston Massacre,* 244 and passim.

"believed Captain Preston": William Palfrey to John Wilkes, October 23–30, 1770, in George M. Elsey, "John Wilkes and William Palfrey," *Transactions of the Colonial Society of Massachusetts* 34 (1943), 425.

Modern historians: Zobel suspected that John Adams managed to "pack" the jury while Samuel Adams was out of the room. Zobel, *Boston Massacre,* 246. Hinderaker, in *Boston's Massacre,* 193, suggested that the Sons of Liberty's supporters in London urged Bostonians to ensure a fair trial.

"I shudder with horror": William Palfrey to John Wilkes, March 13, 1770, reprinted in *Proceedings of the Massachusetts Historical Society,* vol. 6, 424.

Proceedings began: Preston to Gage, Boston, October 31, 1770, reprinted in Adams, "New Light on the Boston Massacre," 338.

206 *only capital trial:* Hutchinson to Gage, Boston, October 28, 1770, reprinted in Adams, "New Light on the Boston Massacre," 337.

"appear'd perfectly unconcern'd": William Palfrey to John Wilkes, October 23–30, 1770, in Elsey, "John Wilkes and William Palfrey," 423. For a description of the courtroom, see Zobel, *Boston Massacre,* 247–48.

already prepared pardons: Gage to Dalrymple, New York, August 13, 1770, reprinted in Adams, "New Light on the Boston Massacre," 326.

Jane Crothers: Married Pvt. Joseph Whitehouse, March 27, 1770. "Boston, MA: Church Records, 1630–1895," Christ Church Records, 84. The Records of the Churches of Boston, CD-ROM (Boston: New England Historic Genealogical Society), 2002.

207   *"great mortification":* Preston to Gage, Boston, October 31, 1770, reprinted in Adams, "New Light on the Boston Massacre," 338.

208   *"the same Jury":* Gage to Hutchinson, New York, November 12, 1770, and Gage to Dalrymple, New York, November 12, 1770, reprinted in Adams, "New Light on the Boston Massacre," 345–46.

"we have not so good:" Hutchinson to Gage, Boston, November 26, 1770, and December 3, 1770, Ibid., 348.

Samuel Adams complained: Boston Gazette, January 21, 1771.

"why the King's troops": Boston Post-Boy, May 29, 1769. See also *Boston Gazette,* March 12, 1770, in which a delegation from the Roxbury Town Meeting brought a petition to Lieutenant Governor Hutchinson, asking him to remove troops from Boston.

209   *"we heartily sympathize":* Boston Evening-Post, April 16, 1770.

"the odious Light": Boston Evening-Post, May 29, 1769.

"The Soldiers still on Tryal": John Rowe Diary, November 28, 1770, "The Soldiers on Tryal at the Superior Court"; then, November 29–December 3, 1770, "The Soldiers still on Tryal," MHS.

210   *"technical evidentiary sense":* Zobel, *Boston Massacre,* 272.

"He spoke to me": Zobel and Wroth, eds., *Legal Papers of John Adams,* vol. 3, 108.

"at home": Ibid.

211   *"no Blow given":* Ibid., 119.

"not so many as": Ibid., 131. Testimony of Joseph Hilyer.

"particularly well": Hemmenway, *Trial of William Wemms,* 41–42.

212   *"the inhabitants had reason":* Zobel and Wroth, eds., *Legal Papers of John Adams,* vol. 3, 156.

"on your conduct": Ibid., 160.

213   *Archibald Gould:* Ibid., 170.

"Man nor Boy nor Child": Ibid., 212.

214   *a "molatto":* Ibid., 192. See also the testimony of Nathaniel Russell and Andrew.

"at the Head of 25": Ibid., 120; also 112–14.

215 *see the trial:* John Rowe Diary, December 4, 1770, MHS.

(gallery had no chairs): Martha J. McNamara, *From Tavern to Courthouse: Architecture and Ritual in American Law, 1658–1860* (Baltimore: Johns Hopkins University Press, 2004), 52.

listened quietly: Supporters of both sides commented on the decorum in the courtroom. See William Palfrey to John Wilkes, October 23–30, 1770, in Elsey, "John Wilkes and William Palfrey," 411, 418, 423, 426 (1943); and Dalrymple to Gage, October 25, 1770, in Adams, "New Light on the Boston Massacre," 336. See also Hutchinson to Hillsborough, October 30, 1770, quoted in Wroth and Zobel, eds., *Legal Papers of John Adams,* 21.

"one of the Council": Hutchinson to Gage, December 3, 1770, in Adams, "New Light on the Boston Massacre," 348–49.

Robert Auchmuty: See Zobel, "Newer Light on the Boston Massacre," *American Antiquarian Society Proceedings* 78 (1969), 119–28.

"the Lawyers have held back": Dalrymple to Gage, Boston, December 3, 1770 in Adams, "New Light on the Boston Massacre," 349.

"necessity of entering": Hutchinson to Gage, December 3, 1770, in Adams, "New Light on the Boston Massacre," 348–49.

216 *"plain English":* Zobel and Wroth, *Legal Papers of John Adams,* vol. 3, 266.

217 *sentiments were "united":* Boston *Evening-Post,* March 12, 1770.

"The sun is not about to stand still": Zobel and Wroth, *Legal Papers of John Adams,* vol. 3, 266.

219 *clarified very little:* Neil York persuasively argues that the prosecution and the defense offer "mutually exclusive" yet "mutually acceptable" versions of events. York, "Rival Truths," 58.

send them by boat: Dalrymple to Gage, December 10, 1770, Castle William, vol. 98, GP.

he sailed for England: He departed for London on HMS *Glasgow. Essex Gazette,* December 11, 1770.

"exactly right": The Adams Papers, Diary and Autobiography of John Adams, vol. 2, 79.

220 *"our children":* Joseph Warren, *An oration delivered March 5th, 1772. At the request of the inhabitants of the town of Boston; to commemorate the bloody tragedy of the fifth of March, 1770* (Boston: Printed by Edes and Gill, by order of the town of Boston, 1772). John Rowe Diary, March 5, 1772, MHS.

Epilogue: Civil War

222 *a civil war:* A recent excellent example is Virginia DeJohn Anderson, *The Martyr and the Traitor: Nathan Hale, Moses Dunbar, and the American Revolution* (New York: Oxford University Press, 2017).

223 *like a bad divorce*: I thank Rosemarie Zagarri for this excellent metaphor.

a merchant who had died: Boston Gazette, October 21, 1765.

Hannah and her seven siblings: Boston: *The Inhabitants and Estates of Boston,* reference code 46874.

no stranger to town politics: "To Benjamin Franklin from Jonathan Williams, Sr., 13 December 1771," Founders Online, National Archives, https://founders .archives.gov/documents/Franklin/01-18-02-0174, accessed April 11, 2019. Original source: *The Papers of Benjamin Franklin,* vol. 18, *January 1 through December 31, 1771,* ed. William B. Willcox (New Haven, CT, and London: Yale University Press, 1974), 264–65, fn. 5.

"As to your intention": Gage to Milliquet (at Boston), New York, April 30, 1770, vol. 91, GP. Spellings of Melliquet's name vary.

got married: July 20, 1770, "Marriage Licenses . . . Performed by a minister in Plaistow, NH," *Essex Institute Historical Collections (Historical Collections of the Essex Institute)* (Salem, MA: Essex Institute, 1937), vol. 73, 195.

224 *"when I granted you leave":* Gage to Milliquet (at Boston), New York, April 30, 1770, vol. 91, GP.

"You have been a long time absent": Gage to Milliquet, New York, November 26, 1770, vol. 98; Gage to Milliquet, May 20, 1771, vol. 103; July 8, 1771, vol. 104; September 2, 1771, vol. 106, GP.

"The Bearer": "To Benjamin Franklin from Jonathan Williams, Sr., 13 December 1771," *The Papers of Benjamin Franklin,* 264–65.

225 *exchange his commission:* Melliquet did eventually find another ensign on half-pay who was willing to join the Twenty-Ninth Regiment. "Preferments," *The Scots Magazine* (Sands, Brymer, Murray, and Cochran, August 1771), vol. 33, 448.

the town of Waltham: Proceedings at the Celebration of the Sesqui-Centennial of the Town of Waltham, Held in Music Hall, on Monday, January 16th, 1888 (Waltham: Press of E. L. Berry, 1893), 46.

two of their five children: John Henry, Trinity Church Records, August 27, 1775; Ann Barbara, Dedham Episcopal Church (Dedham Church Records), October 25, 1775.

"one Mr. Mellicut": Provincial Congress Massachusetts, *The Journals of Each Provincial Congress of Massachusetts in 1774 and 1775: And of the Committee of Safety, with an Appendix, Containing the Proceedings of the County Conventions — Narratives of the Events of the Nineteenth of April, 1775 — Papers Relating to Ticonderoga and Crown Point, and Other Documents, Illustrative of the Early History of the American Revolution* (Boston: Dutton and Wentworth, printers to the state, 1838), 551–52.

Glossup: King's Chapel Records, July 6, 1771, *Records of the Churches of Boston;* Nellis and Cecere, eds., *The Eighteenth-Century Records of the Boston Overseers of the Poor,* 116, 134, 138; Boston Overseers of the Poor records, "List of children bound out of the almshouse, April 21, 1756–January 20, 1790," box 9, folder 1, MHS.

226   *"a little clashing"*: Abigail Adams to John Adams, September 16, 1774, *Adams Family Correspondence,* vol. 1, December 1761–May 1776, 152.

Samuel fled: Stark, *Loyalists of Massachusetts,* 369.

"The continuance": Samuel Quincy to Hannah Quincy, January 1, 1777, ibid., 370.

227   *"I have never once"*: Samuel Quincy to Hannah Quincy, March 12, 1777, ibid.

228   *"How horrid"*: Lucy Knox to Hannah Flucker, April 1777, Gilder Lehrman Collection, #: GLC02437.09891, gilderlehrman.org.

INDEX